LIT
ENC

OF

Runes

SIRONA KNIGHT

Sterling Publishing Co., Inc.
New York

Library of Congress Cataloging-in-Publication Data

Knight, Sirona, 1955–
   The little giant encyclopedia of runes/Sirona Knight.
      p.   cm.
   Includes index.
   ISBN 0-8069-4994-5
   1. Runes–Miscellanea. I. Title
BF1779.R86 K56 2000
133.3'3–dc21   00–041283

10 9 8 7 6 5 4 3 2 1

Published by Sterling Publishing Company, Inc.
387 Park Avenue South, New York, N.Y. 10016
© 2000 by Sirona Knight
Distributed in Canada by Sterling Publishing
°/o Canadian Manda Group, One Atlantic Avenue, Suite 105
Toronto, Ontario, Canada M6K 3E7
Distributed in Great Britain and Europe by Cassell PLC
Wellington House, 125 Strand, London WC2R 0BB, England
Distributed in Australia by Capricorn Link (Australia) Pty Ltd.
P.O.Box 6651. Baulkham Hills, Business Centre, NSW 2153,
Australia
Manufactured in Canada

Sterling ISBN 0-8069-4994-5

Contents

PART 1

Symbols and Mythology

The Mystery of the Runes

The runes are magical symbols that convey the story of creation, life, destruction, and rebirth, and these forces constantly occur on many levels of being. Because the mind processes all stimuli as symbols, the runes are extremely useful for personal transformation. They are symbols you can use right now to help create a better and more enriching life.

Initially, runes were a series of sounds, incantations, and bodily postures for communicating with divine powers and connecting with the elements of nature. Gradually people identified these sounds, incantations, and postures with specific signals or symbols, which became concepts that could be inscribed or written down.

A rune bears the primary definition of "secret." In Old Norse, *run* means "mystery." In Old Irish and Scotch Gaelic, *run* means "secret" or "mysterium," as does *rhin* in Middle Welsh. The Proto-Indo-European root of the word rune is *reu*, "to roar," while the modern German cognate *raunen* means "to whisper".

The idea of letters' having magical meaning beyond their literal meaning is not special to runes. Many of the early writing systems had magical meanings—including Egyptian hieroglyphs, which were originally magical pictures—in addition to their literal meanings. It was only later, with the advent of many foreign words, that an early system of writing with twenty-four consonants was standardized for non-Egyptian words, and this became the writing of the early traders.

Technically, the runes are not really an alphabet at all, because in a strict sense the word "alphabet" or the lesser-used "abecedary" refers to a row of characters beginning as do the Greek, Hebrew, Roman, and Gaelic, with the characters alpha and beta or their equivalents—A, B, and so on. Letter rows that use a different order are not alphabets in this sense, and so are called by other names. Runic letter rows begin with the six letters F, U, TH, A, R, K, and because of this are named Futharks. The most ancient of the Futharks is the Elder Futhark with its twenty-four runes. That is the rune row used in this book.

The magical implications of pictures most likely

originated in European cave drawings, dating back to 15000 B.C.E. In these drawings, a picture of an elk was, on one level, a picture showing what the animal looked like. This was the literal meaning. But beyond this, the drawing also embodied the essence and spirit of the animal—in the case of the elk, a fast creature with protective horns that are very dangerous if you get in too close.

As with Egyptian hieroglyphs, many of the early writing systems lost their magical element as they became a form of notation. Traders were continually coming across new cultures that had new foods and goods. It became important that the writing system be adaptable enough to handle this influx of new words.

The primary traders of early history were the Phoenicians, who had a reputation for roaming the world aboard their ships, providing a link between many different cultures throughout the world. The Phoenician alphabet came into use around 1200 B.C.E., and had twenty-two characters that were read from right to left. Because they traveled so extensively, the Phoenicians spread their system of writing throughout the known world. It became the source for later writing systems such as Greek, which came into being in the eighth century B.C.E. and had twenty-four characters, just like the runes.

As people used writing more to convey literal rather than magical meanings, specific letters were used to make up recognized words. The magical element of writing waned, and in most cases was lost. The runes are one of those early writing systems that never lost the magical aspect, and those magical meanings go along with their literal letter meanings. Gebo, for example, the seventh rune of the Elder Futhark, looks like an "X," but its letter equivalent and phonetic value are that of "G," and its magical meaning is "a gift"—in particular, the divine gift of life. The "X" depicts the relationship between the giver and receiver and how their paths cross, joining at the point where the two lines come together.

As magical symbols, runes connect with your body, mind, spirit, and the environment, and their inherent nature makes them relevant and useful today. Runes express the process and flow of universal energies. Runic symbols and systems are eternal expressions of deity and nature, making them ideal for use in psychological integration, spiritual growth, and magic. They serve as a direct symbol-language between your conscious and unconscious, so you can interpret their meanings as spiritual, mental, and/or physical.

An inclusive rather than exclusive divination system, runes are universal and nondenominational. Everyone who is comfortable with rune symbols and their meanings can use them. As you work with runes, your conscious and unconscious connect, so that you access the runic energies in a unique way. You personalize the symbols. You connect with each individual rune and with groups of runes differently, until eventually you create a personal meaning for each one.

You can use runes today to explore your Northern European heritage, for meditation, divination, healing, and magic. Runes can also be used as dream tools. For example, by staring at and holding one rune just before you go to sleep and as you awaken, and giving yourself the suggestion to go deep within the rune, you can better understand its full meaning and discover its immediate and long-term value in your life.

The runes are as applicable today as they were thousands of years ago. When you use them as divination tools, runes can still help you to find answers to personal questions, to better understand the influencing factors, and to foretell future events. Runes reconnect you with your inner resources and wisdom. When you use runes, you increase your self-awareness, relieve stress, gain a sense of personal empowerment, heal, and clear out blockages in your life.

Runes make ideal meditation tools. For example, to move from one rune to another in meditation, practice pulling a different rune each day for twenty-four days. Focus as much as possible on that rune's energy throughout the day by carrying the symbol in your pocket or purse. You can also write the symbol on paper, and tack it on the refrigerator, bulletin board, or anywhere you can see it easily.

Runes also provide a medium for creativity. Using rune readings and casting methods helps you access and tap into archetypal images, ancestral memories, and the creative source, as well as your innermost feelings and intuitions. Rune readings are also a great way to meet people and get to know them better. When you work with another person, you express your thoughts and impressions as you pull each rune. You communicate your ideas and share your experiences.

In whatever way you employ the runes, now is the time to remember how to understand and speak their sacred language. According to runic lore, rune magicians never actually die, but are reborn generation after generation, keeping and carrying the mysteries of the runes with them. You, too, can learn the secrets of the runes as they are reborn in each of us, through the divine within.

The History of the Runes

Both the origin and age of the runes are hotly debated topics among scholars, and have been for years. The similarity of runes to the Latin and Greek alphabets, both in number and shapes, suggests that the runes came from these alphabets, but as more information comes to light, the age of the runes keeps being moved further back. At this point they are being connected to some of the earliest writing systems.

Traditional symbols of the Northern peoples, runes are said to have been passed on by the mythical Hyperboreans, the fabled peoples of the Northernmost Isles. Some scholars say runes originated in the second century B.C.E., when the Cimbri and the Teutons invaded the Italian peninsula and came into contact with the North Etruscan and Latin alphabets. Other scholars believe that runes were formulated by the Goths in the first and second centuries C.E., on the Baltic coast. As early as the first century C.E., the Roman scholar Tacitus describes runes' being used in divination practices. He writes that during the full moon, a priest, priestess, or the head of the household would inscribe runes on strips of wood cut from a fruit-bearing tree, then close his/her eyes, turn to the north, invoke the goddesses and gods, and cast the runes on a white cloth.

Some of the more recent theories about the origins of the runes are:

1) The Elder Futhark is of the same origin as the ancient Turkish inscriptions of the Gokturk alphabet.

2) The runes were introduced to Scandinavia during the same period that spiral ornaments were introduced to Crete—somewhere between 1800 and 400 B.C.E. Evidence shows that the Goths were already familiar with the art of runes before they left Scandinavia, between 200 B.C.E. and 200 C.E.

3) The Norwegian runes are identical with runes used in Semitic-language areas, such as Trojan

Asia Minor and Canaan (Palestine) as far back in history as 2000 B.C.E. To this conclusion, some scholars postulate that the runes were not inspired by the Greek and Latin alphabets, but that they all developed from the same original, Oriental writing systems. Some of the first Norwegian runic inscriptions were written in a Semitic language. New archeological finds show that many people from the Mediterranean Sea area, especially Semitic people from the island of Crete, often traveled north on trading tours.

No matter where they originated, runes were a primary means of passing down information through the generations. Historical evidence indicates that initially they were a series of sounds and postures related to natural and divine forces, which later evolved into the letters of the alphabet used by the earliest Germanic tribes of Northern Europe. Prior to 200 B.C.E., tribes all the way from Romania to the British Isles, France, and northernmost Scandinavia had all developed the use of runes.

One of the key reasons that runic lore has been kept intact for these thousands of years is that some of the Northern European peoples were extremely isolated, particularly in the fjords of Scandinavia. It was especially in these places that runes thrived. The invading Romans and Christians did a thorough job of disrupting the traditional spirituality of the Northern European peoples, but because of basic geography, much of it remained intact.

As a writing system, the runes have characteristics that suggest both their origin and age. Because runic characters were carved in wood and stone rather than written, the original symbols contain only straight lines. Not until later did curved lines come into play. For example, the letter "R," which normally has a curved half-circle on top, was written in runic characters as two straight lines that form a sideways "V."

Another interesting aspect of runic letters is that they do not have horizontal lines. This was because they were often cut into wood, and the grain of the wood was horizontal. Using carved lines that were either vertical or diagonal, there was less chance that the lines would be mistaken for the grain of the wood. A perfect example of this is the Ingwaz rune, which appears as a diamond and, as such, has only diagonal lines. Theoretically, it is the same as a square, the difference being that a square has two horizontal lines. Basically, a diamond is a square that has been tilted, so that its angles line up on a vertical and horizontal axis.

The basic differences between carving and writing are particularly pertinent in the case of runes. Writing involves having both a writing implement and a writing medium, some form of paint or ink. Carving, in contrast, merely involves having an implement to carve with, which, in its most primitive form, could be as simple as using the finger to carve shapes in wet sand. Early hunters were already using knives and other stone tools, so it makes sense that they would also begin using these tools for writing and documenting events. Carving letters into wood, rocks, and bones seems a logical step for a hunter. It was a way of linking the beginnings of language together with the knowledge, magical or otherwise, that needed to be passed down to each subsequent generation.

The runes also depict archetypal shapes that exist as patterns throughout nature. You can see rune symbols in almost everything. For example, the Kenaz rune, which looks like a sideways "V," looks like the "V" formation of geese, ducks, and other birds as they fly through the sky. Another way to connect even more deeply with the runes is to become aware of their shapes in everything—animate or inanimate.

Runic Artifacts

The use of runes reached its pinnacle between 800 C.E. and 1300 C.E. The oldest manuscript with runic symbols is the "Abecedarium Nordmannicum," from the ninth century C.E. A fourteenth-century Danish manuscript written entirely in runes is the "Codex Runicus," containing the laws of the province of Sconia. In the Thirty Years' War in the seventeenth century, the Swedish forces used runes as a code to confuse Austrian intelligence. From the fifteenth to eighteenth centuries, people used runes primarily in house markers and monograms, and by the nineteenth century, only scattered pockets of "rune singers" remained in the remote areas of Scandinavia.

Early runic artifacts have been found in a wide area stretching across Europe. Archeologists found at Kylver, on the Baltic island of Gotland, a rune row carved on an early fifth-century stone; it is the earliest known runic artifact containing a complete runic row. At Vadstena in Ostergotland, Sweden, a stamped gold talisman with runes carved in it was found dating from the middle of the sixth century. A runic artifact found at Briza, near Sarajevo in Bosnia, dates back to the first half of the sixth century and contains nineteen of the twenty-four runes from the Elder Futhark. At Arum in the Netherlands, a wooden magical sword that dates around 600 C.E. carries the inscription "return, messenger," carved in runes. Found in the Thames River in London was a stunning ninth-century English single-edged iron sword; it contained the entire Anglo-Saxon rune row inlaid in brass and silver wire.

In Blekinge, Sweden, there exist veins of quartz that appear to have long lines of runes running through them, standing out from a granite rockface. Called Runamo, the place was considered sacred in the twelfth century, and people referred to the quartz band of runes as an earth dragon. In 1833, Finnur Magnusson of the Royal Society of Denmark spent ten months studying Runamo before having a vision as to its meaning and writing down a poem entitled "Fornyrdislag" in the Old Norse metrical form. Geologists have since proven that Runamo is indeed a natural phenomenon, revealing that the shapes of the runes are natural archetypes even within the very stones of the Earth.

The Scandinavian settlement in Greenland lasted about 500 years, the last contact with it being around 1408 C.E. The Norse also came to North America at some time around 1000 C.E. They called it Vineland, "the land of vines." The most interesting North American runic artifacts include the Kensington Runestone, which was discovered in 1898 in the state of Minnesota. Found under a tree stump, the giant slab of stone weighs about 200 pounds. It has an inscription carved in Late Scandinavian runes in a numeric system similar to Roman numerals. The inscription tells of an expedition by Goths and Norsemen to Vineland. A second runic artifact, found in 1952 by Ronald Mason near Winnetka, Illinois, was a horn. On one side of the horn is a carving of a man pointing to the sun, and on the other side is Odin's son, Vidar, fighting the Fenris Wolf at Ragnarok. Beneath the carving is a panel with runes describing the scene. Scholars have argued over the authenticity of both these American artifacts, particularly because the dates and locales suggested by the artifacts do not support current theories regarding the migration patterns of the Norse peoples. At the same time, evidence does exist that points to their authenticity.

Rune Mythology

In their original order, runes reflect the story of Creation, according to the perceptions of the early Norse peoples. As our universe began, the story goes, so did the runes. They embody the forces that create, sustain, and destroy *all* the patterns of the universe. This *all*, referred to in this book as the "Oneness," is a term that means the infinite wholeness of everything. Nothing exists outside of Oneness. Religions have personified Oneness in many ways, as both male and female, but ultimately Oneness is the union of everything that was, will be, and is.

Norse mythology plays an integral part in the understanding of the runes. Traditional information regarding rune mythology comes from two collections of Old Norse writings known as the *Eddas*. The first, known as the *Elder* or *Poetic Edda*, is a collection of thirty-four Icelandic poems dating from the ninth to the twelfth centuries. The common belief is that this collection was put together by an anonymous person around 1250 C.E. The poems use alliteration and a simple strophic (rhythmic) form as their only formal devices. Most of the poems of the *Poetic Edda* deal with mythology, and they can be divided into two sections, mythical and heroic.

The second collection of writings is called the *Younger* or *Prose Edda* and is the work of the Icelandic poet and historian Snorre Sturluson. Scholars have suggested that this collection was intended as a handbook for aspiring poets who wished to become court poets. The *Prose Edda* includes a preface on the creation of the world, mythological stories, rules governing poetic style, and an analysis of the ancient poems. These writings explain the creation of the Nine Worlds, including Earth, and also the mysteries of the runes.

In the beginning, before the world was created, the only thing that existed was Ginnungapap, essentially primordial stuff that, in the Norse version, was likened to a yeasty rime. On one side of this rime was Muspelheim, which emitted the element of fire and heat; and the other polarity was Nifelheim, representing the forces of fog, ice, and cold. Like bread or beer, the yeasty rime mixture, or wort (root or herb), within Ginnungapap began to be affected by the heat and cold, much as the yeast in bread and beer is affected by the level of hot and cold, the perfect balance providing the optimum environment for the yeast to grow. Too much heat and the yeast dies; too much cold and the yeast goes into stasis. Much like the Earth, which, in providing the perfect environment—not too hot, not too cold—produced the essential prerequisites for life, the yeast mixture in Ginnungapap continued to grow. Within its form sprang a giant cosmic cow known as Audhumla. The cow licked the yeasty rime, and by so doing freed the first of the giants. More giants took form and inhabited the rime, and they became known as the "rime giants."

The number of rime giants grew until Odin, the son of Bor and Bestla (daughter of a giant), and his two brothers, Vili and Ve, slayed the great giant Ymir. They then placed the giant's body at the hub of Ginnungapap, where they fashioned all of creation from it, including Midgard (Middle Earth) and eight worlds that split off in each of the eight directions. Worms and other creatures that gathered to feast on Ymir's brain were transformed into the dwarfs and elves that inhabit the worlds of Svartalfheim and Alfheim, respectively. From Ymir's blood, Odin and his brothers made the sea and the lakes, from his flesh the earth, from his hair the trees, and from his bones the mountains. His teeth and jaws were used to make the pebbles and rocks. The other rime giants fled to one of the lower worlds, Jotunheim, where they reside still, representing in rune mythology the forces of chaos. The third rune, Thurisaz, particularly embodies the energy of the giants.

At this point in the Norse creation myth, the first man, Ask, a human-shaped ash tree, and the first woman, Embla, a human-shaped elm tree, appeared. Odin and his brothers then gave Ask and Embla the gift of life, symbolized in the runes by Gebo, the G-rune.

Odin was also the god who gave the runes to humankind. In a shamanic initiation, he climbed Yggdrasil, the World Tree, and hung suspended between the Nine Worlds for nine days and nights. Wounded by his own blade, he went without food and water, and, after taking a magic potion, discovered the runes. At the moment of his discovery, Odin received complete wisdom directly from the source. The runes gave Odin power over all things. In an instant, he understood the potential of the runes as a sacred tool and body of divine knowledge.

Odin's discovery of the runes represented a shaman's journey between the realms that make up the levels of existence. Like Odin, you can use the runes to enter each of the "nine lays of power," and learn to harness and direct these boundless energies. From the Nine Worlds of the World Tree come the energies that affect all life.

Each of the Nine Worlds of creation has a position on Yggdrasil. Alfheim, home of the elves, and Asgard, land of the gods and goddesses of the Aesir, lie above Midgard. Svartalfheim, home of the dark elves or dwarfs, and Hel, home of Hella and those who die from natural causes, lie below Midgard. The other four worlds are Nifelheim in the north, Jotunheim in the east, Muspelheim in the south, and Vanaheim in the west.

In Norse mythology, there are several families of gods. The family of the Aesir, the human gods, has members that include Odin, Frigga, Thor, Tyr, and Heimdall. The Vanir, who live in Vanaheim, are the nature gods, and include Njord, Frey, and Freyja. In the "Encyclopedic Listing of Runes" (pages 35–195) you'll find more information about the Norse gods and goddesses and how they relate to the rune meanings. For example, Tiwaz, the T-rune, receives both its name and meaning from the god Tyr, who embodies law, justice, and war. The depiction of Tiwaz is an arrow or spear pointed upward.

Rune mythology also tells of "Ragnarok," a time when the three "evil" forces in the world finally gained power and brought about the end of the world. These three forces were:

1) the Fenris Wolf, who finally devoured the sun and moon and killed Odin,
2) the giant serpent, who came up out of the ocean, creating earthquakes and natural catastrophes, and
3) Loki, the god of chaos and trickery, who finally, through his malicious nature, brought about the darkness and the end of the world.

After the catastrophe of Ragnarok, a handful of deities survived, plus two human beings who hid in the trunk of the World Tree. These two people then began the human race again, and life was reborn. The last two runes, Dagaz and Othala, symbolize this period of rune mythology. Dagaz represents the light of the sun, while Othala represents the DNA coding that all humans have, which enabled them to begin the human race again.

PART 2

Encyclopedic Listing of Runes

THE runes came from the gods, since it was Odin, the god of Wisdom, who first discovered their magic after a shamanic initiation. In the *Volsunga Saga*, the Valkyrie Brunnhilde, one of Odin's daughters, placed shaved and sheared runes into the hero Sigurd's (Siegfried's) chalice of mead. When Sigurd drank the contents of the sacred cup, he absorbed the wisdom of the runes. According to Norse legend, runic energies are dispersed throughout the cosmos, some in Asgard with the gods of the Aesir, some in the underworld with the giants, dwarfs, and Norns. These energies also stream through the upper world of the elves and Midgard, where we humans live.

Each rune contains three aspects:

1) the symbol, what it depicts and means,
2) the name and what the word means, along with its letter value, and
3) the energetic force that the rune embodies and why it is considered a living symbol.

Rather than being static, runes represent dynamic universal forces that are constantly changing and evolving.

Traditionally, the runes provided a way to pass information from one generation to another. They told the story of the origin of the cosmos and how the cosmic energies came into being. By understanding these underlying energies, we can better understand how they affect our lives. The first three runes—Fehu, Uruz, and Thurisaz—represent creativity, structure, and protection, which are the three basic elements required for universal life and general well-being.

Because the runes represent all the cosmic energies that weave together the three *aettir* (families), they actually form an ancient treasure map, leading to divinity. When we come to know the runes and how to use them, we are following Odin's quest, a quest motivated by his insatiable thirst for knowledge, coupled with the wisdom of how to use that knowledge. The runes are Odin's stepping stones for moving across the "rainbow bridge," going up to Asgard, and becoming one of the gods. In any case, the runic path leads to greater awareness and a more divine state of being.

The Elder Futhark's Three *Aettir*

The 24 runes of the Elder Futhark are divided into three equal groups of eight, called the *aettir*. The first runes of each of the three *aettir* are Fehu, Hagalaz, and Tiwaz, also called the Mother Runes. The lineage of the runes is passed down through these three primary runes, since all other runes stem from them.

In Old Norse, the words *aett* (singular) and *aettir* (plural) mean generations and families, denoting that the information was passed down through the family structure—in particular, through the lineage of the Mother Runes. The word *aett* also linguistically relates to the number eight, which in German is *acht*.

As illustrated within each *aett*, the division of eight is one of the most common universal patterns. The eight-fold nature of each *aett* corresponds to the division of the sky and the plane of the Earth into eight parts. The traditional year-cycle of Northern Europe is also sectioned into eights, marked by festivals on the solstices, equinoxes, and the four cross-quarter days. In a modern context, the working day is divided up into three eight-hour sections, or *aettir*: the day shift, the swing shift, and the graveyard shift. While the term "graveyard" is associated with the dead, it also denotes eventual rebirth. In a metaphysical context, the three *aettir* represent expectation, desire, and merging, which are the three basic elements of any magical pattern.

Polarities exist between the different runes; for example, the first two runes of the first *aett*, are Fehu (fire) and Uruz (ice). Polarities also appear within each rune. For example, the first rune, Fehu, basically means mobile wealth, which on the positive side deals with riches, knowledge, and the means to do great things, but on the negative side can encourage greed, jealousy, and keep you from achieving your personal goals. Working with these energetic polarities is what the runes are all about. By understanding their inherent polarities, we begin to understand how we can employ these energies to enrich our lives and the lives of others.

The first *aett* is about creation. The second *aett* is about the so-called human elements, while the third *aett* is about reaching the frequently talked-about state of goddesshood and godhood, where all energies become integrated into One. Each of the three *aettir* ends on a positive note: 1) Wunjo, the Golden Age; 2) Sowilo, the sun itself; and 3) Othala, symbolic of the overall leap to the next level, where the circular process of the runes begin all over again, on a new, higher plane of consciousness. When Odin took up the runes from the abyss, he purposefully moved from one rune to another (from one *aett* to the next), until he gained the sacred wisdom of all of them.

The following section outlines what the runes are about and the unlimited ways we can use them to create positive goals, thereby enhancing every aspect of our existence. Energetic patterns shape who we are, what we do, and what we will become, given our present path. By changing the present, we can alter the future. Each action set in motion creates waves of energy that move within the whole of Oneness. A reaction or response then takes place in order to balance the energy of the initial action. This balancing is important in the scheme of things, and even more crucial is the integration of the polarities that exist at every turn.

As we move through the runes, it becomes possible to integrate their aspects into the whole of our being. By working with the runic energies and truly understanding their innate wisdom, as did Odin, we return to the divine-ness from which we originated, thus completing the circle of the runes and, on an even grander scale, the circle of Oneness.

The First *Aett*

The first four runes of the first *aett* illustrate the different polarities of energy. Fehu represents the primordial fire (heat) and raging flames of Muspelheim, while Uruz represents the eternal ice (cold), frost, and mist of Nifelheim. The interaction between fire and water (ice), and hot and cold, plays out in everything that exists, representing the polarities inherent in the universe.

The polarities of fire (creativity) and ice (structure) first meet in the abyss of the Ginnungagap. From this meeting came the first being, the cosmic cow called Audhumla. She symbolizes the first feminine creative principle in nature and the first incarnation of the Mother Goddess. Both Fehu (cattle) and Uruz (oxen) were bovine creatures, and can be viewed as complementary opposites in this context, for Fehu represents the creative force of fire and Uruz the structure of ice (frozen water).

The giant troll Ymir emerged from the same matter as the cosmic cow. From him came a son and a daughter, and from them all the giants. These beings are embodied in the third rune of the first *aett*,

Thurisaz. The cosmic cow then licked away the ice from the frost-covered stones until Buri appeared. He was the first of the Aesir Gods, and Odin's grandfather. The fourth rune, Ansuz, symbolizes this event.

The Aesir then began to consolidate their power, taking control of the creative process by killing Ymir. They created the Earth from his corpse, and set the paths of the sun and moon in motion along with the cycles of night and day. Raidho, the fifth rune, represents this cyclic principle.

The sun and moon were also celestial torches, and are linked to the sixth rune, Kenaz. This rune also represents the knowledge gained by the Aesir through creation.

The nature deities called the Vanir enter into the picture at this point, in particular the goddess Freyja, who later teaches Odin the art and craft of love magic.

THE GODDESS FREYJA AND THE GOD FREY

The ruling goddess and god of the first *aett* were Freyja and Frey. Their names mean "the lady" and "the lord." Freyja ruled over the plant life of the Earth, the trees and animals of the forest, natural love, female sexuality, and magic. She was also the goddess of love between men and women, and she was often called upon for assistance in love affairs. She wore a magical necklace called Brisingamen, made of amber or quartz that she obtained from four dwarfs. She traveled through the worlds wearing a cloak of falcon feathers or in a chariot pulled by cats or bears.

The Norse god Frey ruled over fertility, male sexuality, prosperity, marriage, and sacred kingship. His father was Njord, the god of the wind and sea, and his mother the goddess of Earth, Nerthus. Considered the god of growth and the fruitful rain, Frey was called "Veraldar Gudh" in Sweden, which means "God of the World."

So far, the progression of the first *aett* has moved from the elements to the giants, and then finally to the Aesir. Once the Aesir created Midgard (Earth) and Asgard (home of the gods and goddesses), they set the stage for the next course of events. These events came in the form of the seventh rune, Gebo, embodying the gift of life. This gift was bestowed by Odin and his brothers Vili and Ve, who gave it to the two human-shaped trees, as mentioned before: Ask (the man) and Embla (the woman), the first human couple. From this couple came humankind, who eventually took control of Midgard. Wunjo, the eighth and last rune of the first *aett*, symbolizes the completion of the first stage of Creation. In Northern Mythology, this period, known as the "Golden Age," was a "Garden of Eden"–type time of bliss before the advent of evil in the world.

FEHU (fay-hoo)

Sound: "F"

Depiction: Looks like the horns of a cow or two arms reaching skyward (the goddess stance)

Runic Position: 1st *aett*, 1st rune

Original Meaning: Cattle, which first meant mobile wealth and the power that came from it. Today, mobile wealth comes in the form of money, which buys goods that can be kept, bartered, or sold.

Key Words: Prosperity, mobile wealth, abundance, fertility, unstructured creativity, the primal fire

Tree: Elder

Herb: Nettle

Gemstones: Ruby, garnet, red cat's-eye, rose quartz, blood agate, carnelian, jasper

Color: Red

Runic Half-Month: June 29–July 14

Hour of the Day: 12:30 p.m.–1:30 p.m.

Other Names:
The Germanic name: Fe (Fehu)
The Norse name: Fé
The Anglo-Saxon name: Feo, Feoh
The Icelandic name: Fé
The Norwegian name: Fe

Description: The name Fehu means "cattle." In early herding cultures, such as the Norse, cattle could be kept and milked, thus providing a continuing source of food. In addition, cattle could be sold or bartered for other goods or killed for meat. Their hides could be used for clothing and their bones and horns for tools.

The first letter of the Hebrew, Greek, and Gothic alphabets also means cattle, illustrating the importance of these animals for ensuring the survival of early societies. Because of their importance as a form of wealth, cattle were carefully guarded to promote their health and fertility. The wealth aspect of the Fehu is characterized when the giant in "Jack and the Beanstalk" says, "Fee, Fi, Fo, Fum, I smell the blood of an Englishman." The runic "fee," which is an English version of the root Fehu, refers to his riches.

Basically, the giant is singing the Fehu *galdr*, when up pops Jack. The beanstalk corresponds to the World Tree, and Jack even trades the family cow for the beanstalk seeds.

The F-rune rules the basic force of fertility, containing the mystery of both creation and destruction. It denotes the harmonious functioning of these two extremes, leading to a dynamic evolutionary power within Oneness. Wealth, for example, can either create or destroy things, depending upon the situation. This destructive quality of wealth can bring out people's worst nature. On the positive side, we live, we learn, and in the process we evolve to higher levels of awareness. As we do, we begin to realize that riches and wealth come in many forms.

God/Goddess: Aesir/Vanir—The Aesir were the human gods and goddesses, such as Odin, Frigga, and Thor. The Vanir were the original nature gods and goddesses, such as Njord, Frey, and Freyja. Originally, the Vanir and Aesir were separate, but after a great deal of conflict and warring, they exchanged members. That is when Frey and Freyja became members of the Aesir.

Power Animals: Falcon, boar, cat, bear, cow,

tiger, horse, sow, ant, deer, hare, bee, bull, hedgehog, ewe, snake, sparrow, mouse, goat, ram, lion, monkey

Element: Fire

Number: 1

Astrology: Aries

Tarot: The Magician

Mythology: Audhumla, the primal cow, licked the frosty salt-covered stones, thereby freeing a tall handsome man named Buri. The gods of the Aesir were descended from Buri. Because of the cow's association with Fehu, it is the eldest of all the Elder Futhark runes. Along with the Aesir, the gods of humankind, this rune is also associated with the Vanir, the gods of nature. More specifically, Fehu relates to the early Vanir deities Njord, Frey, and Freyja. Njord and his twin sister, Nerthus, were parents to Frey and Freyja, and directly related to the natural wealth of the Earth, whereas Frey and Freyja were fertility deities, associated with livestock, especially newborn calves in the spring.

Coming directly out of the creation of the universe, Fehu is the raw archetypal energy of motion and expansion in Oneness. In mythology, this force flowed from Muspelheim, the southern world of flames, and acted as the source of the cosmic fire that produced Midgard, our human world. The cosmic fire illustrated by Fehu represented not only creation but also destruction, again reflecting the energetic polarities inherent in all things.

Magical Qualities:
Strengthens intuitive abilities
Channel for transferring, projecting, and sending runic energy
Draws the celestial energies of the sun, moon, and stars into your personal energy field
Increases monetary wealth
Increases your wealth of knowledge
Increases the fertility of your life goals and plans

Galdr Song:
Fehu, fehu, fehu
F f f f f f f f f f
Fu fa fi fe fo
Of ef if af uf
F f f f f f f f f f

Meaning in Divination: A mobile form of

power, closely related to the Germanic concept of "hamingia," which translates as good luck and guardian spirit. The "hamingia" was a field of energy around the body that could move at will—on its own. From this perception, Fehu embodied the directed, expansive power that moved energy outward from people and objects. It was manifested in healing energy, primal expansive motion, and prayers or blessings.

The two lines extending upward look like the horns of a cow and also like a person with his/her hands raised and outstretched—traditionally a pose used by priests and priestesses for prayers and blessings. In this way, Fehu symbolized communing with the gods and goddesses, where a person's field of intention moved outward (and inward) into the many dimensions of Oneness. As mobile wealth, this rune also represents money and the things it can buy.

The energy of the F-rune is the unbridled creative fire that has no boundaries, and thus no real structure or form. This energy intimidates some people because it seems uncontrollable. But if you merge with this Fehu energy and become one with it, a great burst of creative fire results, which you can use to create and fuel your personal magical patterns. With

Fehu, you need to be careful not to burn yourself out, but instead feel the runic energy in every cell of your body, until you become energized physically, mentally, and spiritually.

URUZ (ooo-ruse)

Sound: "U" or "OO"

Depiction: Represents the great European wild ox, the auroch, and the drizzling rain

Runic Position: 1st *aett*, 2nd rune

Original Meaning: The primal forming force that gives structure to the primal fire. Together they form the forces of creation.

Key Words: Patterning force, structure, formation, wisdom, and inner strength

Tree: Birch

Herb: Sphagnum

Gemstones: Emerald, green agate, malachite, aventurine, green beryl, chrysoprase, jade, green tourmaline

Color: Dark green

Runic Half-Month: July 14–July 29

Hour of the Day: 1:30 p.m.–2:30 p.m.

Other Names:
The Germanic name: Uraz (Uruz)
The Norse name: Ur
The Anglo-Saxon name: Ur
The Icelandic name: Ur
The Norwegian name: Ur

Description: Now extinct, the auroch was a wild ox whose main attributes were strength and ferocity. Uruz as the mother of manifestation represents form, structure, pattern, and order. While Fehu represents the active element of creative fire, Uruz is the energy that sustains this fiery life, and begins to weave it into the fabric of Oneness. The ice of Uruz is structured water, melting with the warmth of the sun, and thus giving life.

As with wealth, strength also has its positive and negative polarities. On the positive side, being strong—particularly in your will and intention—can help you through the most difficult situations. On the negative side, too much strength can reduce your flexibility, making it harder for you to adapt and change when the need arises. In the case of the auroch, it became extinct by the thirteenth century.

The message here is that you need to be strong, but strength alone will not sustain you or keep you alive. As more and more species become extinct every hour, we can see that it is imperative to be able to adapt to changing times. It is also crucial to understand that our strength as humans is innately connected to the strength of nature. When we destroy nature, we weaken and destroy ourselves.

God/Goddess: Vanir—The family of gods who live in the upper world of Vanaheim. Associated with the Earth and sea, the Vanir rule the forces of nature. Some of the main figures are Njord, the god of the wind and sea, and of summer, and Frey, Njord's son, god of sunshine and spring. The goddess of love, Freyja, is Frey's twin sister. She wept for her husband, Odur (akin to Odin), when he went wandering the Earth in the form of the sun. Her tears formed drops of amber in the sea and drops of gold in the stones.

Power Animals: Ox, auroch, bison, bull, cow, horse, whale, dolphin, manatee, boar, sow, goat, ram, buffalo, bear, alligator, anaconda, baboon, sea eagle, gorilla, lion, hippopotamus, dinosaur

Element: Water

Numerological Value: 2

Astrology: Taurus

Tarot card: Strength

Mythology: Just as Odin moved from one rune to another in Creation, one rune sets the tone for the next. Like the Fehu rune, Uruz takes its meaning from the great cow, Audhumla, representing the formation of all things. Fehu was the fire that creates and destroys, and Uruz was the drizzling rain and thawing ice that falls upon the Earth and begins the primal order of things. As Audhumla licked the stones of salt, it began the primal pattern that is mirrored in Oneness. Audhumla herself came from the dripping rime that was created when the world ice met the world fire.

As Fehu provided the creative fire that drives the forces of Oneness, Uruz provided the structure for this creativity. Together they formed the basic forces that created this world, continue to sustain it, and will eventually destroy it. In a real sense, this sequence of birth, life, and death plays itself out not only on a lifetime level, but in every day of our lives. Every time we get up in the morning, move through the day, and then go to sleep at night, we are essentially acting out this basic sequence. In an esoteric or shamanic sense, this sequence brings transition, growth, and knowledge.

Magical Qualities:
Draws energies together to create a magical pattern
Heals both physical and mental ailments
Knowledge and understanding of the self
Magical strength and power
Increases business opportunities
Accesses the lays of power or streams of energy within the Earth
Brings energy together and helps you realize your goals.

Galdr Song:
Uruz, Uruz, Uruz
U u u u u u u u u
U u u u u R r r r r
U u u u u u u u u

Meaning in Divination: Embodying the cosmic order, the Uruz rune contains an element of growth that is gained by overcoming obstacles. Uruz is the force that moves you to assert yourself in the world.

The U-rune is the primal power and, in terms of divination, it stands for beginning to seek new life goals and increasing the energy present in old ones. Thereby, this rune helps to make things more stable and balanced, heal illnesses, and settle disputes.

The U-rune provides an excellent vehicle for getting in touch with your strengths and, in turn, your weaknesses. By examining the energetic patterns that take place every second of the day, you can learn to influence this energy to your benefit. Everything is energy, and energy has pattern, and pattern has structure. The Uruz rune embodies the concept of pattern, and thus in a very basic sense has to do with the way Oneness is structured.

As Fehu provided the creative fire to get patterns started, Uruz begins to give form and structure to them. It's important not to be too rigid as you structure your goals, but to remain flexible enough to adapt to situations and your surroundings. When setting up any goal, you first enter the Fehu phase, where the initial idea bursts forth like a flame in your mind. From this point, you move to the Uruz phase, where the magical pattern starts to take shape and you begin laying out the steps needed to create a successful outcome.

THURISAZ (thur-ee-saws)

Sound: "Th" (the unvoiced "th" as in thorn)

Depiction: Thor's hammer or a sharp thorn on brambles

Runic Position: 1st *aett*, 3rd rune

Original Meaning: Protection, the enemy of unfriendly forces, a thorny vine, such as blackberry, that provides a defense against invaders

Key Words: Protection, destruction, defense, polarity, action, regeneration

Tree: Oak

Herb: House leek

Gemstones: Bloodstone, garnet, red jasper, obsidian, onyx, black tourmaline

Color: Red

Runic Half-Month: July 29–August 13

Hour of the Day: 2:30 p.m.–3:30 p.m.

Other Names:
The Germanic name: Thyth (Thurisaz)
The Norse name: Thurs
The Anglo-Saxon name: Thorn
The Icelandic name: Thurs
The Norwegian name: Thurs

Description: Named after a race of giants, Thurisaz is a power of defense and destruction symbolized by brambles, thorny bushes that fence in livestock and protect boundaries. Depending on how it is used, Thurisaz can represent an active defense or an attack against adversaries.

The rune is used as a source of protection, particularly from unwanted energies and malicious people.

It appears in the variant shape of "Y" in pub and inn signs in England, such as Ye Olde Pub.

God/Goddess: Thor was the strongest of all the Norse gods: his footsteps were thunder itself and he carried a hammer called Mjollnir that could level a mountain with one blow. To wield this hot weapon, he needed an iron glove named Iarn Greiper, a magic gauntlet that enabled him to catch Mjollnir without harm when the hammer returned to him. Another of his magical tools was Megen-giord, a girdle or big belt that when worn doubled his power. Thor rode through Midgard in a wagon drawn by two goats named Tanngniortr and Tanngrisnr. Because the heat of his presence was so great, Thor could never use the Bifrost Bridge, a bridge between Asgard and Midgard. Instead, he had to wade across the many rivers. Thor was married twice, first to the giantess Iarnsaxa, who bore him two sons, Modi (courage) and Magni (strength), and second to Sif, a beautiful golden-haired goddess who bore him a son, Lorride, and a daughter, Thrud. The Norse Thunder God lived in Asgard in Thrudheim, the Land of Strength. His spacious palace, called Belskirnir, had 540 halls. Widely worshipped by the common people, he was called upon to protect the fertility of the land. Hammer-shaped amulets, Thor's symbol, were worn well into the Christianization of Scandinavia. Thursday gets its name from him.

Power Animals: Goat, ram, dragon, hound, cat, tiger, lion, leopard, porcupine, mosquito, Tasmanian devil, wasp, bear, elephant, mongoose, rhinoceros

Element: Fire

Numerological Value: 3

Astrology: Mars

Tarot card: Justice

Mythology: Thurisaz is a symbol of lightning and thunder, equated with Mjollnir, the hammer of Thor. This weapon was the destroyer of the etins (giants) and the protector of Midgard and Asgard. Thor was related to the giants—called "thursars"—in his gigantic size and brute strength, as well as in his lineage, because his grandfather, Odin's father, was a giant. The Aesir constantly strove to maintain their protective enclosures in the world, and the power of this rune was invaluable in this effort. The giants were not morally evil, but were detrimental to the established and instinctual life urge exemplified by the Aesir, Vanir, and humankind. The thorn protected the rose, just as the hammer Mjollnir protected Midgard, Vanaheim, and Asgard, the middle and upper worlds.

Thursars were giants who went by several names, including "rime-thurses," or frost-giants. They were the enormous, ancient, and wise creatures who fought against the gods. They represented primal forces, elemental in nature. On one pole, the Thurisaz-rune represented the powers of the hoarfrost, who were the giants from Nifelheim, the cold land; on the other pole, the fire-giants from Muspelheim, the fire land. In Norse Mythology, as in Greek cosmology, the giants came first. Ymir, the first giant, a huge troll, was shaped by the cold but brought to life by the heat. He was created at the same time as the cosmic cow, Audhumla, was released by her licking the rune, and was sustained by her generously flowing milk, essentially beginning the cycle of life.

Magical Qualities:
Actively protects from enemies and harm
Overcomes unfriendly situations
Love magic
Awakens your will and helps you take action
Awareness of the separation and commonality of
    all things
Projected energy and applied power

Galdr Song:
Thurisaz, thurisaz, thurisaz
Th th th th th th th th th th
Thur thar thir ther thor
Thu tha thi the tho
Th th th th th th th th th

Meaning in Divination: Thurisaz embodies the life–death polarity, and has the potential of melding the two polarities of kinetic energy into one pattern of action. This rune can warn you to not rush headlong into things but think them through first. Thurisaz is either active energy directed outward or passive Thurisaz energy contained and directed inward. It acts mostly as a carrier, and combines well with various other runes to ensure success when you're doing works of magic.

Also associated with the forces of regeneration and fertilization, the TH-rune breaks down barriers, setting the stage for new beginnings. In faerytale, it is the thicket that protects Sleeping Beauty's castle, and, traditionally, the hedge surrounding sacred enclosures. In magic, sleep spells were cast using the thorn or the spindle, and, as in "Sleeping Beauty," this rune also symbolizes the thorn of awakening.

The first two runes of the first *aett*, Fehu and Uruz, embody an unconscious or unmanifested dynamic force. As Thurisaz enters the *aett*, this runic force moves to the edge of consciousness. Its energy is neither totally unconscious, as with the first two runes, nor totally conscious, as with the following rune, Ansuz, which governs consciousness. In this sense,

Thurisaz remains on the edge, between the unmanifested and the manifested. Slightly submerged, this rune resides in the levels of the unconscious mind that are easily accessible. A negative side of this rune appears in the shadows of the unconscious mind. It represents the repressed, shadow aspects of your being, which when not dealt with can fester and become potentially dangerous.

ANSUZ (awn-sooz)

Sound: "AA" (Ah)

Depiction: The wind-blown cloak of Odin

Runic Position: 1st *aett*, 4th rune

Original Meaning: Name of Odin, the Allfather of the Aesir

Key Words: Order, rebirth, consciousness, knowledge, wisdom, mental agility, communication, creative expression, and reason

Tree: Ash

Herb: Fly agaric

Gemstones: Sodalite, aquamarine, sapphire, lapis lazuli, labradorite, jade

Color: Dark blue

Runic Half-Month: August 13–August 29

Hour of the Day: 3:30 p.m.–4:30 p.m.

Other Names:
The Germanic name: Aza (Ansuz)
The Norse name: Oss, Ass
The Anglo-Saxon name: Aesc (Os, Ac)
The Icelandic name: Oss, Ass
The Norwegian name: As

Description: Ansuz is sometimes referred to as the "god rune," because it is Odin's rune, associated with the spoken word, song, poetry, and magical incantation (*galdr*), especially as an expression of magical force. Ansuz also symbolizes the divine source within human beings, an energetic force in the conscious mind that influences all intellectual activities.

Often a favorite of bards, Ansuz derives its name from the ash tree, one of the most sacred trees in the Northern Tradition. The World Tree, called the Yggdrasil, is an ash tree. It is the cosmic axis that links all the worlds of creation together, illustrating its sacredness. Also, the ash and, in turn, the runic power of Ansuz, was instrumental in the creation of the first man, named Ask.

God/Goddess: Odin—Known by over 200 different names, Odin was the "Allfather," who first helped the forces of creation by slaying the giant troll Ymir.

He did this with the help of his two brothers. They went on to fashion all the realms of being from the giant's remains. Odin's curiosity about life often drove him to do things that took him into precarious situations, which didn't seem like good ideas at the time but later turned out to be masterful strokes of genius, such as hanging on Yggdrasil for nine days and nights.

Asynjur—They are Norse goddesses who belong to the Aesir. Protector of housewives and marriage, Frigga is the second and principal wife of Odin, and the primary goddess in this group. A collection of keys hangs from her girdle, showing her status as a housewife. She is a sky goddess and weaver of the clouds. Friday is named in her honor.

Power Animals: Wolf, raven, horse, vulture, eagle, hawk, falcon, bear, tiger, cheetah, cat, hound, fox, butterfly, parrot, mockingbird, cockatoo, emu, snake, turkey, bat, scorpion

Element: Air

Numerological Value: 4

Astrology: Pluto

Tarot card: Death

Mythology: After the emergence of Audhumla, the cosmic cow, Ymir, the giant, as well as the other giants and gods, came the first man and woman, Ask and Embla, human-shaped trees—the ash and the elm, respectively. Ansuz embodies two of several spiritual gifts given to Ask and Embla by the gods Odin, Vili, and Ve (the threefold aspect of the god Odin). These gifts were *ond* or *anda* (breath, spirit, life force) and *odhr* (inspired mental activity, inspiration, genius).

While the giants and the Thurisaz rune symbolize chaos, the Ansuz rune symbolizes order and the Aesir, the gods who descended from Odin. Because of its connection to the Aesir, the Ansuz is Odin's rune, reflecting his role as the numinous god of magic and ecstasy. The poetic mead of inspiration, and the vessel that contained it, are both known by the name "Othroerir" (the exciter of inspiration), a concept closely associated with Odin and this, the A-rune.

Magical Qualities:
Increases magical powers and intuitive abilities
Gets in touch with divine power and knowledge
Communicates with the divine within
Inspiration in the creative arts (speech, song, and writing)

Assists in times of transformation
Shapeshifts and works with power animals

Galdr Song:
Ansuz, ansuz, ansuz,
A a a a a a a a
A a a a a a s s s s
A a a a a
A a a a a a a a a

Meaning in Divination: On a practical level, Ansuz is the counterbalance to Thurisaz. The divine order that stays firm no matter how difficult conditions may become stands as a counterbalance to the chaos inherent in the universe. Just as Thurisaz is used to fetter and protect, Ansuz is used to unfetter and release. As stated in the fourth spell in the ancient Norse poem "Havamal," the Ansuz rune can be used for releasing the chains that bind us. This is also true for psychological fetters, such as anxieties, fears, and phobias.

Because of its connection to the Aesir, Ansuz is the receiver and container, as well as the transformer and expression of spiritual power and divine knowledge. This energy comes from the Aesir. Humankind expresses it through acts of a divine, religious, or magical nature. The polarity in this rune may provide the answer to your prayers as a gift of knowledge from Odin, or it may be a trick of Loki. Opportunity or temptation, which is it? Ansuz can help decide between the two.

With the energy inherent in Ansuz, you can begin to give definite form to your goals and aspirations. Use Thurisaz to protect your magical works and patterns, and Ansuz to set the stage for bringing them to life. By merging with Ansuz, you touch divine energy both within and without.

RAIDHO (rye-tho)

Sound: "R"

Depiction: A wheel under the chariot as half of the solar wheel

Runic Position: 1st *aett*, 5th rune

Original Meaning: The solar wagon and chariot of Thor, carrying the sun across the sky

Key Words: Circular flow, rhythm, movement, travel, progression, riding, journey

Tree: Oak

Herb: Mugwort

Gemstones: Carnelian, rutilated quartz, golden topaz, ruby, purple-red amethyst, aventurine, sugilite

Color: Red

Runic Half-Month: August 29–September 13

Hour of the Day: 4:30 p.m.–5:30 p.m.

Other Names:
The Germanic name: Reda (Raidho)
The Norse name: Reid, Reidr
The Anglo-Saxon name: Rad (Radh)
The Icelandic name: Reid
The Norwegian name: Reid, Reidr

Description: The word for "wheel" in Dutch is *rad*, which is also the Anglo-Saxon name for the R-rune. From this comes the basic meaning of Raidho, which stems from the wheel and its motion. As the wheel allows the forces of creation to flow, Raidho is the cosmic law of right and archetypal order in Oneness. This flow is represented by such natural phenomena as the daily and yearly path of the sun, as well as the cycles of nature that emanate from the solar pattern.

Another meaning arising from the Dutch, Anglo-Saxon, and Germanic words for Raidho—"Rad" and "Reda"—is the concept of counsel and advice. Also, the words in Dutch and German for knight are *ridder* and *ritter*, respectively, implying shining conduct and chivalrous behavior.

God/Goddess: Forseti—The god of justice and law, Forseti stills all strife. He lives in the magnificent palace of Glitnir (shining), which reputedly had a silver roof supported by massive gold pillars. Forseti is the supreme judge of Asgard, and settles all disputes between the Aesir. He is the son of Baldur (light) and Nanna (purity), and his name means "presiding one."

Power Animals: Horse, goat, cat, boar, sow, ox, cow, starfish, antelope, falcon, eagle, cheetah, hawk, kestrel, sow bug

Element: Air

Numerological Value: 5

Astrology: Sagittarius

Tarot card: The Chariot

Mythology: Raidho represents the forces that move the energies of Oneness in a circle. This circular flow is embedded in both the daily and annual solar wheel, and links together the eight major festival days of the year. Because of this connection, Raidho is the rune of divination and ritual or magical ceremony, helping divine energy to flow from one place to another. When you "ride the wagon" in the right (sunwise or clockwise) direction, it can carry you to magical places.

In a mythological sense, the spiral journey of the sun, and its annual course from north to south and back again, was seen as the procession of Nerthus, the Earth Mother, and Frey, who as the gods of fertility, personified spring. Nerthus was also called Hertha, and it was thought that she rode in a cart pulled by oxen through the area of the Baltic Sea every spring to promote fertility. Frey would ride (Raidho) through the skies in a chariot drawn by two boars, and sometimes on the back of the golden-bristled boar, Gullinbursti.

Extending this analogy, the wheeling of stars around the cosmic axis can be thought to be the chariot of Thor or Freyja. Pulled by two he-goats, Thor's brazen chariot racing across the sky caused thunder. Freyja's chariot was drawn by large male cats. These chariots and any other cosmic transportation are denoted by the R-rune, demonstrating primal forces controlled by conscious thought.

Magical Qualities:
Use in ritual, particularly with the Great Days and
   Full Moons
Moves runic energy toward a specific destination
Increases your connection to the cyclic flow of life

Uses sunwise movement for personal empowerment in magic

Works with the runic streams of energy

Connects with the transforming powers of the God and Goddess

Expands your conscious thought processes

Galdr Song:

Raidho, raidho, raidho,

R r r r r r r r r

Ru ra ri re ro

Rudh radh ridh redh rodh

Rut rat rit ret rot

Or er ir ar ur

R r r r r r r r r

Meaning in Divination: This rune represents the path of the initiate's journey through the Nine Worlds of Yggdrasil. Raidho embodies the intentional channeling of runic energies, which move according to natural laws, traveling along the road that leads to the best result. The concepts of rhythm and dance also are important to Raidho. This rune deals with the cycles of existence and how each leads to another, much as each rune leads to the next. In this context, reaching the goal is not an end, but a transformation and new beginning.

The R-rune is the wagon rune, representing the elements of earth, water (ice), air, and fire, as well as the different states of matter: solid, fluid, gaseous, and transforming. It can be used for shamanic traveling to other realms of consciousness, such as the elfin world of Alfheim. Also because of its connection to the eight spokes (divisions) of the wheel of the year, this rune symbolizes repetitive motion, such as that used in magic. The best way to work with Raidho is to use the natural flow of energy, directing it toward specific patterns. The negative polarity of the R-rune is that sometimes you find yourself going around in circles and not getting anywhere. Remember that each cycle (circle) is part of a larger cycle. By keeping the larger picture in perspective, you lessen your chances of moving aimlessly in circles.

KENAZ (kane-awz)

Sound: "K"

Depiction: Flame of the torch

Runic Position: 1st *aett*, 6th rune

Original Meaning: The controlled fire, cremation, and the internal fire

Key Words: The rune of knowledge, the internal or controlled fire, guiding light

Tree: Pine

Herb: Cowslip

Gemstones: Citrine, fire opal, carnelian, golden topaz, amber, beryl

Color: Gold

Runic Half-Month: September 13–September 28

Hour of the Day: 5:30 p.m.–6:30 p.m.

Other Names:
The Germanic name: Chozma (Kenaz)

The Norse name: Kaun
The Anglo-Saxon name: Cen, Ken
The Icelandic name: Kaun
The Norwegian name: Kaun

Description: Kenaz illustrates a flaming brand, a fiery chip of resinous pine wood that people in earlier times used for light. In esoteric terms this means that the K-rune brings inner enlightenment. Its name stems from the Old Norse word *kenna*, meaning "to perceive." In the twelfth-century Icelandic poem "Alvismal," also called "The Lay of Alviss," the dwarf Alviss illuminates Kenaz. He says that humans have literal names for everything; the gods are interested in how things function; the giants, in how they can use them; while dwarfs and elves view things in terms of poetic "kennings." Kennings is a technique in which a poet uses eloquent descriptions as a method of perceiving objects and situations in new ways, adding a multidimensional texture to things. In this way, humans view trees as wood; the gods see them as objects that protect the land; the giants view them as fuel for burning; and the dwarfs and elves perceive them as willowy, intelligent beings that adorn the Earth. A poetic view of trees is seem in Yggdrasil, the

World Tree, from which branch the Nine Worlds of existence.

Kenaz embodies the primitive fire and the spiritual being filled with light, making it the rune of spirit and mind. It is the fire rune, but unlike the raw and archetypal power in Fehu, Kenaz symbolizes a fire controlled by humans. Ritually, Kenaz is the fire of creation, sacrifice, the hearth, and the forge-fire that is controlled by humans for a specific purpose. Metaphysically, the fire represents transformation and regeneration. From the fire of Kenaz come the ability and the will to generate and create. Because of this, the K-rune is the rune of creative artists and craftspeople. (A related Dutch word, *Kunst*, literally means "art" or "craft.")

God/Goddess: Freyja—A blue-eyed, blond-haired Norse goddess of fertility and physical love, she married Odur, the sunshine. The most beautiful of the goddesses, Freyja made sure the reproductive urge never died in marital relationships. Sometimes called Valfreya, she was also the leader of the Valkyries, female riders who honored the bravest fallen warriors. Early Christians banished her to the mountains as a witch.

Power Animals: Cat, salamander, lion, falcon, hawk, eagle, owl, tiger, chimpanzee, bobcat, cuckoo, peacock

Element: Fire

Numerological Value: 6

Astrology: Venus

Tarot card: The High Priestess

Mythology: From the Ansuz rune came the gods, the Aesir, and from the Raidho rune (the circular cycles that affect everything.) From Kenaz came fire, the fire of spirit as well as the fire that lights the darkness. It was fire coming into contact with ice that created steam and water, providing the perfect fertile environment for the creation and development of life. Kenaz in particular refers to human fire, and because of this it is called the "human rune," or rune of humankind.

Magical Qualities:
Creative inspiration
Strengthens your abilities in all realms
Regenerates and heals
Helps in personal transformation

Manifests through polarities
Useful in love and sexual relationships
Increases fertility
Increases personal insight

Galdr Song:
Kenaz, kenaz, kenaz,
Ku ka ki ke ko
Kun kan kin ken kon
Ok ek ik ak uk
K a u n n n n n n n

Meaning in Divination: Kenaz brings about change and transformation, making it the emotional root of creativity. This change becomes accessible through the controlled power of the psyche combined with the contained energy of nature, resulting in the achievement of a tangible objective. From these polarities comes a union that results in manifestation.

Because of the working of polarities, including that of male and female, Kenaz is the rune of human passion, lust, and sexual love as positive attributes. This aspect of the rune is part of "seirdr," which is a form of love magic. Odin was the only man ever to have been taught this knowledge; he learned it from Freyja.

Also, the rune is important in relationship to kin, especially with respects to clan tradition, a bonding of the energy of the living and dead members of the kinship group. This bonding creates an energetic link that moves beyond earthly existence. In addition, the concept of kin can be expanded to include a wider grouping, such as like-minded people of similar origins.

Kenaz is the fire that brings life to your goals and aspirations. Akin to a pregnancy, Kenaz is the point at which your creations begin to take on a life of their own. When you pull this rune, it is time to nurture your magical patterns, all the while building up the life force, so that, like children, the patterns can thrive on their own.

GEBO (gay-bow)

Sound: "G"

Depiction: The crossing of two forces

Runic Position: 1st *aett*, 7th rune

Original Meaning: The exchange and resulting interaction between the human and the divine

Key Words: Connection, gift, exchange, interaction, balance

Tree: Ash/Elm

Herb: Heartsease

Gemstones: Sapphire, aquamarine, fluorite, azurite, lapis lazuli, sodalite, rose quartz, amethyst, jade, kunzite

Color: Deep blue

Runic Half-Month: September 28–October 13

Hour of the Day: 6:30 p.m.–7:30 p.m.

Other Names:
The Germanic name: Geuua (Gebo)
The Norse name: Gipt, Giof
The Anglo-Saxon name: Geofu (Gyfu)
The Icelandic name: Gjof
The Norwegian name: Giof

Description: Gebo symbolizes a gift that originates and results in the connection between people. Personified by the Norse goddess Gefn, "the bountiful giver," Gebo links the human world with the divine, since one aspect of the gift derives from interaction between humans and the divine. The concept of giving that is inherent in the G-rune is not one-sided, but actually a two-way exchange: The gift is given with the understanding that a gift is to be given in return. Therefore, Gebo is the rune of giving and receiving. Through this system of give-and-take, everything balances out. The preservation of balance is the important idea here. It applies equally to positive and "negative" gifts.

Ways that the Gebo rune has been used traditionally vary from people using the Gebo "X" to sign their name or mark the treasure on a map, to people using the Gebo "X" in correspondence to denote kisses. From this last use comes another aspect of Gebo, that of a contract, a partnership, particularly between lovers. The rune was also imprinted on stone or wood and used as a boundary marker.

God/Goddess: Odin—His role here was as the giver of life to the original humans, Ask and Embla, who, until Odin and his two brothers gave them life, were human-shaped trees, the ash and the elm. The three gods endowed these two wooden logs with the qualities of wit, breath, hearing, voice, vision, and other human characteristics.

Gefn—One of Frigga's handmaidens, she sold her hymen for a jewel but continued to retain her virginity. She is considered a form of the Earth Goddess. All women who die as virgins are passed into Gefn's care.

Power Animals: Raven, wolf, hound, eagle, bear, cat, falcon, lobster, oyster, chimpanzee, firefly, eel, bull, cock, iguana, stag

Element: Air

Numerological Value: 7

Astrology: Pisces

Tarot card: Lovers

Mythology: While Kenaz is the rune of humankind, Gebo is the rune of deity—that magical power present in the Ginnungagap (energetically charged void) before the formation of the worlds. Gebo represented the gifts given to humans by the gods. For example, in the Icelandic poem "Volsunga," the three gods Odin, Vili, and Ve encountered the two trees, Ask and Embla, on which each god bestowed the gift of life. Gebo also embodies the gifts that humans give to the gods in return for the gift of life. There is no part of us that is not divine, stemming from the goddesses and gods. In turn, there is no part of the Goddess and God that is not part of us. We are one. In Gebo, this relationship flows both ways.

Magical Qualities:
Magical initiation
Love magic
Sacred sexual expression
Mystical union of the Goddess and God
Increases harmony in relationships
Reconciles polarities
Harmoniously connects runic streams of energy
Accesses divine wisdom

Galdr Song:
Gebo, gebo, gebo,
Gu ga gi ge go
Gub gab gib geb gob
Og eg ig ag ug
G a a a a f f f f f f f

Meaning in Divination: On the highest level, the gift transcends both giver and receiver. When including the Gebo rune in a sending (sending runic energies toward a goal), remember that every gift demands a gift in return. The law of compensation dictates that any displacement or movement of energy has to be compensated for in some way. With Gebo, the movement is a gift that moves from giver to receiver and sets up a chain of energetic patterns that culminate in a balancing. In this sense, the giving inherent in Gebo resembles the barter system, where one person might trade bread in exchange for jam, and as a result both parties have bread and jam. It is a mutual exchange, benefiting both.

Through the exchange between humans and the divine, an aspect of Gebo revolves around the sacred mystery of the two (or many) into One. The power of the G-rune binds people together through an act of will, in order to create a specific result. An example of this is sacred sexual expression, which is the exchange of energetic polarities in a way that produces an intended and desired result. When doing magical work, you can also use Gebo to bind two or more runes together. In magic, Gebo represents the reconciliation and merging of opposing energies, such as male and female.

WUNJO (woon-yo)

Sound: "W"

Depiction: The weather vane or tribal banner

Runic Position: 1st *aett*, 8th rune

Original Meaning: Relationship and interaction of beings descended from the same source

Key Words: Joy, pleasure, hope, delight, kinship, fellowship, wonderment

Tree: Ash

Herb: Flax

Gemstones: Diamond, golden topaz, amber, citrine, rutilated quartz, clear quartz, herkimer diamond

Color: Gold

Runic Half-Month: October 13–October 28

Hour of the Day: 7:30 p.m.–8:30 p.m.

Other Names:
The Germanic name: Uuinne (Wunjo)
The Norse name: Vend
The Anglo-Saxon name: Wynn
The Icelandic name: Vin
The Norwegian name: Wynn

Description: Wunjo means joy, that elusive state of harmony that sometimes exists in the chaotic world. This rune deals with the wights, the spirits in all things. For instance, every tree has a wight or spirit that resides within it. Wunjo is the midpoint between opposites, where alienation and anxiety disappear. It is the rune of fellowship, comradery, shared aims, and general well-being.

With Wunjo, joy can be found by coming into balance. One example is the weather vane, which moves in harmony with the prevailing currents of air. This is akin to the joy found in the ecstatic shamanic state of bliss, that place where the spirit can journey and experience pleasure and peace outside the body. The W-rune represents the energetic harmony of two people who make honor and integrity their first consideration. In this way, the individual can best maintain his/her freedom.

God/Goddess: Frey—He was the sunshine, and as such his day of power was the winter solstice, when the sun begins to grow brighter and the days longer.

Wodan—Another name for Odin, it is he who ruled the light half of the year, from the winter solstice to the summer solstice.

Uller—God of winter, archery, and the hunt, he ruled the dark half of the year, from the summer solstice to the winter solstice. His weapon was a longbow made of yew, the best wood for a bow, and he lived in a yew grove in Asgard. He was the son of Sif and stepson to Thor.

Power Animals: Boar, wolf, raven, horse, stag, hound, lion, bluebird, dolphin, dove, hummingbird, elephant, kingfisher, cat, bee, spider

Element: Earth

Numerological Value: 8

Astrology: Leo

Tarot card: The Sun

Mythology: Wunjo is referred to as the "Golden Age." One of Odin's 200 other names was Oski, "fulfiller of wishes." Contained in this title was the name Wuldor, who is Uller, stepson of Thor.

Also from Wunjo comes the concept of the glory twigs, symbols connected with acts of magic and the realization of true will. Glory twigs in Anglo-Saxon are named "Wuldortanas." Twigs from trees are still used for runic divination.

Magical Qualities:
Strengthens social links and bonds
Increases your sense of joy and happiness
Binds runes toward specific purposes
Accesses your ancestral family ties, which can be
    on many energy levels
Links runic energies together into one

Galdr Song:
Wunjo, wunjo, wunjo,
Wu wa wi we wo
Wun wan win wen won
Wo we wi wa wu
W w w u u u u n n n n n

Meaning in Divination: The depiction is akin to the weather vane on old barns, showing which way the wind blows. "Wend" also means to change the direction of something, to turn and run with—or against—the wind. Wendrunes are runes written backwards. Because of its ability "to turn things around"—to change situations to your advantage—Wunjo is the ideal rune to turn the tide and ensure victory.

The W-rune stands for the mystery of the harmonious existence of varied, but complementary energies. It binds different energetic fields together, and is therefore an invaluable rune in magic. Also, because it is connected to wishes, it is one of the most magically charged runes. In the Thurisaz rune, this power is no more than a potentiality, while in Wunjo it becomes fully realized. When used correctly, Wunjo puts you in touch with great power, and helps you to actualize your goals and aspirations.

Wunjo brings good fortune, joy, and reward. Because of this it is perceived as the happiness rune. It also symbolizes Oneness, including both the divine and material worlds.

The Second *Aett*

While the first *aett* illustrates the emergence of order from chaos and the establishment of cosmic patterns, the second *aett* deals with the energies that stir, weave, pull, and disrupt these cosmic patterns, and as a consequence create change. Ruled by the Aesir god Heimdall (light) and the giant Asynjur goddess Mordgrud (dark), the second *aett* represents the dynamic powers of transformation, which serve as a counterbalance to the forces of creation. Heimdall guards the Bifrost, the bridge between Asgard and Midgard, while Mordgrud guards the gold-paved bridge over the River Gjoll, which leads to Hel, one of the Nine Worlds.

The "Golden Age" embodied in Wunjo, the final rune of the first *aett*, refers to a time when gold was considered simply an object of beauty, with no monetary value. Objects were made out of gold for enjoyment. A woman named Gullveig (Goldlust) introduced the negative side of gold to the Aesir, the side of greed and corruption, very much like the introduction of the glass bottle that causes nothing but problems in the popular film *The Gods Must Be Crazy*.

Hagalaz, the first rune of the second *aett*, symbolizes transformative, and often disruptive, energies relating to both Gullveig and Urd, who is the Norn of the past and guardian of the well. The second rune, Naudhiz, embodies the third Norn, Skuld. The third rune, Isa, embodies the second Norn, Verdandi. These three runes deal with aspects of time, particularly time relative to itself—for instance, the past in relation to the future, and youth in relation to old age.

Everything reaching its deepest descent into matter, with only one way out, is expressed in the fourth rune, Jera. The quest for knowledge moved Odin to sacrifice himself on Yggdrasil, represented by the fifth rune, Eihwaz. He then gave his eye in trade for a drink from the sacred well of Mimir to gain knowledge of the past, present, and future. This sacrifice is symbolized by the sixth rune, Perdhro. After realizing he could only view but not change time, Odin descended to the realm of the dead and conjured up the volva (wise woman) named Heid (a variation of Freyja). They made love and from their union came the Valkyries, represented by the seventh rune, Algiz. The eighth rune, Sowilo, symbolizes the return of consciousness.

The first half of the second *aett* is a continuation of the first, in that all the runes up to the fourth one,

Jera, symbolize the creation process. At Jera, the wheel of time turns, and Odin, through his sacrifices, initiated the process of the return of consciousness. Sowilo, the sun, illuminated the energies of other runes in the second *aett*, much as the sun illuminates the Earth.

Generally in mythology when deities were represented by three beings, they symbolized aspects of the whole. The threefold (triple) goddess was an example of this. In Norse mythology, the three Norns were all aspects of time: what was, what is becoming, and what will be. Also called the three fates, the Norns wove the fabric of birth, life, death, and rebirth. Urd spun the thread of existence. She passed the spun thread to Verdandi, who wove it into the present pattern of existence, the Web of Wyrd. This energetic web was like a fabric composed of vast numbers of threads "woven by decrees of fate." Verdandi passed the woven web to Skuld, who pulled apart the design and threw the untangled threads back into the void. In the English version, these Norns were called the "Weird Sisters," like the three witches in William Shakespeare's play *Macbeth*.

HAGALAZ (haw-ga-laws)

Sound: "H"

Depiction: The connection of two realms of being or the primal snowflake (in its 6-branched form)

Runic Position: 2nd *aett*, 1st rune

Original Meaning: The icy egg or yeast of primal life and pattern within Oneness. Also the movement downward and inward, into the underworlds of the Norns, to learn their wisdom

Key Words: Transformation, change, evolution, merging, harmony, protection, the past

Tree: Yew/Ash

Herb: Lily of the valley

Gemstone: Clear quartz, diamond, moonstone, opal, clear calcite, geode

Color: Gray or White

Runic Half-Month: October 28–November 13

Hour of the Day: 8:30 p.m.–9:30 p.m.

Other Names:
The Germanic name: Haal (Hagalaz)
The Norse name: Hagall
The Anglo-Saxon name: Hagall (Haegl)
The Icelandic name: Hagall
The Norwegian name: Hagall, Hagl

Description: Embodying eternal cosmic harmony, the name Hagalaz means "hailstone," representing transformed water. The layered nature of a hailstone was recognized for its potential for transformation, as well as its ability for destruction. In the Hagalaz rune, the destructive potential for hail out of season was balanced by the potential for transformation, bringing new fertility and growth as the ice thawed.

The H-rune represents the mysterious framework of the world. Hagalaz forms a cosmic model that contains the potential energy of Oneness, born from the dynamic generating, and constantly evolving, unity of fire (energy) and ice (antimatter).

Known as the crystal rune, because Hagalaz in an alternate form is the six-branched snowflake, Hagalaz refers to rock crystal, diamond, or snow crystal in the material world, and the crystal spirit in the meta-physical world.

Considered the pure energy of frozen light, all runes can be projected by shining a light in a certain way through a hexagonal quartz crystal. When light passes through the vertical axis of this six-sided crystal, it projects the six-branched snowflake pattern of the Hagalaz rune. Shining light at a right angle to the crystal creates the Isa rune. Similarly, all the other runes can be projected by shining light at the proper angles. This ties into sacred geometry, revealing the inherent energy and information coded in universal geometrical patterns.

The quartz crystal's sacred power of light makes the H-rune a powerful one for shamans. Because of its shape in the Younger Futhark as the primal snowflake, Hagalaz is also considered the Rune Mother. All of the other runes can be fashioned from its six-spoked form. Hagalaz's shape also echoes the hexagonal lattice underlying the structure of matter, clearly seen in the quartz crystal. This six-sided or six-petaled shape is also represented by the North Star, the guiding star of sailors. The German word *Hachel*, meaning "wise woman," is yet another aspect of Hagalaz.

God/Goddess: Ymir—The primordial giant troll from whom all the realms of being stem was created from the union of the flames of Muspelheim with the yeast waves of ice from Nifelheim. His name means "the roarer," denoting the primal vibration or sound. He was fed by the milk of Audhumla, the cosmic cow, and all the races of rime-giants sprang from him.

Urd—The Norns drew water from Urd's well every day, mixed it with gravel, and sprinkled it on the World Tree, making sure never to over- or under-water it. Urd, or Urdar, is the original Norn and the eldest sister of the three giantesses, the spinner of the thread and ruler over the past. Her name later became "Weird," when she became one of the "weird sisters" in Shakespeare's play *Macbeth.*

Gullveig—A Vanir wise woman who entered the halls of Asgard demanding vengeance for an injury. Gullveig was killed three times but still lived. Attempting to kill her brought about the first war (the Vanir against the Aesir), which the Vanir won. The two tribes exchanged gods and goddesses, and then ruled together. Gullveig symbolizes the Triple Goddess, and represents the negative side of Freyja.

Hella—A giantess, she is the daughter of Loki. This

half-white, half-black goddess rules over the underworld of Hel, and lives in Nifelheim in a hall of misery called Elvidnir. Hella is also the sister of the Fenris
Wolf and the Midgard serpent, the two forces of
chaos that ultimately destroy the world in Ragnarok.

Power Animals: Serpent, dragon, falcon, eagle,
hawk, owl, vulture, whale, dolphin, wolf, spider, bat,
blackbird, butterfly, chameleon, dragonfly, praying
mantis

Element: Water

Numerological Value: 9

Astrology: Aquarius

Tarot card: The World

Mythology: Hagalaz represents the cosmic primal, layered ice egg, filled with crystallized magical
power and cosmic pattern, which was transformed in
combination with fire. The hailstone is the symbol of
the yeasty rime "egg" that contains the seed of Ymir,
the primal rime-giant, formed from the juncture of
the world fire of Muspelheim and world ice of
Nifelheim. This is the potential seed of manifestation.

Hagalaz rules Hel. The dead are part of our past.

After Wunjo and the Golden Age, the creation myth describes the Norns, three giant maidens who came from Jotunheim. With their wolf companions (hounds of the Norns), they were the most powerful of all deities—not even the Aesir could undo what they had done. As previously discussed, these goddesses of fate represent time: Urd, the past; Verdandi, the present; and Skuld, the future. The Norn of the past, Urd, rules over the Hagalaz rune.

Hagalaz is the ninth rune, the number that is most sacred and mysterious in the Northern Tradition. Yggdrasil has nine worlds, Odin hung for nine nights on the tree in order to understand the meaning of the runes, and the god Heimdall had nine mothers; nine sisters, representing the waves, gave birth to him.

Magical Qualities:
Connects runic energies into one
Assists in personal change and transformation
Assesses ancestral memory
Protects from harm
Shamanic journeying
Shapeshifting
Heals past physical, mental, and spiritual wounds
Increases mystical experiences and knowledge

Galdr Song:

Hagalaz hagalaz hagalaz
H h h h h h h h h h
Hu ha hi he ho
Hug hag hig heg hog
Hul hal hil hel hol
Oh eh ih ah uh
H h h h h h h h h h

Meaning in Divination: Hagalaz is the rune of friendship, stability, and bonding. It reveals that from primal chaos, normally thought a destructive force, comes the potential for positive transformation. Every energetic death carries the potential (seeds) for rebirth and positive personal growth. Nine, the number of Hagalaz, is the number of completeness that leads to a birth of greater power and productivity.

Hagalaz is the rune associated with Bifrost, the rainbow bridge guarded by Heimdall and made of fire, air, and water that stretches from Midgard to Asgard. It represents the dangerous path between worlds or experiences that can bring transformation or destruction. Take care not to fall off the bridge, unless you are prepared for the consequences!

The H-rune often relates to conflicting or disruptive forces originating in the unconscious, creating the potential for change. It is also the rune of self-sabotage due to behavioral patterns that came from the past (Urd). Both Urd and Hagalaz are associated with the realm of Hel, which in a metaphysical sense equates to the individual unconscious, and in a holistic sense connects with the collective unconscious. This rune has the capacity for extreme polarities—the ultimate good or complete destruction.

NAUDHIZ (now-these)

Sound: "N"

Depiction: The two sticks (bow and bore) coming together to kindle the need-fire

Runic Position: 2nd *aett*, 2nd rune

Original Meaning: The need-fire, which burns even through the darkest of times, and the darkness, representing the future, which normally remains hidden

Key Words: Need, help, resistance, deliverance from distress, love, passion, shadow self

Tree: Beech

Herb: Bistort

Gemstones: Hematite, obsidian, onyx, smoky quartz

Color: Black

Runic Half-Month: November 13–November 28

Hour of the Day: 9:30 p.m.–10:30 p.m.

Other Names:
The Germanic name: Noicz (Nauthiz)
The Norse name: Naud, Naudr
The Anglo-Saxon name: Nied (Nyd)
The Icelandic name: Naud
The Norwegian name: Naudr, Naud

Description: Naudhiz literally means "need," alluding to the scarcity or absence of things that can't be done without. Needs are constraints that restrict your options. An Anglo-Saxon poem calls Nyd, the Anglo-Saxon name for the rune, a "tight band across the chest." On the other hand, this rune provides the potential power that can release you from your needs. In this release exists the counterpart of need, which is help. The whole idea is to evolve beyond need, and move to the next level—want or desire.

The Norns are shapeshifters. This is why the Naudhiz rune symbolizes the shaping power of the world and humankind. Representing the "spinning tree" or "windy tree"—the source of all fertility— Naudhiz is the cosmic fire, which, when it comes into contact with the cosmic ice, produces the energies of rebirth and transformation.

God/Goddess: Skuld—She is the Norn who rules the future and in turn death. In Norse legend, Skuld's face was always veiled, and she carried the scrolls of fortune with her. She was the invincible elf-queen with the power to raise the dead, as Jesus did in the Christian tradition. Because of her connection to the future, she was the rune "mistress" and the key deity when the runes are used for divination. The story went that if she were approached in the proper manner, she would provide a glimpse into the future.

Power Animals: Wolf, dragon, hound, fox, squirrel, spider, cuckoo, serpent, crow, donkey, firefly, flea, meerkat, moth

Element: Fire

Numerological Value: 10

Astrology: Capricorn

Tarot card: The Fool

Mythology: The Edda *Voluspa* ("The Song of the Sybil") tells how the three gods Odin, Vili, and Ve came to Earth and found Ask and Embla, the first man and woman, faint, feeble, and with no fate assigned them. After the gods gave Ask and Embla life, the Norns (or Nornir) gave them their fate in terms of the past, future, and present. Because of this, Naudhiz represents the breath of life and manifestation, an idea that originated with the creation of the Nornir. With their creation, however, came resistance in the universe. The laws of cause and effect sprang into action, and at the same time, so did the seeds of destruction. In response to that inherent destruction, the Norns also helped sustain the whole of existence by carefully and continuously pouring water from Urd's well onto the roots of Yggdrasil, the World Tree, so that it would not rot or wither and die. The Norns were also known for practicing weather magic, and thus had control over the elements.

In particular, Naudhiz is closely associated with the Norn Skuld, the youngest of the three, who rules the future. She was the one who cut the thread of life when it came to its end. Skuld's face was always veiled, symbolizing the unseen aspect of the future, whereas the faces of Urd and Verdandi remained uncovered.

In addition, Naudhiz is the rune of the goddess of night called Nott. The N-rune also ruled the misty realm of Nifelheim, which means "fog world." Nifelheim, or Nifelhel, was the realm of the dragon

Nidhog, who pawed at the roots of Yggdrasil in an attempt to destroy the World Tree.

Magical Qualities:
Protects
Helps you make better choices
Assists with divination
Increases powers of clairvoyance
Meets and works with your spirit guides and power animals
Understands your needs and desires
Fuels your magical patterns
Overcomes psychological obstacles such as bad habits

Galdr Song:
Naudhiz, naudhiz, naudhiz,
N n n n n n n n n
Nu na ni ne no
Nudh nadh nidh nedh nodh
Nut nat nit net not
Un an in en on
N n n n n n n n n

Meaning in Divination: When referred to in rune poems, Naudhiz represents the concept of necessity, layered with the friction that leads to transformation. Strongly associated with love and the heat of passion, friction produces heat, which in turn produces fire. When used with knowledge and wisdom, the need-fire becomes creative and procreative, but when used unwisely this energy becomes a force for destruction that burns like wildfire, leaving only ashes.

Embodying resistance, Naudhiz is a cumulative synthesis, a product of a thesis and antithesis: distress coupled with the guidance to deal with it and move beyond the problem.

Because Naudhiz contains sexual elements, it is a powerful tool in love magic. It is also an excellent choice for protection, especially spiritual protection.

ISA (ee-saw)

Sound: "I"

Depiction: An icicle or primal ice stream; straight, vertical, and unmoving

Runic Position: 2nd *aett*, 3rd rune

Original Meaning: Primal matter and antimatter moving up and down through the vertical axis, holding everything together in its present structure

Key Words: Stasis, constraint, slow expansion, massive force, gradual integration, delay

Tree: Alder

Herb: Henbane

Gemstones: Milky quartz, clear quartz, opal, moonstone

Color: White

Runic Half-Month: November 28–December 13

Hour of the Day: 10:30 p.m.–11:30 p.m.

Other Names:

The Germanic name: Icz (Isa)
The Norse name: Iss
The Anglo-Saxon name: Is
The Icelandic name: Iss
The Norwegian name: Is

Description: Some runes, such as Uruz and Hagalaz, represent aspects of ice, but Isa is an elemental rune whose basic form, that of a straight line running from north to south, is found in nearly all of the other runes. Isa means ice, and symbolizes static energy. It is the rune that stops all activity. Ice forms because of the loss of energy that turns a liquid into a solid. Although ice is static, it can move en masse. When Isa does move, it is with tremendous force, like glacial ice that moves with a strength that knows no bounds, tearing valleys into the Earth. In this respect, the element of water as ice in this I-rune is stronger than steel.

Static energy in the form of ice is slow moving in relation to a fast-moving environment. Depending on circumstances, Isa energy can provide a strong structure in a hostile world, or it can be a millstone around your neck when you need to make a quick change.

God/Goddess: Rime—Thurses, the original race of giants who ruled until Odin and his two brothers slew the rime-giant Ymir and created all the worlds of existence.

Verdandi—The Norn who wove the thread of life into the present pattern of existence, creating the Web of Wyrd.

Skadi—Goddess of snow, she demanded two things from the Aesir after they caused the death of her father: 1) that they make her laugh, and 2) that she be free to choose a mate from among them. Loki made her laugh, and she mistakenly chose Njord for her mate, later taking a new mate, Uller, the sky god.

Power Animals: Polar bear, whale, walrus, elephant (mammoth), manatee, bald eagle, sea gull, turtle, anaconda, water buffalo, reindeer, clam, moose, penguin

Element: Water

Numerological Value: 11

Astrology: The waning, crescent moon

Tarot card: The Hermit

Mythology: Isa embodies primal ice, the icy

stream (or glacier) that flows from Nifelheim, the misty ice world. World ice was antimatter that combined with matter, the energy flowing from Muspelheim, the fire world, in order to create Midgard, the middle world where humans exist.

Isa is akin to the force represented by the rime-giants. It is a stillness and lack of vibration, a concept as primal as the concept of "spirit." Ice and fire were the forces that created the world and, in turn, they were the energies that would ultimately destroy it. As the poet Robert Frost wrote in his poem "Fire and Ice": "Some say the world will end in fire, and some say ice." Isa ruled Jotunheim, the world of the giants, the frost giants in particular. The giant Norn Verdandi, who presided over the present, ruled the I-rune.

Magical Qualities:

Works with concentration and intention

Looks at the form of patterns

Slows down energy without stopping it

Balances and integrates your ego

Understands the polarities of energy and what they can do

Increases your awareness of synchronicity

Helps you understand potential dangers

Galdr Song:

Isa, isa, isa,

I i i i i i i i i

I i i i i i s s s s s s

S s s s s s i i i i i i

I i i i i i i i i

Meaning in Divination: Isa is the polar opposite of the first rune, Fehu, the primal fire that began creation. The positive side of Isa is that there are times when stasis can be helpful in assimilating information—particularly when a lot of input is directed your way, and you need time to evaluate it. The negative qualities of Isa are stagnation and procrastination. When they take over, the energy around you feels frozen in place, and it needs to start moving again.

Isa symbolizes the force of attraction, gravity, inertia, and entropy in Oneness. Because of this centralizing and concentrating effect, it represents the individual ego, the energy that holds the ego and self together during stressful times. It is the place where the past and the future come together, molding the present into form.

JERA (yar-awe)

Sound: "Y"

Depiction: The sacred union of heaven and earth, the dynamic rotation of the summer–winter cycle

Runic Position: 2nd *aett*, 4th rune

Original Meaning: Signifies the life cycle or cycle of the sun

Key Words: Cycles, right action, completion, fertility, natural law, continuation

Tree: Oak

Herb: Rosemary

Gemstones: Emerald, malachite, aventurine, green tourmaline

Color: Green

Runic Half-Month: December 13–December 28

Hour of the Day: 11:30 p.m.–12:30 a.m.

Other Names:
The Germanic name: Gaar (Jera)
The Norse name: Ar
The Anglo-Saxon name: Ger (Jara)
The Icelandic name: Ar
The Norwegian name: Jara, Ar

Description: The word *jera* means "year" and refers to the cycles of existence. Jera cannot act against the natural order of things. The Old Norse name *ar* relates to the word *ari*, meaning "eagle," symbolizing the swift flight of the archetypal sun. Numerically, it is the twelfth rune and a powerful number with respect to time, in that there are twelve months in a year and twice twelve hours in a day.

Jera embodies the completion of a cycle, and represents the dynamic rotation and changes in a cycle. This is displayed in the eternal contrast of opposites that make up the whole. It is used in magic for a good harvest, because of its association with fertility.

God/Goddess: Frey—Originally one of the Vanir nature gods, Frey controlled the weather (sunshine and rain), and was associated with the winter solstice. He ruled Alfheim, the land of the elves. His horse, called Blodug-hofi, could race through water and fire.

Gullinbursti, his golden-bristled boar, given to Frey by the dwarfs, pulled his chariot and ship. *Skinbladnir*, Frey's magical ship, would travel on land, sea, or in the air. Though it was large enough to hold all the gods and goddesses, Frey's ship folded up and fit into his pocket when not in use. His sword, when unsheathed, swung itself if a wise man wielded it and fought opponents on its own power. Frey's wife was the beautiful giantess Gerd. After seeing her from Odin's throne, Frey sent Skirnir, his servant, to bring her back to him. Frey lent Skirnir his sword and horse. Only after Skirnir threatened Gerd did she agree to go with him. Frey was killed by the fire giant Surt at Ragnarok.

Power Animals: Eagle, boar, horse, hound, bear, squirrel, grasshopper, chipmunk, cow, deer, duck, hare, ladybug, peacock, swallow

Element: Earth

Numerological Value: 12

Astrology: The Sun

Tarot card: The Emperor

Mythology: In the poem *The Voluspa*, Gullveig is

"Thrice burned, thrice reborn, often laid low, she lives yet." The three previous runes related to the Norns, who in their roles of past, future, and present represented aspects of time. The fourth rune of the second *aett*, Jera, represents time as a whole.

This rune is associated with cosmic fertility and the Vanir god Frey. He was called Argud in Icelandic, which means "year god." This related to his role as god of sunshine. He wooed Gerd, daughter of the frost giant Gymir, and when the two of them consummated their relationship in the forest of Barri, they brought the barren forest to life with the merging of the ice-covered earth and the fire of the sun. Symbolically, this story depicted the world emerging from the ice of the third rune Isa, into the fire of Jera, much as the seasons move from winter to spring every year.

Magical Qualities:
Understands the circular flow of Oneness
Works with natural patterns, such as seasonal cycles
Increases creativity and fertility
Increases harmony
Learns how polarities work together to make the whole
The power of manifestation

Galdr Song:

Jera, jera, jera,
J j j e e e r r a a a
J j j j j j j j j
Ju ja ji je jo
Jur jar jir jer jor
J j j e e e r r a a a

Meaning in Divination: Jera embodies dynamic form, representing the change toward completion. One of the two "central runes" in the scheme of the Elder Futhark, Jera affirms the cyclical nature of this world, including the twelvefold cycle of the sun. It deals with the sun's yearly path, as Raidho deals with the sun's daily path and guiding force. Sowilo, the eighth rune of this *aett*, is the archetypal sun.

Because of its relation to the annual cycle, Jera symbolizes natural law and the fruitfulness of effort. If the magical pattern is set up in accordance with natural laws, and the energy is with you, your harvest will be abundant. A plentiful harvest can happen only if the right things have been done at the right times.

EIHWAZ (eye-waz)

Sound: "E" and "I"

Depiction: The vertical column of the World Tree

Runic Position: 2nd *aett*, 5th rune

Original Meaning: Yew, in the form of the World Tree, as the giver of life and death

Key Words: Communication, death, regeneration, knowledge, dreaming, magic

Tree: Yew

Herb: Mandrake

Gemstones: Lapis lazuli, sapphire, blue topaz, herkimer diamond

Color: Dark Blue

Runic Half-Month: December 28–January 13

Hour of the Day: 12:30 a.m.–1:30 a.m.

Other Names:
The Germanic name: Ezck (Eihwaz)

The Anglo-Saxon name: Yr (Eoh)
The Norwegian name: (Eo)

Description: Eihwaz represents the vertical axis of the world that twisted through the massive trunk of Yggdrasil, the World Tree. Because Yggdrasil was represented by a yew tree, Eihwaz is one of the most powerful and magical runes.

The yew tree is an evergreen known for longevity, but it also contains a toxin known to affect the central nervous system. Because of this, early rune users cut staves from yew trees, thus combining longevity with toxicity—again illustrating energy that has the polarities of death and regeneration. The stave of Britsum is a preserved runic talisman that was carved in yew wood some time between 500–650 C.E. Its inscription is interpreted as "Always carry this yew! Strength is contained in it!"

God/Goddess: Odin—He was the god of nobility and warriors, not the common man. Many heroes' genealogies begin with Odin, including that of Sigurd (Siegfried). Odin had two watchdogs, the wolves Geri and Freki, whom he constantly fed, and two ravens, Hugin and Munin, which represented thought and memory. Odin sent his ravens out each day to gather news from the world and bring it back to him. Odin was destined to be swallowed by the Fenris Wolf at Ragnarok, but even though he knew his fate, he still chose to do battle, exemplifying the warriors' code of honor.

Power Animals: Eagle, spider, horse, wolf, raven, serpent, dragon, jaguar, dolphin, eel, salmon, butterfly, dragonfly, lizard, kingfisher, hound, moth

Element: All the elements

Numerological Value: 13

Astrology: Scorpio

Tarot card: The Hanged Man

Mythology: Eihwaz came into being when Odin, in his quest for knowledge, hung from the spinning Yggdrasil and discovered the runes and their meanings. The word for the World Tree, Yggdrasil, means "Ygg's horse." Ygg was another name for Odin and horse was a metaphor for the gallows. After coming back from the shamanic experience of hanging from the tree, Odin had not only gotten the runes, but also—as the "wild hunter"—the ability to travel between the realms of life and death.

Eihwaz was also associated with Uller, god of hunting and archery, who ruled Asgard during the cold part of the year. The son of Sif and an unnamed frost giant, Uller was also god of the Wild Hart. His home in Asgard was called Ydalir (yew grove), because the yew is best for bows.

Magical Qualities:
Understands the knowledge of the cosmic or World
  Tree
Releases you from the fear of death
Develops your creative and magical abilities
Increases your divination skills
Communicates between different realms of aware-
  ness
Practices lucid dreaming
Communicates with your ancestors

Galdr Song:
Eihwaz, eihwaz, eihwaz,
Iwaz iwaz iwaz
E e e e e e e e e
Iwu iwa iwi iwa iwu
Iwo iwe iwi iwa iwu
E e e e e e e e e

Meaning in Divination: As the axis that grows through and connects the three realms of the upper-world, Midgard, and the underworld, Eihwaz is a life-giving energy and a powerful stave of protection and banishing. Tiwaz, which is the first rune of the third *aett*, also moves through the three realms, but with an emphasis on separation. With Eihwaz, the emphasis is on communication and the connections between the three realms—in other words, moving through the thresholds. As with the World Tree, the roots grew down into the underworld, the straight line of the trunk was the Earth, and the top branches and leaves were in the upperworld, home of the gods and goddesses.

Eihwaz is ideal for working with different planes of being, including the realm of dreams. When you use this rune as a divination tool, it may reveal a new or different stage or course in life. It can also be used for protection and to move someone's energy out of your space. The number thirteen is the most power-ful magical number; it only began to be considered unlucky with the advent of Christianity.

PERDHRO (perth-row)

Sound: "P"

Depiction: The dice cup as a device for casting lots

Runic Position: 2nd *aett*, 6th rune

Original Meaning: Divination as an indicator of Orlog, the primal laws

Key Words: Birth, wisdom, kinship, manifestation, chance, luck

Tree: Beech

Herb: Aconite

Gemstones: Moonstone, obsidian, clear quartz

Color: Black or Silver

Runic Half-Month: January 13–January 28

Hour of the Day: 1:30 a.m.–2:30 a.m.

Other Names:
The Germanic name: Pertra (Perthro)

The Anglo-Saxon name: Peordh (Pertra)
The Icelandic name: (Perd), (Plástur)
The Norwegian name: (Pertra)
The Dice Cup

Description: The dice cup of Perdhro symbolizes the cosmos, and the lots within the cup represent the energies that affect an individual's life. It is also related to a game piece, such as a pawn in chess, reflecting the game aspect of life. On one hand, there are known quantities and a basic way the game progresses—in the form of birth, life, and death. On the other hand, there are a multitude of uncertainties within the game. Perdhro also deals with the interaction of what is called "free will" (the human element in the game) and what is thought to be pre-determined. This includes such things as heredity (genotype) and social upbringing (phenotype).

Perdhro is also pictured as an overturned cauldron, which is a symbol of knowledge relating to the clan in particular, and the wisdom that is passed down through the ages. Therefore, Perdhro is the rune that represents memory, problem-solving, and magical knowledge. In the ancient traditions, it is said that reaching the next level of spiritual development is a matter of remembering who you are. Perdhro is the rune to help you do this. It reveals things concealed from your view, those things hidden within the cauldron, thus bringing them into your physical reality.

God/Goddess: Nornir—The Norns, the three sisters who tended Urd's Well at the base of Yggdrasil. Some said that each person had three personal Norns who decided his or her fate.

Frigga—Probably the most important of the Aesir goddesses, she was the wife of Odin and identical to her mother, Fyorgyn, the Earth herself. Frigga dressed in the plumage of hawks and falcons, and came before any of the other goddesses. This quiet Mother Goddess spent her days in her sea-hall home. In an effort to save her divine son, Baldur, she was inadvertently responsible for his death.

Mimir—The wise son of Bolthorn, he was both a god and giant. His head was cut off by the Vanir when he was sent to them as a hostage, but Odin preserved it so he could seek knowledge from it. He placed the head next to Mimir's Well, and visited it to gain wisdom about the secrets of the universe.

Power Animals: Falcon, hawk, wolf, hound, water snake like the anaconda, spider, chameleon, hen, clam, oyster, cricket, dinosaur, frog, tortoise, kangaroo

Element: Water

Numerological Value: 14

Astrology: Saturn

Tarot card: The Wheel of Fortune

Mythology: After hanging on the World Tree, Odin went to the well of Mimir, where he sacrificed his eye in order to gain the wisdom of the runes, along with total knowledge of the past, present, and future. The well contained the accumulated knowledge of all his ancestors, collective energy that could be tapped into for wisdom and guidance.

Together, the three Norns controlled Perdhro, as this rune was the embodiment of Urd's and Mimir's Wells. Frigga, Odin's mate, spun the raw material that made the thread which the three Norns wove into the web of a person's fate. Consequently, the Norns also controlled the powers of cause and effect; whatever medium received an action transmuted it into a dynamic (but essentially unaltered) form and returned it to whence it came. The Norns also controlled time, since the cause and effect sequence took place through time and duration, as the past over-lapped into the future to bring about present reality.

Magical Qualities:
Perceives your fate—past, future, and present
Understands the nature of cause and effect
Taps into infinite Oneness
Seeks the wisdom to make things work for you
Understands the power of future sight
Knows where your patterns are going to lead

Galdr Song:
Perdhro, perdhro, perdhro,
Pu pa pi pe po
Purdh pardh pirdh perdh pordh
Po pe pi pa pu
P p p e e e r r r th th th r r r o o o

Meaning in Divination: Perdhro symbolizes the "Orlog," the energy that controls your fate. Underlying this idea is the notion of cause and effect or action and reaction. From this give-and-take comes synchronicity and divination, central concepts within the runes. By becoming aware of the syn-chronicity in your life, you can evolve and become more knowledgeable about the energies that move, influence, and propel you forward. The perception of Perdhro is a paradox—constant change that always remains the same. Once again, it is the polarities of energy that give this rune meaning.

The rune of time and duration, Perdhro can eventually help bring all your goals and aspirations to fruition, particularly if you take the necessary steps. Perdhro embodies the great pattern, containing the potential for cosmic manifestation.

It is also the rune of balance maintained within Oneness. Whenever this balance is altered, energy is displaced, and it then moves again to balance itself. In your magical practice, make an effort to become aware of the consequences of your life patterns so that they come out the way you intend. Work with the energy of Perdhro to gain wisdom and divination ability. As a vessel, the P-rune holds the energy of the runes as a whole.

ALGIZ (all-geese)

Sound: "Z"

Depiction: Elk antlers, branches of a tree, a swan in flight

Runic Position: 2nd *aett*, 7th rune

Original Meaning: Protective force, the three Valkyries

Key Words: Spirit, protection, sanctuary, refuge, power, divinity

Tree: Yew

Herb: Angelica

Gemstones: Rainbow tourmaline, fluorite, agate, jasper, diamond

Color: Rainbow

Runic Half-Month: January 28–February 12

Hour of the Day: 2:30 a.m.–3:30 a.m.

Other Names:
The Germanic name: Algis, Algiz, or Elhaz
The Anglo-Saxon name: Eolh
The Norwegian name: Elgr

Description: Algiz represents the power of human spirit moving and evolving toward godhood and goddesshood. Literally, this rune means "elk," referring to the four cosmic harts that continually nibbled at the nettles of the World Tree. The rune embodies both the elk, because it looks like its horns, and Yggdrasil, because it looks like the trunk and three branches of a tree. Like Eihwaz, this rune is associated with the yew tree and yew bow.

This rune is often used for protection and for the successful outcome of magic. The Old German *alhs* means "temple" or "sanctuary," traditionally a place where all spiritual knowledge and magical tools were housed. Thus, it was a place that was strongly protected against invaders. This rune is written both upward, looking like the divine triad pointing skyward, and downward, with all three lines moving down into the Earth. When the A-rune is doubled, it looks like the snowflake form of the Hagalaz rune. In the Elder Futhark, only the upward form is used. The exception to this would be using the doubled, tripled, or quadrupled Algiz form for bindrunes (see page 217).

God/Goddess: Heimdall—He was the protector of Asgard, guarding the rainbow bridge, Bifrost. At Ragnarok, he would sound his horn Gjallar, and then Heimdall (light) and Loki (darkness)—ancient enemies—would kill one another. Until then, he dwelt in the sacred mountains. He was able to see in the dark for a hundred miles in every direction, had incredible hearing, and never needed sleep. Nine sisters, signifying the waves, gave birth to him. As Rig, he begat Thrall, Carl, and Earl, representing the three classes of humankind: slave, free-persons, and nobles.

Valkyries—There were nine times nine (81) Valkyries, called the "Divine Valkyries." There are other Valkyries called the Vaetter maidens, who were half mortal and appear only to those with second sight. In the thick of battles in Midgard, Odin dispatched his "fetch maidens," the helmeted Valkyries, who rode on horses and wolves or shapeshifted into ravens. They selected the bravest of the fallen warriors and transported these chosen dead, known as the Einheriar, over the rainbow bridge to Valhalla, to live among the gods of Asgard. The Valkyries would serve these warriors mead, which flowed endlessly from the udder of Odin's goat, Heidrun. They would feed them meat that came from the boar Saehrimnir. The meat was prepared by boiling it in the cauldron Eldhrimnir. The boar would magically come back to life before the next meal. After eating, the warriors would go outside and fight each other to the death, and then they would be brought back to life before the next feast. The Valkryies sometimes opposed Odin, teaching magic to the heroes they wanted to save, as Brunnhilde did with Sigurd (Siegfried).

Power Animals: Elk, reindeer, swan, goose, stag (hart), ram, wolf, raven, horse, cat, bat, owl, crab, lobster, badger, wasp, goat, boar, crane, blackbird, hound, bear, porcupine, wolverine, cock, cougar, starfish, eagle, hawk, magpie, mongoose

Element: Air

Numerological Value: 15

Astrology: Cancer

Tarot card: The Moon

Mythology: Algiz is depicted as Tyr's hand. It is the hand that he sacrificed to bind away the Fenris

Wolf, the embodiment of the powers of chaos and darkness that was to end the world. As one of the oldest rune symbols, Algiz represented the three faces of the god and goddess, as well as the three polarities of energy: positive, neutral, and negative. Other mythological references to the number three include the runes themselves, which are divided into the three *aettir* and the three realms of existence on the World Tree: upper, middle, and lower.

Algiz was the embodiment of the human spirit as it strove toward divinity. Also called Elhaz, Algiz represented the three upper worlds on Yggdrasil:

1) Alfheim or Lightalfheim, home of the elves,
2) Vanaheim, the home of the Vanir, and
3) Asgard, home of the Aesir.

By reaching toward the upperworlds of light as illustrated in the A-rune, a person could commune with elves, gods, goddesses, and beings of nature, thereby attaining divine wisdom.

Magical Qualities:
Protects and defends from harm
Moves toward the completion of your patterns
Taps into the divine threefold and ninefold patterns

Understands your divine connection
Communes with the elements
Increases your regenerative powers

Galdr Song:
Algiz, Algiz, Algiz
Z z z z z z z z z z
Uz az iz ez oz
Oz ez iz az uz
Z z z z z z z z z z
M m m m m m m m m

Meaning in Divination: Algiz is a primary rune of protection. Along with Thurisaz, the A-rune provides a line of defense that starts with trees and is followed by a line of thorny bushes, guaranteed to stop—or at least slow down—any invader. In an energetic sense, "invader" means anyone you don't want in your physical or energetic space. In magic, part of initiating or creating something involves protecting your fledgling, much as you would your own child.

Along with protection, the energy of Algiz represents the movement upward toward the divine from which we originated. In terms of magic, it means having your energetic patterns take flight and move toward a successful outcome.

Turned on its side, Algiz looks like a flying swan or goose. The polarity involves protecting yourself while you are in those initial stages of flight, before you master your wings. If you feel yourself being attacked energetically, visualize the Algiz rune standing protectively around you on all sides, above, and below. Then focus on your magical patterns coming to fruition.

SOWILO (so-wheel-o)

Sound: "S"

Depiction: One part of the dynamic solar wheel

Runic Position: 2nd *aett*, 8th rune

Original Meaning: The divine solar wheel or the thunderbolt

Key Words: Partnership, journey, power, transformation, understanding

Tree: Juniper

Herb: Mistletoe

Gemstones: Ruby, carnelian, citrine, golden topaz, cat's-eye

Color: Gold

Runic Half-Month: February 12–February 27

Hour of the Day: 3:30 a.m.–4:30 a.m.

Other Names:
The Germanic name: Sugil (Sowilo)
The Norse name: Sol
The Anglo-Saxon name: Sigel
The Icelandic name: Sol
The Norwegian name: Sol
Old Danish: Sulu
Old German: Sil, Sulhil, Sigo

Description: Sowilo symbolized the sun, which in the Northern Tradition was feminine rather than masculine. Also, the eye that Odin kept at Mimir's Well became the sun, whereas the eye he gave up became the moon. Sowilo can be used for education and understanding. In addition, it counterbalances Isa, the cosmic ice, since ice melts into water that can then be used for growing things.

God/Goddess: Sol—Conceived in a union between the Aesir and the giants, the twins Sol (sun) and Mani (moon) became charioteers for Odin. Sol drove the chariot of the sun, which was pulled by the steeds Arvakr (early riser) and Alsvin (quick-footed). The shield of Svalin protected both Sol and the horses from the rays of the solar orb they ferried across the skies. The wolves Skoll and Hati pursued and would catch the sun and moon during Ragnarok (the end of the world). Originally, Sol was the female goddess of the sun, called "the glory of the elves." She brought the healing, warming sunlight.

Power Animals: Cat, wolf, boar, horse, bear, groundhog, blue jay, camel, cock, salamander, bee, cheetah, lizard, peacock, robin, snake

Element: Fire

Numerological Value: 16

Astrology: The Sun

Tarot card: The Sun

Mythology: Sowilo is associated with the god Baldur, who, in an annual ritual with his twin brother Hodur, ruled the light half of the year. Baldur was slain by Hodur, who then ruled over the dark part of the year. This contrast and polarity between the light and dark times of the year is universal among agricultural and nature-driven cultures.

The sun was said to be the eye Odin kept at the well of Mimir. Unlike many other spiritual traditions, the Norse regarded the sun as feminine. This ancient concept springs from the idea that the warmth and light of the sun is what gives life to all organic beings, and no doubt, to all energetic beings. It is only later that the sun was considered masculine and the moon feminine. In this sense, Odin was really both male and female, as he was both moon and sun.

Magical Qualities:
Illuminates and fuels your magical patterns
Develops your psychic abilities
Is aware of your relationships with other people
Moves in the direction of enlightenment
Expands your awareness of the solar cycles
Helps your patterns come to fruition

Galdr Song:
Sowilo, sowilo, sowilo,
S s s s s s s s s s
S s s s o o o o l l l l
Su sa si se so
Sul sal sil sel sol
Us as is es os
So se si sa su
S s s s s s s s s s

Meaning in Divination: Sowilo represents the energy that leads you through the nine worlds of

Yggdrasil. In a practical sense, it is an aspect of the pattern plus an active course that leads to its fruition. While Raidho represents the circular pattern itself, Sowilo symbolizes the fuel that ignites it. All patterns have a circular or spiral nature. A straight line never truly exists because in space all lines curve, and eventually feed into themselves, becoming a circle. Sowilo is the representation of everything coming full circle, thus the fruition and, in turn, the destruction of all patterns. On one hand the sun is the life-giver, but on the other hand, it can burn, parch, and destroy with its light. It is these polarities that give magical patterns form and movement.

Much like Wunjo at the end of the first *aett*, Sowilo is the culmination of the lessons contained in the second *aett*. It is the coming to fruition of your efforts, whether positive or negative. When your goals progress in a positive way, they propel you to the next level, the third *aett*. But if you fail to build a good foundation, everything may come toppling down around you. Each *aett* is a building block to the next, just as each rune moves you to the next. In terms of time, which is what the second *aett* is all about, we have now entered the third millennium, represented by the third *aett.* Sowilo symbolizes the immense prosperity, for example, in the United States, that embodies the end of the second millennium. From one rune to the next, we progress.

The Third *Aett*

The third *aett* is ultimately the *aett* of divinity, ruled by Tyr, the chief god of order and justice, and the Harvest Goddess Zisa, who is honored on September 28. In this third and final *aett*, humankind either becomes divine or descends into the recesses of destruction known as Ragnarok. This means that within every pattern lies the seeds of its successful cultivation or total destruction, depending on the choices made and the paths taken. Energy is always polarizing, constantly changing while trying to remain the same. It is out of this fluctuating environment that patterns are conceived, planned, and enacted.

The first *aett* illustrates the energies of creation, while the second *aett* denotes the basic forces and polarities that affect physical and energetic patterns. The third *aett* embodies the gods and goddesses as divine teachers, for it is they who ultimately teach humans to master the energies and elements of Oneness. In doing so, humankind becomes divine. This birthright, the gaining of complete wisdom and mastery, is what Odin's quest—and the runes—are all about.

Following Odin's runic path, the first rune of the third *aett* is Tiwaz. The T-rune is known as the rune of Tyr, god of law, justice, and war, energies that comprise the masculine polarity. In contrast, the second rune in the third *aett*, Berkana, represented the Mother Goddess, who possessed the traits of beauty, birth, and nurturing. The third rune, Eihwaz, represented the Vanir and the dual polarities of nature. The fourth rune, Mannaz, represented the human energies associated with the Aesir.

At this point the runic journey centers on the elements, beginning first with Laguz, the water rune, symbolizing the water of life that flows as pure energy. The sixth rune of the third *aett* is Ingwaz, the ancient name for the Earth God, signifying mastery over the element of Earth, with its inherent form and structure. The next rune, Dagaz, which is where the word "day" comes from, relates to the element of fire and, as a consequence, the idea of light and its connection with complete wisdom. The last rune of the third *aett*, Othala, named in honor of Odin, is the rune of completion and Oneness, where everything comes together.

The element associated with the Othala rune, and with Odin, is air. In many spiritual traditions mastery over the element of air denoted mastery over all the elements, thus making them one coherent energy that is aligned with your energy. This alignment or synchronization was characterized by the "Orlog." The underlying concept suggested that upon taking the runic journey and merging with its wisdom, in all its wonder, you could become one with Odin. Even Oneness ultimately gains its name from Odin, in the form of "Woden-ness," meaning the infinite whole brought together as One.

TIWAZ (tea-was)

Sound: "T"

Depiction: The point of a spear or arrow, the world column holding up the skies

Runic Position: 3rd *aett*, 1st rune

Original Meaning: The sky gods, the original gods

Key Words: Justice, order, victory, support, self-sacrifice, faith, loyalty

Tree: Oak

Herb: Sage

Gemstones: Ruby, garnet, jasper, bloodstone, golden topaz, citrine

Color: Bright Red

Runic Half-Month: February 27–March 14

Hour of the Day: 4:30 a.m.–5:30 a.m.

Other Names:

The Germanic name: Tys (Tiwaz)

The Norse name: Tyr

The Anglo-Saxon name: Tir, Tiw

The Icelandic name: Tyr

The Norwegian name: Ty

Description: Tiwaz is the oldest name known for Tyr, god of war, law, and justice. Tyr ruled not through intervention, but by providing direction, consistent leadership, and powerful guidance. He sacrificed his hand between the jaws of the Fenris Wolf in order to save his fellow gods from the forces of darkness. From this act, Tiwaz represented self-sacrifice, and thereby was considered the rune of great leaders.

Tiwaz represented Tir, the Pole Star, which was known as Frigga's spindle. Tir kept its faith well, and was always on course. It represented the guiding principles of the universe, which are constant and can be relied upon for judging your position and the direction you are headed in life. Also because of its depiction as an arrow, Tiwaz symbolized a powerful striking force that could be used defensively or offensively. In love magic, this is the symbol of the male, and its energies are strength, power, and direction.

Invocation of this rune brings those masculine energies into play.

God/Goddess: Tyr—The son of Odin and Frigga, he was the god of battle and martial honor. For his fellow Aesir, and in particular Odin, he sacrificed his hand to the Fenris Wolf so that a magical ribbon fashioned by the dwarfs could bind it until Ragnarok, the end of the world. By doing this, Tyr was also the first oath-breaker. Tuesday gets its name from Tyr's Dag, meaning Tyr's day.

Power Animals: Wolf, falcon, hawk, hound, owl, bear

Element: Air

Numerological Value: 17

Astrology: Libra

Tarot card: Justice

Mythology: The Tiwaz-rune was the rune of the god of heaven, Tyr, and the god of mystery, Mithra (MithOdin). Tiwaz is sometimes called Mithra's rune. Tyr was also the god of sacrifice and the patron of warriors, thus making Tiwaz the rune of warriors—in particular, spiritual warriors. Traditionally, warriors scratched Tiwaz on their spear tips and on the hilts of their swords.

The recording of oaths was done on Odin's spear, and violations of those oaths required a swift and destructive response. Swearing allegiance and the bond of kinship on Odin's spear was to hold that vow forever. Breaking an oath incurred the wrath of the gods for all time.

Magical Qualities:
Increases your faith in the universe
Evaluates and judges what needs to be done
Obtains the successful completion of patterns
Builds your spiritual energy
Develops your personal spirituality
Teaches how to use order to your benefit

Galdr Song:
Tiwaz, tiwaz, tiwaz,
T i r
Tu ta ti te to
Tur tar tir ter tor
Ot et it at ut
Tyr
T i r

Meaning in Divination: Tiwaz embodies the mystery of spirituality and faith, according to the divine patterns of Oneness. Representing the male polarity, Tiwaz energy is characterized as being war-like and aggressive. On one side, it represents law and justice, but on the other side it embodies an unemotional energy that can be stern and not very nurturing. This rune energizes defense and outward expansion, in that male energy seeks to defend what it has, while at the same time aggressively pursuing what it doesn't have yet. This aspect of Tiwaz has to do with the energy that traditionally surrounded the hunt. The format or plan would be set, the hounds let loose, and the rider of the runes would bring about the expected results. All the factors—the plan, the quarry, the well-trained hounds, and a fast horse, as well as the ability to ride—were crucial to the success of the hunt.

By looking into the Orlog, you can see the inevitable outcome of your actions. You can pur-posefully influence this outcome by the choices and decisions you make, but you cannot change it. The ways of magic are the same. Your magical goals must conform to basic universal laws in order to wind up anywhere near their intended mark. Use the energy of the T-rune to move your goals forward, particularly when there seems to be a struggle among the energies present.

BERKANA (bur-kan-a)

Sound: "B"

Depiction: The breasts of the Mother Goddess

Runic Position: 3rd *aett*, 2nd rune

Original Meaning: The divine energy of the birch as Earth Mother

Key Words: Nurturing, rebirth, growth, transition, spirit, concealment, protection, ancestry

Tree: Birch

Herb: Lady's mantle

Gemstones: All gemstones

Color: Dark Green

Runic Half-Month: March 14–March 30

Hour of the Day: 5:30 a.m.–6:30 a.m.

Other Names:
The Germanic name: Bercna (Berkano)

The Norse name: Bjarkan
The Anglo-Saxon name: Beroc
The Icelandic name: Bjarkan
The Norwegian name: Bjarkan

Description: Berkana relates to the great Earth Goddess, the mother of all things, embodying the energies of manifestation in the form of birth and rebirth. Traditionally, planting a birch tree in the front yard of your house was said to protect it from harm. Also, birch wood was frequently used in making magic wands, so that when the wand strikes something, it releases and brings to life the energies contained within. Berkana also represents a rebirth of spirit, analogous to the renewal of life in the spring after the winter thaw. In contrast to the male energies of Tiwaz, Berkana represents the down-to-earth, nurturing, sensitive, feminine energies.

Berkana's numerological value, eighteen, is a double nine. Nine is considered the perfect number magically, because it is three threes, or a "triad of triads." Symbolically, nine is the number of completion and new beginnings, on a higher organic level. Doubling nine into eighteen provides the B-rune with even more of this initiating power. Accordingly, in many cultures, at the age of eighteen a person is legally considered an adult.

God/Goddess: Frigga—She was the second wife of Odin, and mother to Baldur, Hodur, Hermod, and usually Tyr. Ancient poems cite that Odin and Frigga had seven sons who founded the seven Saxon kingdoms in England. Tall and stately, the earth and sky goddess Frigga dressed in long white robes that could turn dark just as the sky does in bad weather. The patroness of housewives, she was permitted to share Odin's throne, and she personified the Earth. Through her eleven handmaidens, she ensured the well-being of humankind, helping lovers, presiding over marital love and fidelity, and administering justice. Like Odin, she had an innate vision of the future, a key to the runes.

Holde—She was a complex goddess who served as a counterpart to Frigga. As the sky goddess, Holde was seen riding on the wind—the snow was the feathers from her bed. Wise women were said to "ride with Holde." As the water goddess, at noon she took the form of a beautiful White Lady, and bathed in a lake from which children were born. It was necessary to dive down a well to reach her home. As an earth

goddess, Holde presided over the spinning and cultivation of flax. In this guise, she was a maternal deity,
goddess of the hearth and home, and also a female
leader of the Wild Hunt. Wherever Holde's procession passed, the harvest would double that year.

Power Animals: All animals

Element: Earth

Numerological Value: 18

Astrology: Virgo

Tarot card: The Empress

Mythology: Traditionally, birch trees are consecrated to the god Thor, and symbolize the return of
spring. Also, the brush part of the "besom broom," a
particular kind of broom for witches that is used for
sweeping away unwanted energies, is often made of
birch. In May Day celebrations, the maypole, symbolic of Yggdrasil, is made from the trunk of the
birch tree.

While Freyja symbolized the energy of the maiden,
Frigga represented the energy of the mother, the second phase of the female polarity. Mythologically, this
energy came in the form of the sacred cow,

Audhumla, from whose udder (the breast) sprang forth the sustenance of life.

Holde, the triple goddess of birth, life, and death, embodied all the elements. One of the most complex feminine figures of the Northern Tradition, her image unfortunately has degenerated into that of an ugly hag. It is now being revitalized.

Magical Qualities:
Works with the feminine energies
Understands the forces of transition
Conceals and protects energy
Revitalizes the spirit and personal empowerment
Gathers and directs the powers of earth, air, and
    water
Increases intuitive ability
Perfects magical skills

Galdr Song:
Berkana, berkana, berkana,
Bu ba bi be bo
B e e e e e r r r r r
Burk bark birk berk bork
Ob eb ib ab ub
B e e e e e r r r r r

Meaning in Divination: Berkana's intrinsic quality revolved around the life, death, and rebirth triad, which brought with it transition. As Mother Goddess, Berkana brought life and was the mother of all manifestation, representing the energies of birth and rebirth on a cosmic, as well as a human, level. At the same time, Berkana embodied the opposite polarity—death—the dark aspect of the Mother Goddess. In a shamanic sense, death symbolizes the death of the old self, and rebirth symbolizes the transition into the new. So, Berkana ruled over the four transitory stages: birth, adolescence, marriage, and death. As a result, the B-rune is also the rune of becoming, of fulfilling your potential, and thus evolving on a spiritual level. It may signify new beginnings or the end of a cycle. The B-rune is for laying foundations, and then cultivating them with the nurturing care of the earth, sky, and water goddess. It can be used to really take "holde" of things in your life.

Berkana also conceals and protects, embodying secret or concealing places, such as caves and lodges. In readings, this means that you can use the energy of the rune to protect or conceal yourself from another, but on the flip side, someone may be protecting or concealing something from you.

EHWAZ (ee-waz)

Sound: "E"

Depiction: Two horses facing one another, two upright trees bound together representing the divine twins

Runic Position: 3rd *aett*, 3rd rune

Original Meaning: The equine aspect of the twin gods or heroes

Key Words: Duality, movement, partnership, interaction, harmony

Tree: Oak/Ash

Herb: Ragwort

Gemstones: Milky quartz, diamond, clear quartz, pearl, amber

Color: White

Runic Half-Month: March 30–April 14

Hour of the Day: 6:30 a.m.–7:30 a.m.

Other Names:
The Germanic name: Eys (Ehwaz)
The Norse name: Ehol, Ior
The Anglo-Saxon name: Eoh
The Icelandic name: Eykur
The Norwegian name: Eh, Eol

Description: Ehwaz embodied the energy of the twin gods, who often ruled as polar opposites. Odin, for example, ruled over the warm part of the year, and Uller ruled over the cold part. Ehwaz emphasizes the harmonious interaction of energies within these polarities, rather than their competitive nature. In the same way that the warm and cold polarities move the Earth through the yearly cycle, polarities move energy by their dynamic interplay.

Ehwaz is the horse rune, and the movement generated by the polarities is symbolic of a horse carrying its rider. As the rune of Sleipnir, Odin's swift eight-legged steed, Ehwaz made possible the journey between the worlds of Yggdrasil. In magic, the rune can confer the ability to move between other realms of reality and states of perception. In this way, it connects to the concept of a "fetch," the spiritual horse, so to speak, that carries a person on the journey between worlds. This journey facilitates soul travel through which information and knowledge can be obtained.

God/Goddess: Freyja/Frey—Originally from the Vanir and the children of Njord (the sea god) and his sister, Nerthus (the earth goddess), Freyja and Frey represented the sacred twins. They were siblings and lovers. Legend had it that Frey incarnated on Earth as Fridleef I, King of Denmark in 40 B.C.E. Associated with spring, summer, and the fertile earth, Freyja departed the Earth during autumn and winter, and her leaving caused the leaves to fall and the Earth to don a frigid mourning cloak of snow.

Power Animals: Horse, hound, boar, cat, goat, falcon, hawk, eagle, bear

Element: Earth

Numerological Value: 19

Astrology: Gemini

Tarot card: The Lovers

Mythology: Odin's horse, Sleipnir, was the product of the god Loki and a powerful stallion named

Svadilfari. This union came about when the Aesir hired a stonemason to rebuild Asgard's stone wall, destroyed in the war with the Vanir. The stonemason's price was to marry Freyja and take possession of the sun and the moon. The gods agreed to the price only after Loki assured them that they would never have to pay, because the stonemason would be given only six months to do the job, and he could not possibly finish on time. Near the end of the six months, the gods realized that the stonemason had used the strength of the stallion Svadlifari in order to complete the job promptly. All that was left to be built was the gate! Odin ordered Loki to solve the problem. Loki's solution was to turn himself into a mare and lure Svadilfari away from the wall, but in order to keep the stallion away, Loki had to mate with the beast. In the end, Loki returned to Asgard with the eight-legged colt Sleipnir, which he presented as a gift to Odin, telling him that without question the steed was the fastest ever. It was upon Sleipnir that Hermod later rode to the netherworld of Hel to ask Hella, protectress of the realm, to return Baldur so that he might become a living god again.

Magical Qualities:
Increases magical power and wisdom
Travels to other realms and dimensions of being
Increases lucid dreaming ability
Increases the swiftness of your personal patterns
Works with polarities of energy
Understands the harmony in relationships
Shapeshifts and works with your power animals
Projects the double

Galdr song:
Ehwaz, ehwaz, ehwaz
E e e e h w a a a a a z z z z z
Ehwu ehwa ehwi ehwe ehwo
Ehwo ehwe ehwi ehwa ehwu
E e e e h w a a a a a z z z z z
(Also try the plural form "ehwo.")

Meaning in Divination: This rune represents a journey in consciousness that is protected, supported, or guided. The emphasis here is on partnerships and working together, and often denotes assistance from another person or energetic helper, such as a "fetch" (a spirit double). This relates to the Valkyries, Odin's servants, who escorted the dead and were called "fetch wives."

Ehwaz relates to partnerships and joint ventures of all types. It can unify two people in a strong, harmonious relationship, either on a personal or a business level. Ehwaz is a great rune for marriage, because it emphasizes cooperative interaction between people. Because of its connection with traveling between different realms, Ehwaz represents the astral or energetic body—the part of your being that can be projected outside your physical body. Ehwaz denotes dream power and astral travel.

MANNAZ (man-nawz)

Sound: "M"

Depiction: Bifrost, the bridge between this world and the divine upper world, marriage between deity and human

Runic Position: 3rd *aett*, 4th rune

Original Meaning: The divine ancestor and sky god

Key Words: Godhood and goddesshood, memory, humanity, order, intelligence, ancestors, sacred union

Tree: Holly

Herb: Madder

Gemstones: Bloodstone, ruby, garnet, amber, rainbow tourmaline, smithsonite, amethyst

Color: Rainbow

Runic Half-Month: April 14–April 29

Hour of the Day: 7:30 a.m.–8:30 a.m.

Other Names:
The Germanic name: Manna (Mannaz)
The Norse name: Madr
The Anglo-Saxon name: Mann
The Icelandic name: Madur
The Norwegian name: Madr

Description: Mannaz symbolizes the divine aspect existing in every human being. Inherent in this is the idea that humankind is the product of divine energy, with the power of intelligence, reason, memory, and tradition. Mannaz represents humankind and all the qualities that make us human, from our earliest ancestors to our progenitors.

God/Goddess: Heimdall—God of dawn and light, the son of Odin and nine giant sisters, he was the divine sentry of the rainbow bridge. Heimdall was born on the horizon, and then nurtured by the strength of the Earth, the warmth of the sun, and the moisture of the sea. As Rig, he visited Earth and entered three homes, and after each visit a son was born. Their names were Thrall, Carl, and Earl and they represented the three classes of people: slaves, free-persons, and nobles.

Odin—He and his two brothers, Vili and Ve (Hoenir and Lodur), gave life to the first humans. Foremost father of the Aesir, Odin was ruler of the Aesir and Midgard. He was the son of the god Bor and the giantess Bestla, and grandson of Buri, the first god; Buri was released from the primeval ice when Audhumla (the cow) licked the ice. Odin gave the breath of life called "Ond," which is the divine spark in humankind and the all-pervasive energy that penetrates and animates everything. Known by over two hundred names, Odin was the wisest and most famous of all the gods.

Power Animals: Wolf, raven, eagle, hound, cow, horse, fly, bear, salmon

Element: Air

Numerological Value: 20

Astrology: Jupiter

Tarot card: The Magician

Mythology: Cosmologically, Mannaz represents the evolving human intelligence. It is the symbol of the god Heimdall, the genetic link between the gods and goddesses and humankind and guardian of Bifrost, the rainbow bridge. In the poem "Rigsthula," in the *Elder Edda*, Rig (Heimdall) brought forth the three levels of social structure: the provider, the warrior, and the priest-king.

Mannaz is the name of a tribal god who was the ancestor of all Germanic people, closely akin to the Celtic God Manannan. Mannaz in turn had three sons—Ingvio, Irmio, and Istio—who gave their names to the three main branches of the West Germanic tribes. In mythological terms, this was analogous to the creation of the three levels of social structure.

Magical Qualities:

Increases mental powers such as knowledge, memory, and wisdom

Perceives the divine and human nature in yourself and others

Works with the social order to perpetuate your patterns

Understands the polarities of personality

Accesses ancestral memory

Understands the concept of incarnation

Galdr Song:

Mannaz, mannaz, mannaz,
M m m m a a a a a n n n n n
Mu ma mi me mo
Mun man min men mon
Um am im em om
Mon men min man mun
M m m m m m a a a a a n n n n n
M m m m m m m m m m

Meaning in Divination: In its perfect state, Mannaz symbolizes the complete human being, one who integrates the wisdom of the runes with the self. Considered a double Wunjo, the rune is associated with perfection and the conscious application of the individual's will. It embodies the idea of this will being directed toward the common good of a entire group.

People are the main influence and focus in the M-rune. It stands for the social order and shows how, through this order, you can achieve your full potential on a human and divine level of being. Understanding this order is essential to creating positive and successful life patterns. When Mannaz comes up in a reading, it can indicate legal affairs and matters of mutual cooperation. The negative polarity can point to a potential enemy or someone who is hindering or undermining you. In addition, Mannaz may indicate worry about your social status, or getting caught up in social hierarchies, such as peer or political groups.

LAGUZ (la-gooz)

Sound: "L"

Depiction: The quick-growing green portion of a leek or a wave of water

Runic Position: 3rd *aett*, 5th rune

Original Meaning: Signifies life energy and organic growth

Key Words: Fluidity, life force, birth

Tree: Willow

Herb: Leek

Gemstones: Aquamarine, azurite, calcite, chrysocolla, fluorite

Color: Deep blue-green

Runic Half-Month: April 29–May 14

Hour of the Day: 8:30 a.m.–9:30 a.m.

Other Names:

The Germanic name: Laaz (Laguz)
The Norse name: Lögr
The Anglo-Saxon name: Lagu
The Icelandic name: Lögur
The Norwegian name: Laukr

Description: The meaning behind Laguz relates to the leek, a hardy and vigorous vegetable. From this association with the leek comes the idea that Laguz embodies the energy that makes living things live, including the source of this life. Contained within this concept are the natural laws and primal forces of life as well as the opposite polarity—death or the cessation of life on this earthly plane.

The L-rune represents fluidity, and is associated with the power of the ocean tides and the force of rivers and waterfalls. Its energy is one of going with the flow, because to struggle with it is to drown in its depths. Most of the human body is made up of water, and water is an element that we require on a regular basis for survival.

God/Goddess: Njord—Father of Frey and Freyja, Njord was the god of the sea and winds, of summer, and calm, friendly weather. He was handsome and usually dressed in a green tunic. At his seaside palace, Noatun, he calmed the ocean storms called up by Aegir, the angry sea god. Swans were sacred to Njord because they first appeared each year at the beginning of summer. Seals were also his favorites because of their playfulness. The sponge is called Njord's glove.

Ran—In contrast to Njord, she is called "the robber," and is the goddess of the stormy sea and the drowned. To drown was to go to Ran, and the wise carried gold on a sea voyage to appease her, just in case the ship went down. Wife to Aegir, Ran had nine giant daughters, the nine waves, called "the claws of Ran." Together, Ran, Aegir, and their nine daughters dragged ships down into the depths of the ocean. On the other hand, Ran could steady any seafaring vessel with one hand. In her mermaid form, she was seen combing her long hair as she reclined on the shore.

Power Animals: Swan, seal, sea gull, duck, whale, dolphin, otter, beaver

Element: Water

Numerological Value: 21

Astrology: Waxing Moon

Tarot card: The Star

Mythology: Laguz represented the primal waters in Nifelheim, which contained the dormant yeast of life. When the yeast became solidified by ice and then energized by the fire of Muspelheim, the potential for life became realized. From water come the basic ingredients for life. Laguz represents the source from which all rivers of energy flow into the ocean, which in this case is Oneness.

In its Old Norse form of *logr*, meaning "sorcery," this rune relates to the goddess Freyja, who introduced the practice of magic to the Aesir when she went to live with them in Asgard. In particular she taught Odin *seidr*, a type of love magic that had previously been practiced only by women.

Magical Qualities:
Increases your living spark by your becoming aware of it
Tunes into the watery flow of life
Becomes familiar with the energies of life and death
Increases the flow of your personal patterns

Understands and integrates your emotions and
  desires
Immerses you in divine knowledge
Washes away negative energies and unwanted patterns

Galdr Song:
Laguz, laguz, laguz,
L l l l l l l l l l
Lu la li le lo
Lug lag lig leg log
Ul al il el ol
Lo le li la lu
L l l l l a a a a a g u u u u u
L l l l l l l l l l

Meaning in Divination: Tied to birth, Laguz is a
potent rune for initiation. It was a Norse tradition to
sprinkle newborn babies with water to show their
worthiness for life. Symbolic of the seed as it meets
water and begins the life process, this rune is also tied
to the leek, an organic entity that links the white
under part with the green upper part. It is a symbol
of the expansion of life in both physical and spiritual
realms, and Laguz is the planting of energetic patterns that sprout quickly from the Earth. Middle

Earth is the third aspect in this triad, which as a whole denotes the fluidity of the life force. From the concept of the river, we understand that everything is connected to the whole, and that within the whole everything is relative.

Also connected to this concept are the tides, which energetically move inward and outward, rising and ebbing on a daily basis. The tides reflect energy's natural flow in an up-and-down, back-and-forth motion that is universal. It is important to remember that, when you practice magic, you need to account for this ebb and flow of energy as it moves back and forth between negative and positive poles. The idea is to accentuate the positive flow while minimizing the negative.

INGWAZ (ing-was)

Sound: "I"

Depiction: A diamond

Runic Position: 3rd *aett*, 6th rune

Original Meaning: The Earth God

Key Words: Energy, gestation, integration, male fertility, protection, castration

Tree: Apple

Herb: Self-heal

Gemstones: Malachite, rose quartz, citrine, golden topaz, aventurine, amber, chrysoprase

Color: Yellow

Runic Half-Month: May 14–June 14

Hour of the Day: 9:30 a.m.–10:30 a.m.

Other Names:
The Germanic name: Enguz (Ingwaz)
The Norse name: Ing, Ingvarr

The Anglo-Saxon name: Ing
The Icelandic name: Ing
The Norwegian name: Ing

Description: Ingwaz symbolizes energy, in particular the channeling of potential energy by bringing it together and integrating the separate elements.

Ingwaz denotes the completion of a pattern or its transition to the next stage. In this form, it is also a fertility rune and connected with initiation, a rebirth that can happen on one or many different levels, including the physical, perceptual, energetic, and spiritual.

God/Goddess: Ing—Ingvio or Yngvi are other names for Frey, the god of sunshine. Ing is also the name of an ancient Germanic Earth God, who is an earlier incarnation of Frey, also the god of fertility and consort-priest to the Earth Goddess. The first of the East Danes to contact the Norse, he is considered the father of all the tribes along the North Sea. These tribes are called the Ingvaeons, which means "those of Ing."

Nerthus—Worshipped by the Danes, she was a goddess of fertility and fruitfulness, who kept a basket in her lap filled with all good things. After she roamed the land, riding on a cart pulled by cows and accompanied by her priest, she returned to her lake sanctuary. There the cart, cows, and the goddess were bathed in the sacred lake by her attendants. These attendants disappeared (and were perhaps purposely drowned) in the lake afterward. Interestingly, Nerthus became Njord in later tales and father to Frey, not only changing names but also gender. A double twist is that some say that Ingun (a form of Ing) is Frey's and Freyja's mother! Later in history, Nerthus was transformed into Freyja.

Power Animals: Cow, goat, horse, ox, dove, bee

Element: Earth

Numerological Value: 22

Astrology: The dark moon

Tarot card: Judgment

Mythology: Similar to Tiwaz, Ingwaz represents a god with the same name, who was the male consort of the Earth Goddess, associated with the rune Berkana. Ingwaz is the old German Earth God of male fertility, the house hearth, and the inglenook (a nook by a large, open fireplace). The rune symbolizes the protection of households. The Ing legend is considered the most ancient of all clues in the death-journey or otherworld-journey.

One of the god Frey's more ancient names was Yngvi or Ing. He was known for taking part in ritual processions and fertility rites of the Ing-Nerthus cult, in which he rode in a wagon. Legend has it that this god of fertility and conquering arrived mysteriously in a ship out of the unknown, stayed long enough to establish a ruling race, and departed just as suddenly and mysteriously over the sea waves.

In the Norse tradition, it was often the women who conducted rites involving sexuality. The Ingwaz-rune is related to the experience of women in the old Nerthus cult, which dealt with the mystery of fecundity and birth. During the spring, the fertile season, the women acted out Ing or Nerthus bringing his carriage from the spiritual world to Earth, traveling across the land, and leaving in the carriage's trail a more fertile Earth. This is the sexual energy of May, symbolizing the proverbial "birds and bees." (Later the Goddess Freyja assumed the role of Ing and Nerthus.)

Magical Qualities:
Useful as a sacred enclosure for magic

Learns the nature of diverse energies

Understands the forces of change, which bring initiation and transition

Understands fertility in terms of complete patterns

Learns to channel energies together into a single, focused intent

Love and sex magic

Galdr Song:
Ingwaz, ingwaz, ingwaz,
I i i i i n n n n n g g g g g
Ung ang ing eng ong
Ong eng ing ang ung
I i i i i n n n n n g g g g g

Meaning in Divination: Although powerful, Ingwaz does not release energy immediately, but instead builds it up and releases it in a single burst, much like the male ejaculation. In ritual this takes place when everyone in the group channels his/her energy toward one intention. The more energy you have to channel, the greater the thrust of energy toward that intention. The more energy you move toward an outcome, the more likely it is that the outcome will be realized, which is why this rune is associated with fertility.

DAGAZ (da-gauze or thaw-gauze)

Sound: "D" or "TH" (voiced)

Depiction: The balance between night and day

Runic Position: 3rd *aett*, 7th rune

Original Meaning: The light of the day

Key Words: Light, enlightenment, polarity, awakening, intuition, well-being

Tree: Spruce

Herb: Clary sage

Gemstones: Lapis lazuli, sodalite, amazonite, azurite, blue zircon, sapphire

Color: Blue

Runic Half-Month: May 29–June 14

Hour of the Day: 10:30 a.m.–11:30 a.m.

Other Names:
The Germanic name: Daaz (Dagaz)

The Norse name: Dagr
The Anglo-Saxon name: Daeg
The Icelandic name: Dagur
The Norwegian name: Dagr

Description: Dagaz means "day," and depicts the interplay and balance between polarities—light and darkness in particular. Dagaz is also the rune of midday (noon) and midsummer (summer solstice), both representing times when the light of the sun is at its height. Metaphysically, these are times of power, strength of mind, and well-being.

As the light of day, Dagaz also represents the moments of sunrise (dawn) and sunset (twilight), and in this context it is the rune of total awakening. What is awakened is the light within yourself, which then becomes one with the light around you. In magic, dawn, noon, and sunset are considered power times—times when the portals between worlds open for an instant, and then close again.

God/Goddess: Odin—The all-seeing, all-knowing, enlightened inventor of the arts, Odin traveled to all Nine Worlds of the Yggdrasil. He was a potent magician, sorcerer, and healer, as well as the forefather of most of the noble families of the north. His son was Baldur, the light. His watch-wolves, Geri and Freki, were always at his feet. Wolves are predators that often hunt at Dagaz times—dawn and dusk— when the light is dim and prey are at a disadvantage.

Power Animals: Wolf, raven, horse, eagle, bear

Element: Fire

Numerological Value: 23

Astrology: The waxing and waning moon

Tarot card: Temperance

Mythology: Dagaz relates to *dvergar*, which are the dwarfs, formed from the maggots and worms in the flesh of Ymir, the giant. The dwarfs, who are less powerful than the Aesir, but more intelligent than humans, live in the lower world of Svartalfheim, which means "dark elf home." Depicted with dark skin, long beards, green eyes, and a short stocky build, dwarfs had caps and cloaks that could make them invisible at will. Related to the dark–light polarity of the Dagaz rune, dwarfs could not come out during daylight because if they did, the light would turn them to stone.

In the "Lay of Alviss," the underground dwarf asks

for the hand of Thor's daughter Thrud. Thor puts thirteen questions to Alviss that he must answer in order to win Thrud: what is the name of the world, sky, moon, sun, clouds, wind, calm, fire, sea, trees, night, wheat, and beer—in all the worlds of the Aesir, Vanir, giants, dwarfs, and elves. Alviss knew the answers to all the questions, but answering them occupied so much time that the sun had already entered the room. Alviss had to run out in a hurry or be turned to stone.

The polar opposite of Svartalfheim is Alfheim, which lay between Asgard and Midgard, the land of the white (or light) elves. This land represents the bright aspect of Dagaz. Frey, the sun god, was the lord of Alfheim. Often coming to the aid of the Aesir and Vanir against their enemies, the elves could enter Midgard any time they desired. Gentle and kind, with no ill will or greed, and as light as air itself, they possessed supernatural powers and were considered divine helpers.

Magical Qualities:
Understands the powers of darkness and light
Uses the sun's fire to fuel magical patterns
Knows how to move through the dark without fear

Merges with the cycle of light
Spiritual enlightenment

Galdr Song:
Dagaz, dagaz, dagaz,
Dh dh dh dh dh dh dh dh dh dh
D a a a a a a g a a a a z z z z
Du da di de do
Dh dh dh dh dh
Odh edh idh adh udh
Od ed id ad ud
D a a a a a a g a a a a z z z z

Meaning in Divination: Dagaz embodies the ritual fire of the hearth and the mystical light that can be used in magic. The Dagaz rune is related to daylight and is the rune of divine light. Pulling the D-rune can indicate a need for protection from people doing negative work against you.

Dagaz refers to that shamanic state in which polarities of energy come together—"the razor's edge." This may be a time of enlightenment and awakening. It means not only the harnessing of the powerful fire energy that gets things done, but the wisdom to best use these energies. Fire energy can get things done or really burn things up. When used with wisdom, it can help your plans come to fruition, in much the same way that the sun provides the sustenance, the flame, that sustains all life. The more sunlight, the more life: the ratio is proportional. There is a saying that the branch the sun shines on most bears the most fruit. In this context, the Dagaz rune may indicate a need to get outside into the sunshine, to energize yourself so that your life can become more fruitful.

OTHALA (oath-awe-la)

Sound: "O"

Depiction: The womb and legs of the goddess standing

Runic Position: 3rd *aett*, 8th rune

Original Meaning: Immobile property associated with heredity

Key Words: Ancestry, prosperity, inheritance, DNA, family

Tree: Hawthorn

Herb: Gold thread

Gemstones: Diamond, emerald, ruby, clear quartz, amber

Color: Deep yellow

Runic Half-Month: June 14–June 29

Hour of the Day: 11:30 a.m.–12:30 p.m.

Other Names:
The Germanic name: Utal (Othala)
The Norse name: Odal
The Anglo-Saxon name: Otael (Ethel)
The Icelandic name: Odal
The Norwegian name: Odal

Description: Othala symbolizes the sacred land, including the interaction and bond that people have with the land. The people of northeastern Germany and the Netherlands called this rune "Eeyeneerde," meaning "own earth" or "own land." By comparison, Othala refers to ancestral heritage in the form of family, clan, and tribal land. Early Europeans perceived land as wealth that was never sold, but instead was handed down from generation to generation. Also, as each successive generation died and was buried, in many ways its energy returned to the Earth. This vitalized the Earth with ancestral power that could be called upon by future generations in time of need. This is analogous to the concept of the "sleeping king" or "sleeper"—a great leader who sleeps within the land, often in a mountain or cave, waiting for the time when he is awakened to come to the aid of humankind.

Fehu is wealth that you can trade and sell, whereas Othala represents wealth that is immobile and can be neither sold nor given away. Like the wealth of information coded in human DNA, Othala influences every aspect of your being. It symbolizes the sovereignty of the land.

God/Goddess: Odin—Odin was the All father who was procreator, the original couple, and the energies of Oneness. At some point Odin was all things and, as all things, he was both male and female. It was not until later that he became a male god.

Power Animals: Eagle, wolf, raven, bear, hound, sheep, cow, swine, cock, hen, horse, bee, salmon, peacock, ibis, octopus, owl

Element: Air, the mastery of all elements

Numerological Value: 24

Astrology: The full moon

Tarot card: The Moon

Mythology: The oldest literal meaning of Othala is "noble" or "prince," denoting regal status. Odin is the god of Othala as he quests for all wisdom. This is the ultimate quest because, as with the grail cup, it offers the possibility of everlasting immortality. When you understand and come to know the polarities of Oneness, you can control the powers of life and death. But as Odin found out, you cannot change the Orlog.

Othala represented either Odin's final destruction at the hands of the Fenris Wolf, or his ascension into the divine state of being all things at all times. Othala is the moment and place when all the elements of Oneness are reconciled and balanced, and if your magic has endurance, you reach your intention and actualize your dreams. If you aim for divinity, then divine is what you will become: action follows thought.

Magical Qualities:
Understands the implications of the whole
The wisdom and integration of all things
Uses the lessons of the past to better deal with the
    future
Is at one with the source of everything
Works with the elements of the sacred land
Communicates with the sleepers
Achieves goddesshood or godhood
Increases your lucid dreaming ability

Galdr Song:
Othala, othala, othala
O o o o o o o o o o
O o o o o
Othul othal othil othel othol
Othol othel othil othal othul
O o o o o

Meaning in Divination: The O-rune is the rune of Oneness. Tap into Oneness and you tap into everything, by virtue of the fact that everything is connected together into one giant web. Oddly enough, the Internet could be called a representation of Othala, because it shows the interconnectedness of everything as it moves in the whole of Oneness. When you experience Oneness or, as the Norse might say, "Wodan-ness," you have wisdom about everything that was, will be, and is. Energy is always on a one-to-one ratio, for this is the essence of the Orlog, the energy that brings everything together into One. Orlog also begins with the letter "O."

When you reach the state of Othala, your desires manifest according to your intention, and you become wise like Odin. Othala may represent everything coming to divine fruition or, on the other pole, being completely destroyed, as in Ragnarok. It is all or nothing as the third *aett* closes, in what can only be termed the divine forces of Oneness. If you travel wisely through the runic stream, you become one with everything and become a divine being. If you resist the Orlog and refuse to heed the wisdom of the runes, you go down in a hail of destruction, to rise once again in the primal fire of Fehu. All paths hopefully lead you to the divine state of affinity with Oneness, at which level anything is possible. Be careful what you dream, because it will become reality.

PART 3

Traditional Runic Practices

Runes of Tradition

Nine mighty songs I learned from the great
son of Bale-thorn, Bestla's sire;
I drank a measure of the wondrous Mead,
with the Soulstirrer's drops I was showered.

Ere long I bare fruit, and throve full well,
I grew and waxed in wisdom;
word following word, I found me words,
deed following deed, I wrought deeds.

Hidden Runes shalt thou seek and interpreted
   signs,
many symbols of might and power,
by the great Singer painted, by the high Powers
   fashioned,

graved by the Utterer of gods.
For gods graved Odin, for elves graved Dain,
Dvalin the Dallier for dwarfs,
All-wise for Jotuns, and I, of myself,
graved some for the sons of men.

Dost know how to write, dost know how to read,
dost know how to paint, dost know how to prove,
dost know how to ask, dost know how to offer,
dost know how to send, dost know how to spend?

The ancient Norse poem "Havamal" (translated by Olive Bray) is from the *Elder* or *Poetic Edda*. Considered the words of Odin the High One, this poem explains the purpose of eighteen different runes in such a cryptic way that rune users still disagree about the true meaning of the verses. What is clear in the verses is that the only way to fully access the power of the runes is to know how to write, read, paint (redden), and prove them, as well as ask, offer, send, and spend them.

Runes belong to the Northern Tradition, which encompasses the Norse, Germanic, and Celtic peoples. The first uses of runic symbols were for magic and divination; they were, for example, carved on magical wands called *gandrs*. The ancients carved runic letters into wood, stone, metal, and bone, and used these sacred symbols as family marks and hex signs on wooden caskets, grave markers, and gravestones, and as protective amulets and talismans. The letters were also used as decorative and symbolic art. Some sixth-century coins, for example, bear runic inscriptions.

Special writing boards, called *vaxapjalds*, were used for writing runes. These boards, found at the Hopperstad stave church in Norway, were written about in the sagas. The *vaxapjald* was a hand-held writing board. One of its surfaces was covered in wax. The runes were cut into the wax, but could be erased by smoothing out the wax surface before writing a new message on the board.

Before printing presses, runes were also carved on wooden calendars known as *rimstocks*. Wooden rune staves were used on two kinds of "clog" almanacs. Important days of the year, names of visitors, new births, and other vital information were all cut into a flat, square almanac, which was hung next to the fireplace.

Warriors cut the Tiwaz rune on their sword hilts, blades, and scabbards to empower them. They invoked the Norse god of victory, Tyr, while cutting the runes onto the sword's hilt and guard. Like swords, spears were sacred to Tyr and also were given names. The runes were inlaid in spear mounts as well as on shield heads. A warrior's weapons were considered divine gifts, and they were buried alongside the warrior for his protection in the next world.

Eventually, the runic symbols were put to everyday use—in writing, decoration, record-keeping, and business. They were used as a stamp of ownership on personal property, such as houses, trade goods, wagons, livestock, cutlery, and jewelry, and woven into tapestries and rugs. In addition to being branded, clipped, or painted onto animals, runes were cut into the beaks and feet of domestic birds such as geese and ducks. Wooden runic tags were fastened onto sacks or painted on merchants' goods to identify them. Other examples of objects that bear runic descriptions are hair combs, saddle buckles, musical instruments, as well as carts and boats.

The most widespread use of runes across Europe were as "hof" marks, symbols for specific groups. These are still used today as trademarks and family signs. By adding marks such as dots, small circles, or double crosses next to the original mark, the personal marks of other family members could be created. This made it possible to identify individual property within the family group. Unlike heraldry, personal marks were not maintained by law, but were a matter of personal choice.

Buildings with Runes

The Vikings traveled to many foreign countries, carrying the runes with them. Because of this, runes are found in buildings throughout the world. They are inscribed on crosses and used to decorate stained-glass windows. Freemasons used rune-based symbols as their personal marks on churches, castles, and bridges in Central Europe.

Patterns in timber-framed buildings throughout Europe often contain runes, in an attempt to tap into and harness their energies. This building method is still employed, primarily because it has proved so durable and structurally sound. The runes commonly used for spiritual house protection are Ingwaz, Dagaz, Othala, Gebo, and Jera. They are found in contrasting brickwork and roof tiles, carved or painted on the outsides of buildings, and cut into ceiling rafters. Dagaz, Othala, and Jera appear on window and door frames. Ingwaz, Othala, Jera, and Gebo are used in walls, while structural frames are marked with Ingwaz or Gebo. Ingwaz is often depicted with a six-petaled flower pattern carved in its center, symbolizing the Midnight Sun at midsummer, when the powers of light prevail over the powers of darkness. Iron wall anchors that tied walls to structural beams were made in the shape of the protective Eihwaz and Gebo runes. Iron nails symbolized the power of the Norse thunder god, Thor.

Runes can also be seen elsewhere in buildings. For example, the straw and reed thatching in roofs in English cottages and houses sometimes integrate runes into their pattern. In the United States, the Pennsylvania Dutch hex signs are of runic origin. They decorate buildings and barns across the countryside. Customarily, each building has seven hex signs to protect it from harm.

Runes As Alphabets

For thousands of years, people have used signs to represent objects, feelings, and actions. A series of lines painted in red ochre on the front of a mammoth skull dating back 14,000 years resembles runic and alphabetic characters. In Europe, 7,000 years ago rock carvings included pre-runic symbols that may have had the same meaning as later runes, such as the cross and the solar wheel.

Alphabets stem from ancient rock carvings and picture-writing but, unlike runes, they are used to represent language sounds, not energies. For example, in Greek mythology, Hermes, the messenger god, was inspired to create the alphabet after seeing a flock of cranes flying. He realized that their different shapes could be arranged to represent sounds. Unfortunately, while the phonetic values of letters have remained intact, their original magical sound associations have been lost.

Like other Western alphabets, such as the Greek alphabet, the runes were given to humankind by the gods. It was the god Odin who gave the runes to people for the first time. He gave them to us so that we would have a means of communicating with the divine—the divine within and without. Each rune has a name that is a meaningful word, and usually the name begins with the sound that the rune represents. In this way the rune, its name, and its phonetic value are all intimately connected.

Runes have several layers or levels of personal as

well as universal meaning. Their depth of meaning can only be truly appreciated by using them. Because of this, runes match—and in some ways—outdistance, the Hebrew, Enochian, Greek, and Phoenician as one of the great esoteric alphabets of the world, even though they were not designed in an alpha format. Every runic letter is a storehouse of knowledge and meaning that can be written by anyone, but its energies can be fully understood and accessed only by those who study them. They represent the fundamental structure of creation, life, death, and rebirth.

The oldest name written in runic script, "Blithgund," was found on a weaving implement. By the third century, the runic alphabet was the only one used in Scandinavia. However, it fell out of use in middle Europe with the expansion of Christianity thanks to the legally enforced preference for Latin. It is interesting that as late as 1611, though people were persecuted and put to death by Christians for using runes, there were still attempts to get runes adopted as the official alphabet of Sweden. Runic tradition has been impossible to destroy, and recently there has been a resurgence of interest in the runes and their magical uses.

Arranged in rows, runes are unlike alphabets in

that they don't follow an alphabetical sequence. Rune rows are called "futharks" because they begin with the runes Fehu, Uruz, Thurisaz, Ansuz, Raidho, and Kenaz—"F," "U," "TH," "A," "R," "K." The oldest-known full rune row, the Elder Futhark, is considered the most powerful of all rune rows. This is the rune row that provides the basis for this book. Like the Greek alphabet, the Elder Futhark has 24 runes in a specific sequence.

Other rune rows have more or fewer runes in them, but are still ordered according to the *aettir*. For example, the Frisian Futhark, frequently used for magic, has 28 runes. The Anglo-Saxon Futhark has 29 runes, while the Northumbrian Futhark has 33 runes divided into four *aettir*, plus a final rune, "Gar." During the eighth century, the Younger Futhark, with its 16 runes, emerged from Scandinavia. The Danish Futhark and Swedish-Norse Futhark were adapted from the Younger Futhark. Mixed runes, Gothic runes, dotted runes, and Armanen runes are futher rune row variations.

As you can see, runes have evolved over time. By the thirteenth century, they were being written on parchment by scribes, and the runic shapes became more rounded. The runic system has a dynamic and evolving nature, and its archetypes are constantly being expressed in fresh ways. This makes perfect sense when you consider that runes are visible representations of the innate energies in life and the cosmos.

Writing Runes

If you don't already have a personal mark, choose a couple of favorite runes, and draw them together. Then add a couple of other symbols and one of your initials. Using this mark on your personal property to designate ownership will also empower the object. You can use the runes that spell out your name as personal power symbols. They are your birthright. Check the meanings of the runes in your name to get in touch with the runic energies present in it. You can write your name in runes on personal property, scratch the symbols on the underside of your automobile, use them as house marks, embroider them into a sampler or quilt, trace them on a fogged window, and even write them on the beach in the sand. Use your imagination, for their uses are limitless.

One way to improve your knowledge of the runes and the words that stem from them is to choose a word in English that derives from the runes, for example, "gift" from Gebo, "lake" from Laguz, "ride" from Raidho, or "day" from Dagaz. Take a few minutes to think about how the word relates to your own life. For instance, if you examine "day" from Dagaz, ask yourself if you are a day or night person. What do you do with your days? What do dawn (daybreak), day time, and dusk (day's end) hold for you? Are some days of the week better than others? This practice connects you even more with the energies of the runes.

The following list of alphabetical correspondences can be used as a handy reference guide when writing with runes. Keep in mind that it is sometimes best to go with the sound rather than the literal correspondence. Let your intuition guide you.

Alphabetical Correspondences to the Elder Futhark

A–Ansuz

B–Berkana

C–Kenaz

D–Dagaz

E–Ehwaz

F–Fehu

G–Gebo

H–Hagalaz

I–Isa or Eihwaz

J–Jera or Isa

K–Kenaz

L–Laguz

M–Mannaz

N–Naudhiz

NG–Ingwaz U–Uruz
O–Othala V–Wunjo or Uruz
P–Perdhro W–Wunjo
Q–Kenaz X–Kenaz plus Sowilo
R–Raidho Y–Jera
S–Sowilo Z–Algiz or Sowilo
T–Tiwaz Final E, Z, or R–Algiz
TH–Thurisaz and Dagaz

Runes are never written using lowercase letters—only uppercase, and no curves, only straight lines. This makes them very easy to learn and write. For instance, my son learned how to write rune symbols at the same time he learned the alphabet, yet he mastered the runes more quickly.

The runes are often written as a continuous link of text, without spaces between the words or sentences. To separate words or sentences from each other, use notations such as one, two, or three dots or a small Gebo "X."

Runes can also be written in every direction—right to left or left to right. For example, "you" could be written as ⟨runes⟩ or as ⟨runes⟩.

They can be written with the first sentence proceeding right to left, and the second sentence proceeding left to right. Sometimes runes are written as a mirror image, upside down, in vertical rows, or bound together.

For example, SOL could be ⚡ or ⚡ .

ULF could be ᚢᚠ or ᚠᚢ .

Runes can also be cut or written on just about anything. For example, you can carve runes into stone by cutting many points close together, until you have a complete line. A chisel and hammer, preferably consecrated, work well for this purpose.

Secret Runes

Blessed with the most complex cryptology of any ancient writing system because they were used for magic, and also because they were against the law in many places due to political and religious pressures, runes were often written in code. This secrecy also prevented others from altering the inscription, and thereby the magical effect. In fact, writing runes in code is so effective that there are still several cryptic stones in Scandinavia yet to be deciphered.

One group of coded runes that is considered to possess powerful magic is called wendrunes. These runes are written backward, from right to left, with their shapes reversed. Runes written upside down are also called wendrunes.

Other codes substitute one letter for another by shifting the entire alphabet one rune in either direction. This creates a row of seemingly meaningless letters, and it can be used to encode a person's name. You can substitute runic characters in many ways, either rune by rune or in rune groups.

Code sticks were the key to deciphering secret runes. They were frequently used to exchange coded messages. These sticks are similar to the sett-sticks of the plaid weavers of Scotland that encode the tartan colors of the clans.

Number symbols are another simple way to write runes in code. If you number the Elder Futhark 1 through 24, you can use the number rather than the letter for writing messages. For example, the word "rune" would be encoded as "5, 2, 10, 19." You can shift one letter in either direction to make this method more complex, or you can reverse the numbering sequence, making Othala number 1 and Fehu number 24.

Another encryption method, called Lonnrunor, which means secret runes, is still employed today. Using numbers to represent the runes of the Elder Futhark, their *aett*, and position within the *aett*, Lonnrunor offers more flexibility because it allows for a two-tier numbering system. First the *aettir* are numbered: The upper row, first *aett*, ruled by Freyja and Frey, is numbered 1; the middle row, second *aett*, ruled by Heimdall and Mordgud, is numbered 2; and the lower row, third *aett*, ruled by Tyr and Zisa, is numbered 3. Next, the runes are numbered consecutively 1–8 within their respective *aettir*. In this Lonnrunor method, the name "Sirona" would be written as: 2:8, 2:3, 1:5, 3:8, 2:2, 1:4. You could also reverse the *aettir* in Lonnrunor, numbering the first *aett* as 3 and the third *aett* as 1. The second *aett* would remain number 2 in this variation. To make secret runes even harder to decipher, the rune numbers can also be reversed or changed within the three *aettir*.

Secret runes encoded in Lonnrunor are usually written on branch runes, which are upright staves with side branches or twigs that point upward. On one side of the stave, the branch number corresponds to the *aett* number. On the other side of the stave, the number of branches corresponds to the number of the individual rune in that *aett*. A stave with three branches to the left and six branches to the right refers to the sixth rune of the third *aett* (Ingwaz in the Elder Futhark). To further hide the meaning in branch runes, twigs or branches were added in odd places, or parts of a rune were omitted, such as the bottom or top of the rune.

While the side branches on branch runes point upward, hook runes ("hahalrunar") point downward, but the principle is exactly the same. Tent runes ("tjaldrunar") correspond to *aett* and rune number, but are based on an X-shape, without the vertical stave. The lines that correspond to the *aett* and rune are written on the legs and arms of the "X." Tent runes are read sunwise (clockwise), from left to right. "Iis" runes are made up of unconnected single lines, short ones to denote the *aett* number and long ones to signify the rune within the *aett*. The "Lagu" runes are exactly the same as the "Iis" runes, but use the Laguz rune in place of single lines. Other secret runic code systems use combinations or groups of dots and lines, and alternate short and long lines attached to an upright stave, similar to the Irish Ogham tree alphabet.

The runic code practice called "klopruna" uses sounds in numerical groups corresponding to the *aett* and rune in the same way as Lonnrunor codes use numbers. Kloprunes, a binary alphabet that was the forerunner of Morse Code, were sent by knocking on walls, clapping hands, or using drums, bells, and whistling over long distances. In ancient and medieval times, hunters sent kloprune messages with horns. Candles, flaming torches, and flashlight beams were also used to send secret kloprune messages at night. Lights were shown in groups on either side of a board, with those on one side corresponding to the *aett* and those on the other side corresponding to the rune within the *aett*. Lighted kloprunes were used to send signals at night to ships.

You can learn to send kloprunes to a partner. First, decide on the runic code you will be using. Next, select a simple word that you will be sending in kloprunes, and write it down on a sheet of paper. You can spell out anything but, to begin with, select something short and easy to send. Position the sheet so that only you can see it as you send the runes by clapping hands, knocking on wood, or whistling. Duration, sequence, and volume are all important, since each rune is designated by a series of sounds, long or short and loud or soft. Ask your partner to write down the kloprunes as you send them. After you finish sending the runes, see how closely the word on your sheet matches the word your partner has written down. Remember, you can create runic shortcuts by using certain runes as abbreviations, for example, Mannaz as an abbreviation for human, Gebo for gift, or Dagaz for day. You will find that your kloprune skills greatly improve with practice. Children especially enjoy sending kloprunes, and the activity can be made into a family game, while travelling, for example. You can also teach your child how to whistle his or her name using kloprunes.

Bindrunes

Bindrunes consist of two or more runes superimposed on each other and sharing a common stem. This fuses their energies into a single shape, exhibiting a single runic force and creating a powerful magical effect. Widely used for talismans and charms, bindrunes are always joined together in some way, sometimes at the base of their stems, forming a wheel, other times side-by-side or combined into a single rune. Generally, the runes in bindrunes appear in their upright shape.

Historically used as contractions in inscriptions, bindrunes either save space or reduce the number of runes in the inscription to a more magically auspicious total. Today bindrunes are employed in rune magic to create a magical symbol that encompasses more than one rune.

The most powerful bindrunes are made of three-rune combinations, and are also key names in the Northern Tradition. Clearly demonstrating the union between spirit and science, the number three is actually locked into our very DNA. The genetic code that tells the cells in your body how to arrange (or bind) amino acids to form protein chains is written in words (codes) that are three letters (three bases) long. So it's no wonder the number three frequently appears in all spiritual traditions. The "three" pattern, like other numerical patterns, is inherent in our bio-chemistry.

In three-rune bindrunes, sometimes the name is thought to have more significance than when the three runes are used in combination. Most of the time, the runes and bindrune name they create are related in a harmonious and powerful whole. You can use the following simple bindrune formulas to access and amplify the universal runic energies:

- Wunjo, Othala, Dagaz make WOD. This bindrune of divine inspiration, spelling the name of Woden/Odin, invokes the powers of the Norse god of wisdom and can be used to transform a negative situation into a positive one.
- Ingwaz, Naudhiz, and Gebo make ING, the name of the Earth God of fertility and increase. This bindrune can be used as a fertility talisman.
- Sowilo, Othala, and Laguz make SOL, the name of the sun goddess, who provides the strength and energy to deal with change.
- Ansuz, Sowilo, and Kenaz make ASC, the name

of Yggdrasil. This is a bindrune of pure power, survival, and longevity.

- Ansuz, Laguz, and Uruz spell the word ALU, which symbolizes the water of life, literally translated as "ale." This bindrune signifies a change for the better, and can be used in magic for protection and divine inspiration.
- Othala, Naudhiz, and Dagaz make the bindrune OND, the universal spirit of everything, which can help overcome problems.
- Berkana, Ansuz, and Raidho make BAR, meaning bear, conferring the strength and power of the animal.
- Uruz, Laguz, and Fehu make the bindrune ULF, signifying the wolf and all its cunning, stamina, and wisdom.
- Wunjo, Laguz, and Kenaz make the bindrune WLK, which is an alternate, more ancient bindrune for wolf. It represents Odin's companion wolves, Geri and Freki, and also the tracking ability of the wolf.
- Tyr, Othala, and Raidho make the bindrune TOR, signifying the Norse god of thunder, Thor, who can be called upon for protection.

You can create your own bindrune by simply spelling your name out in runes, and fashioning the staves together in a harmonious whole. Use your first, middle, and last initials to do this, using the basic three-rune bindrune formula. As you already know, the number three is magical! Use this bindrune symbol to focus and amplify your energetic field of intention. One way to do this is to *galdr* your name while gazing at the bindrune. Be creative. There isn't any right or wrong way to make a bindrune, so just work the symbols in any way you want. The only guideline is to keep the rune symbols upright as you connect them. If you change their positions you alter their meanings and energies.

Rune Categories

Rune masters divide the runes into categories depending upon their use. Some runes are more practical, while others are more protective. The following are examples of the different rune categories:

- **Alerunes**—These runes are used for protection in both the physical and spiritual realms. Rune masters employed alerunes for binding and constraining spirits and for warding off harm. These runes are Ansuz, Laguz, and Uruz. Alerunes were used to block enchantments by writing them on the back of hands and on drinking cups. Naudhiz was then scratched on the fingernail to activate the alerune power.

- **Biargrunes**—Related to the birch, these runes call upon Berchta, the goddess of childbirth, to ensure a safe birth. Used not only by expectant mothers, biargrunes also protect babies after they are born. The primary biagrune is Berkana, symbolizing new beginnings.

- **Brunrunes**—Weather magic runes that related to sailing, farming, and hunting were utilized to anticipate and control foul weather. "Surf runes" or "fountain runes" connect you with the powers of water flowing in the seas as well as in springs, rivers, streams, and lakes. They were cut on amulets and charms to control the ocean waves. Vikings also carved them on the stern, rudder, or steering oars of their ships as protection on long voyages.

- **Hugrunes (Hogrunes)**—Runes of the mind, hugrunes are named for one of Odin's companion ravens, Hugin (memory). Traditionally written on the chest and other parts of the body, Kenaz (guidance), Algiz (divine inspiration), Mannaz (memory and mental ability), and Ansuz (inspiration) are hugrunes of thought, cognition, communication, and intellectual abilities. Those who employed these runes were made the wisest of all. They are powerful devices for mental concentration in the Northern Tradition.

- **Limrunes**—Healers used limrunes, which drew upon the healing energies of trees, to cure the sick and restore health. In the past, limrunes were carved into the south face of trees.

- **Malrunes**—These runes enhance memory, mental ability, and speech. Stemming from the word *mal*, which means speech, they are found in the title of many Norse texts such as the "Havamal." The power of malrunes is accessed through the spoken and written word. Used in the word-magic of poetry and magical invocation, a malrune is any rune whose magic can be accessed by speaking, singing, or chanting. Effective in all places where words are important, especially in legal actions, malrunes were written on walls, chairs, furniture, and pillars.

- **Ramrunes**—Used magically, ramrunes are

empowered by magical ritual. Named after the male sheep, these are runes of strength and power.

- **Sigrunes**—Used to gain success and victory, these runes embody the solar energies of the Sowilo rune, and were often marked on tools, clothing, weapons, and musical instruments. When writing these runes, do the "Hammer sign" (see page 396) twice to invoke the god Thor.
- **Swartrunes**—These are black runes, and are used to speak with the dead.
- **Trollrunes**—Used in divination, trollrunes help bring you in touch with otherworldly realms. The ancient teachings said that prophecy originated with the trolls, who could foretell the future. As earth spirits, trolls represented the elements in nature. Trollrunes are used in enchantments.

PART 4

The Spiritual Uses
of Runes

Runes as Spiritual Symbols

Neurophysiologists have found that shamanic visions such as Odin's have a scientific basis. Evidence points to the fact that runes relate directly to human neural circuitry through what are called phosphenes. Like patterns of radiant energy, phosphenes are geometrical images that stem from the brain's visual cortex and neural system. Phosphenes resembling alphabetic letters and runic symbols often appear during altered states of awareness, including meditation and magic. You can see these patterns of energy when you shut your eyes. This amazing discovery implies that runic shapes are embedded in our biochemistry and DNA coding.

Because of our shared biochemical connection to the runes, everyone can tap into and access his/her energies, regardless of culture, belief, or spiritual path. Runes can be used by all who value them as a tool for self-discovery and a channel to the divine.

Reaching far beyond their fortune-telling origins, runes are being employed by many people as tools for getting in touch with the divine and, in turn, with themselves. The resurgence of interest in runes is not a fad, but part of a widespread trend. More people are using runes as a form of do-it-yourself therapy for unlocking the secrets of the self, in an effort to find meaning and direction in daily life. No longer considered merely mystical, runes tell us more about our everyday experiences, including what led up to these experiences, what the possible results will be in the long run, and what energies can be applied to reinforce or transform the course of events.

In addition to using runes for spiritual empowerment through casting and reading, you can also employ runes in meditation, dreamwork, and visualization. This chapter will explore rune divination, provide several easy methods for reading runes, suggest ways to use runes in dreamwork and meditation, and do ceremonial rune casting, complete with instructions on how to make a rune reading cloth.

Divination

Few practices of humankind have greater antiquity than divination, a practice performed by cultures throughout the world and by people in every walk of life. An example in medieval Iceland were the "spae-wives," who traveled the land foretelling people's futures.

The idea of knowing the unknown appeals to people as much today as it has in the past. Part of the unknown that rune divination seeks to discover is within ourselves, which is why runes and other divination systems can lead us further on the road to self-exploration and growth.

A way to touch and communicate with the divine, within and without, divination is the art of knowing the unknown, whether in the form of future events, influencing factors, signs, impressions, or messages. People have employed almost every conceivable instrument or phenomenon for the purposes of divination, from oracles such as the one at the Temple of Apollo at Delphi, to the tracks of animals and bird augury. Ancient shamans cleverly fashioned the wisdom regarding the powers of the world into divination systems and games as a means of passing on information and sending coded messages from one millennium to another.

Runes are one of the oldest divination systems we know. The Roman historian Tacitus (98 C.E.) noted that Germanic tribes cut slips from fruit-bearing trees. After inscribing the slips with sigils (symbols), the runecaster would face north, invoke specific gods and goddesses, and then cast three to nine runes upon a white cloth. From the runes on the cloth, the rune-caster would take three of the slips and interpret the divine messages revealed in them.

Contemporary rune divination gives tangible results that you can see and appreciate. Like the runecasters of ancient times, you, too, can learn how to cast and read runes. There are no prerequisites for working with runes besides an open mind and honest effort. Familiarity with other forms of divination is not needed, as runes form a valid system of divination in their own right, much like the Tarot or the I Ching. At the same time, an expanded knowledge of other divination systems is always helpful, and it is a good idea to experiment with different ones, choosing those that work best in certain situations. But more important, to really gain the optimum benefit from rune divination, you need to study Northern mythology, work with the elements, and understand the primary archetypes, focusing on the specific mythological patterns of the Norse gods and goddesses. Like everything else, the more you practice using the runes, the more proficient you will become.

One of the primary concepts to keep in mind when using runes is the "wyrd," the inherent interconnectedness of all things. The wyrd reflects the far-reaching implications of one's thoughts, feelings, and actions. The best analogy is that of the spider's web. When anything touches any part of the web, the vibrations affect the entire structure and everything contained within it. Your every breath, thought, feeling, action, dream—affects everything and everyone around you, just as their thoughts and actions affect you. Make an effort to be mindful of this Oneness when working with the runes.

As one of the most accurate and available methods of divination, runes represent the whole in a unified way. Runic divination is much like holding up a mirror to yourself or to the person for whom you are doing a reading. Because of your intent, and the fact that your mind is focused on a particular question when you mix the runes, they order themselves to reflect the reality of the questioner. As you pose a question, with your entire mind focused on it, the runes that you pull are not actually random selections but choices made through your intent. In this way, rune readings work deeply with both the conscious and the unconscious. In successful divination, you become a son or daughter of the moment, the Goddess and the God, and as you read you are divine!

Why consult the runes? There are two primary reasons:

1) You are facing a specific problem that you can't figure out, and you are looking for clarity and guidance for future decisions.
2) You are trying to figure out what life is all about, examining the path you are on and the influences that are going to come into play in the future.

By consistently practicing divination, you gradually become more sensitized to being in the right place at the right time, making the appropriate choice and gesture. You become more attuned to who and what you truly are. Because of this, you make decisions that are correct for you and more positive for everyone else.

You can use runes for divination purposes in basically two ways:

1) rune readings based on specific rune layouts, and
2) ceremonial runecasting, the traditional method.

No matter which rune divination method you use, the purpose is to awaken your intuition and your receptive abilities. At best, you establish a channel of communication with the runes and the energies they represent. As you do this, you allow them to speak and sing to you. In this way, working with runic energies becomes an unfettering of your natural abilities and a process of remembering.

The meanings of a rune can often be obscure. Your task is to determine how the essence of the rune applies to the question being asked. At first, it is best to stick with the accepted interpretations of the runes, starting with the corresponding key words. Afterward, through practice, meditation, and study you can go deeper into their more expanded meanings and uses.

By tradition, there is always an exchange in rune divination between the runecaster and the runes. At the very least, this exchange can be your undivided attention and a receptive mind. Remember, a gift demands a gift—as exemplified in the Gebo rune. A divine gift from the gods, the runes are tools of sacred knowledge and wisdom. Use them respectfully.

PREPARATIONS FOR RUNE READINGS

To do readings you will need a set of Elder Futhark rune cards, wood squares, or stones. Refer to Part 6 "Contemporary Rune Practices" for more information on how to make or select a set of runes or rune cards. Some experts feel that rune lots need to be of the same size, shape, and material, so that you are not able to identify them individually. This has not been my experience, for one of my favorite rune sets is made of odd-sized and odd-shaped hematite stones. Just select a set of runes or rune cards that you feel personally drawn to.

You need to keep your runes in a bag, pouch, box, or other container that has a wide enough opening so that you can put your hand inside and mix the runes easily and completely. Because it holds the runic symbols, the rune pouch represents the entire cosmos.

Before doing a reading, arrange the setting so that

it induces a harmonious state of mind, body, and spirit. I suggest you clear out the area by smudging (sage and cedar) or burning incense. You can also clean the energies of the area by visualizing a bright royal-blue light flooding through the space like a blue wave of water, washing everything clean. A clean area encourages clear and concise answers to your questions.

Physical conditions such as distracting noise, constant interruptions, and unpleasant odors can disrupt the natural flow of a reading. High-voltage lines, ELFs (electromagnetic fields), and even electronic equipment can all negatively alter rune readings; so can adverse weather. It is customary to avoid doing rune readings when the weather is volatile, for example, when it is raining, especially cloudy, or very windy. This isn't always possible, especially if you live in an area where it rains a lot or is windy most of the time, so use your intuition and good judgment when choosing the best time to do runecasts.

Your state of mind also greatly affects a reading. Make an effort to calm and balance your emotions as well as to let go of distracting thoughts. Take a few minutes and get into a meditative state of mind. Begin by letting go of the tensions and worries of the day by breathing deeply. Bring energy and bright light into your body as you inhale, and let go of any negative thoughts and feelings with your exhaling breath. Breathe in to the count of three, hold your breath for three counts, and then exhale completely to the count of three. Do this three times before mixing the rune stones or cards. This breathing exercise is useful when casting the runes: before, to focus the energies, and afterward, to cleanse the energies and disperse them.

Like your mind, how your body feels and your general physical condition have an impact on readings. Do not do readings when you feel ill or are under the weather. Again, depending upon the situation, you may have to do a reading under adverse circumstances, but do be aware that wrong conditions can greatly reduce the success of a rune reading.

When doing a runecast for another person, make certain that person is rune-friendly and genuinely curious. In addition, make sure the people who are present during a reading are all as harmonious as possible. In this way you can avoid a lot of potential problems with critics, cynics, and skeptics—people who can negate and block the energies in rune divination.

Timing also makes a difference in the divination process. Some people feel that special days such as New Year's Day, birthdays, anniversaries, and weddings are auspicious days for runecasting. One practice that has been carried forward by several traditions is doing readings on the Eight Sabbats, which are the quarter and cross-quarter days of the year—winter solstice, Imbolc (February 2), spring equinox, Beltane (May 1), summer solstice, Lughnassad (the first week in August), autumnal equinox, and Samhain (Halloween). Divination is also practiced on the full moon.

Norse tradition states that a rune reading should take place "in the face of the sun, and the eyes of the light." Again, use your own judgment, as there may be times when you prefer to do readings during the dark hours of the night and early morning.

THE RUNE CLOTH

You need to keep your runes clean. This is best done by wrapping them in a rune cloth before placing them in their pouch or box. The rune cloth, customarily a 9-inch (22.5 cm) square white cloth, protects the runes, and also forms a surface boundary for runecasting. The size represents the Nine Worlds of

Yggdrasil. The side of the cloth you place the runes upon needs to be white or ivory. The opposite side of the cloth can be of any pattern and color.

Using a natural material such as linen, silk, cotton, or hemp, you can leave your rune cloth as it is, or draw, paint, and embroider runic symbols on the back of it. You may feel a few specific runes are appropriate. For example, you could inscribe Ingwaz in the middle of your rune cloth to symbolize a doorway. Frequently, all 24 runes of the Elder Futhark are drawn in a circle around the edge of the cloth. Other symbols such as astrological signs and the four directions—North, East, South, and West—may also be used on runecasting cloths.

You can even make your rune cloth into a pouch to hold your runes. For example, using a 9" square cloth, sew thick ribbon or cord on each of the four corners. When you're not using the cloth, put your runes in the middle of it and gather together and pull up the ribbons on the four ends. Wind the ribbons around the top of the bulk of the runes so as to form a bag. Tie the ends together in a bow, so that you can easily untie the bag when you want to use your runes.

However decorated, your rune-reading cloth covers the surface in front of you. Then you place the runes upon the cloth in the specific layout of your choosing. The rune cloth offers a focal point, from which you move into divine Oneness, an energy that contains no boundaries or separations. The only boundaries exist in our own minds as we dissect things and move them onto their "proper" categories.

EIGHT-POINT RUNE READING CHECKLIST

1. Whenever you seek divine guidance, expect (have faith) that it will be provided and that its intent will be for your greatest good.

2. Find a quiet spot suitable for readings, a place where you will not be disturbed. Before you begin, clear out any negative energy from the space, and then gather all the materials you will need: casting cloth, runes or rune cards, a cushion to sit on, and so forth.

3. Get into a receptive state of mind, calling in any divine powers that you connect with. When doing this, sit facing north, the direction of the ancestors and deities in Norse mythology.

4. Take your time carefully forming a question in your mind. It's crucial that you do not change

the question midway through the reading. The question needs to be something that you really want an answer to. The greater your desire and curiosity, the better for the divination. Ask your question clearly and simply. You can do this aloud or silently. When doing personal divination, it's a good idea to write the question down, placing it next to the casting cloth for reference. You might keep your questions in a notebook together with a record of the runes you pulled. It can be useful to refer to later on.

5. Once the question is firmly fixed in your mind, begin to gently mix the runes. Keep your attention focused on the question the entire time you mix the runes, almost as if placing the question into the runes themselves.

6. Continue to mix the runes until you feel compelled to take up certain runes or rune cards. Continue to stir and pull runes out until you have the correct number in front of you for the layout you are using. Generally you lay the runes out in a horizontal row, facedown, in front of you, from left to right in the order they were pulled.

7. Take the runes, one by one, in order, and place

them in their proper positions in the layout, turning them faceup as you do so and reading their meanings. Think about how you can use the information within these runes to create positive ways to deal with upcoming events.

ᚦ. When you finish with the reading, give thanks in your own way for the guidance and information given.

RUNE READINGS

More formal than runecasting, which is described later in detail, rune layouts and spreads involve laying rune stones, squares, or cards in meaningful patterns on a white casting cloth. You can use any kind of rune—stones, cards, clay or wooden squares—for readings. I have seen rare amber and gold, as well as sterling-silver rune sets, being used for divination. If you use rune cards, mix them, a few at a time rather than shuffling them. Most rune cards cannot withstand continuous shuffling, and will eventually bend and tear.

When you selected your rune pouch or bag, you made sure the opening would be large enough so that you could easily reach inside, mix the runes, and pull them out.

To mix them, you can:

scramble them in their pouch or box,
place them facedown on a cloth and, at random,
    take them up like dominoes, or
you can spread or "wash" them around, facedown,
    on the casting cloth before making your selec-
    tions.

In this book, the specific rune row used for divination is the most popular and well-balanced Elder
Futhark, with its 24 runes. The Younger Futhark (16
runes), Anglo-Saxon (29 runes), and Northumbrian
(33 runes) may also be used as divination systems.

When doing a reading, you customarily address a
particular question or issue, examining the past,
present, and future influences involved. Though
always perceived as changeable and mutable, the
future represents the direction you are headed if you
follow your current path to its eventual end. When
you look at it this way, a reading becomes more like
a process of evaluation than a form of fortune-telling.
With an open mind, you can "read" the way your life
is progressing, looking at the influencing energies,

much as you would read a book. This can be simultaneously simple and complex. For this reason, when interpreting the runes, you need to be flexible. It's important to recognize all the potential possibilities, adjusting each rune's influence accordingly and keeping aware of preconceived notions or expectations you may have.

Most important, divination is not just a matter of discovering future influences, of finding out what's going to happen next month, or what's wrong with things. It's also a means of offering practical help in solving problems and personal dilemmas. Because of this, it is necessary to allow time for the information you receive during readings to sink in. Keep in mind that the runes may illuminate details of the situation you haven't previously been aware of; surprises may occur. This is why it is recommended that you write your readings down, so you can look them over for additional insights at a later time. Sometimes when you do a reading, you are too close-in, and it's difficult to get a clear perspective. Time can help with this.

You can use runes both for personal divination and to do readings for another person. When doing a reading for another person, you are a mediator between the questioner and the runes, using the runes themselves as focal points. Have the person come up with the question and its phrasing. When using rune cards, have her or him mix them and then hand the cards back to you to lay out. When using rune stones, squares, or staves, mix the runes yourself while thinking about the person's question. The reason you do not have the other person mix rune stones or squares is that runes hold a great deal of personal energy. They need to be kept personal and be touched only by you.

Symbolizing the powers of the universe, each rune contains both positive and negative polarities. This brings us to the question of reversed meanings for runes. Some people claim that if the rune appears in an upright position, positive qualities will most likely prevail, and when it is reversed or upside down, the negative qualities come into play. However, this is not necessarily the case. Also, some non-invertible runes exist—runes that have the same meaning either way—such as Gebo, Isa, Jera, Eihwaz, Sowilo, Ingwaz, and Dagaz.

Today, many of the rune card decks specify

reversed meanings for the runes, but these reversals are more Tarot-like than rune-like. Also, a reversed meaning is somewhat redundant as each rune contains all polarities and is a whole within itself.

RUNE LAYOUTS

You can use a number of runic layouts derived from the Northern Tradition as well as from Tarot spreads. Some are simple, others more complex. The ones presented here range from a single rune to a 24-rune layout. You can also use any one layout without following any particular sequence or order. To begin with, try one basic reading. As you progress, you can add other questions, preferably with a maximum of three simple readings or one more complex reading during each sitting.

The following sampling of my favorite rune layouts includes traditional, contemporary, and innovative ones. For your convenience, a layout diagram, description, and step-by-step instructions are provided for each one.

BEFORE EVERY RUNE READING

1. Get yourself into a meditative frame of mind.
2. Think of a specific question, something that is important to you at this time. Take a moment to form the question in your mind. Stay completely focused on the question and do not change your focus or the question at any time during the reading.
3. Journal the question.
4. As you focus on the question, carefully mix your rune stones in their bag or holder or mix your cards. Continue thinking about the question and mixing the runes until you sense intuitively that the time is right.
5. Pause for a moment, focusing on your question, and take a deep breath.

The One-Rune Pull

This simple form of rune reading provides a quick answer to a specific question. Pull a single rune from your rune pouch. Look at it. If you pulled it out sideways, turn the stone once sunwise (clockwise) to orient it. When working with rune cards, mix the deck, and then draw a single card, laying it facedown. Turn the card over from right to left, as you would turn the pages of a book, to make sure you keep the original upright or reversed orientation of the card.

Read the meaning of the rune. The answer to your question may be an obvious yes or no. Take a moment to evaluate the meaning of the single rune in relation to your question. Journal the rune you selected. If it doesn't make any sense at all, then ask another question or try again later when you feel more receptive.

The One-Rune Pull also works well for yes and no questions by simply interpreting an upright pull as "yes" and a reversed pull as "no." If you pull one of the runes that is the same either way, then either interpret it or pull another rune.

When doing the One-Rune Pull reading for another person, you, the reader, pull the stone or square out of your rune bag. As mentioned before, your runes are personal, for only you to touch and use. This is especially true with runes made of stone, wood, or metal, as they actually become energetically imprinted.

When using rune cards, have the questioner mix the cards and pull one out. This is the only rune reading method in which the questioner pulls the card. Most of the time the questioner simply mixes the deck, making an effort to imprint the rune cards with the energy of the question, and then the reader lays out the cards.

The Two-Rune Draw

Follow the basic procedure (page 246), and when you sense it is the right time, draw out two runes. Sometimes the runes you draw will seem to stick to your fingers. The meanings of the two runes will either reinforce and complement one another or they will oppose one another. If they oppose, a stalemate of energies or a sort of limbo is created, depending on their context in regard to the question.

The Three Norns

| 1 | 2 | 3 |

Named after the three mysterious goddesses of fate, this rune reading gives an overview of the past, future, and present influences at work in relation to a specific question. As mentioned before, the Three Norns, or Three Maidens, were sisters, two of whom wove the fate of the world, and a third who, by the end of the day, unraveled it.

The Norns possessed mysterious powers and tended Yggdrasil (the World Tree), determining fate. Fate is a key factor in Norse spirituality, but instead of a helpless predestination, fate meant a destiny created by earlier actions. Traditionally, a Norn is present at each person's birth to declare his/her fate. While this means that one's fate is known at birth, remember that it is constantly being unraveled! The Three Norns layout works off the concept that each person's fate is constantly being spun and unwound by the hands of time. The Norns represent the perceived order of time: past, future, and present. This perceived order is a linear view that sees time as separated into these three distinct areas: what has happened, what will happen, and what is happening. These separations are a way of discussing the dimension of time, but they are not necessarily real. As with the Celts, Native Americans, and Vedic culture, the Norse spiritual tradition views time as being fluid and flexible, thus defying "normal" separations. The runes allow a person to move beyond past, future, and present, to a place where time is fluid and all is One. In this place, personal and divine information become more accessible.

After following the basic beginning sequence outlined on page 246, slowly pull three runes, one at a time, from your rune bag or three cards from the deck, placing them in a horizontal row on your rune cloth. If the runes are facedown, flip them over from right to left as if turning the pages of a book.

Rune #1:

The first rune to the left corresponds to the Norn Urd, representing what has been—all the past actions and events that affect the question.

Rune #2:

The middle rune corresponds to the Norn Skuld.

Signifying the future and that which is to become, the Skuld rune points to the likely outcome to your question if you continue on your present path, or at least one of the possible end results. In some instances, the Skuld rune may signify the fate of the questioner.

Rune #3:

The third rune corresponds to the Norn Verdandi and that which is, as well as the path you, or the person you're reading for, are currently on. It reflects all those influences in the present that relate directly to the question. The Verdandi rune frequently points to a choice that needs to be made.

The Triple-Rune Challenge Layout

3

2

1

After following the procedure outline on page 246, slowly draw out three runes, one at a time, from your rune bag or spread out three cards from the deck, placing them faceup in a vertical row, from bottom to top, on the rune cloth.

Rune #1:

The first (bottom) rune indicates the present state of affairs—where you find yourself right now.

Rune #2:

The middle rune signifies the challenge ahead of you and the action that you may take.

Rune #3:

The topmost rune represents the best possible outcome.

The Body, Mind, and Spirit Reading

| 1 | 2 | 3 |

While thinking about where you find yourself right now, mix the runes for a minute or two, and pull the first three that come. Place them facedown in a horizontal row on the casting cloth. Take the first rune, turning it over as you would the pages of a book, and then turn over the second and third runes. Read these three runes in combination with one another. They form a holistic picture of your physical, mental, and spiritual condition.

Rune #1:
The first rune, to the left, represents your present physical condition.

Rune #2:
The second rune (in the middle) reflects your present mental condition.

Rune #3:
The rune to the right signifies your present spiritual condition.

The Four Dwarfs Spread

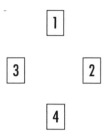

Ideal for discovering how you really feel about a relationship, job, spiritual path, or any emotionally charged issue, the Four Dwarfs Spread describes the four primary underlying desires in relation to your question.

Based on the tale of the magical Brisingamen necklace, this four-rune spread represents the four dwarfs, who in Norse Mythology become the four directions: north, east, west, and south. One day when Freyja, the Norse goddess of love, happened to find the stone threshold of the subterranean world open, she went in and found the four dwarfs, Alfrig, Dvalin, Berlingr, and Grer, forging the magnificent golden necklace called the Brisingamen. The necklace was more wonderful than anything Freyja had ever seen, and she asked to buy it. The dwarfs told her they would part with the necklace only if she would lie with each of them for a night. When the four-night exchange was complete, Freyja was the owner of the magical Brisingamen.

The story of the Brisingamen represents Freyja's shamanic journey, on which she joins with the elements and, by doing so, perpetuates the seasonal cycles. The priceless necklace represents the stars, as they progress through the night sky, and also the undying fertility of the Earth.

Begin this reading by getting into a receptive state of mind. Take a few deep breaths, calm yourself, and focus your attention on an emotionally charged question, something you really care about. Next, mix the runes slowly, and then pull four runes, putting them facedown in a row on the rune cloth in front of you. Turn the runes faceup, one at a time, and place the first rune at the top, at the north point of the layout as shown in the diagram. Position the second rune at the right-hand, east point; the third rune in the left-hand, west position; and the fourth at the bottom, south point.

Rune #1:

The topmost rune denotes your past desires in regard to the question. The past desires of your ancestors may also be reflected in this rune.

Rune #2:

The rune to the right reveals your present desires and exactly how you feel about the question right now.

Rune #3:

The rune to the left describes the desires and feelings of others, and how these desires affect your question.

Rune #4:

The bottom rune symbolizes your heart's deepest desire, that which you keep hidden from the world. This heart's desire will grow and blossom within the next four months, if the fourth rune is positive.

The Five-Rune Spread

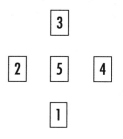

This spread represents the four basic directions, surrounding a center rune. Follow the basic instructions on page 246, and then mix your runes as usual and draw them, placing them facedown on the casting cloth. Place the runes according to the diagram as if they were the four points on a compass, with a central fifth point. Position the first rune at the bottom of the cross, the second to the left of center, the third above center, the fourth to the right of center, and the fifth in the center of the layout. Turn them over one by one.

Rune #1:

The bottom stone represents the basic influences that surround the question.

Rune #2:

The second rune indicates any problems and obstacles that may affect the outcome of the question.

Rune #3:

The top rune denotes the positive influences at work, in regard to the question.

Rune #4:

The fourth rune reflects the immediate outcome.

Rune #5:

The center rune suggests the key future influences.

The Persona

| 1 | 2 | 3 | 4 | 5 |

This simple five rune reading can assist you in better understanding yourself or another person. Follow the instructions on page 246, and while you mix the runes, focus your attention on yourself and your life, or on someone else you are curious about. Pull the first five runes that come, and place them faceup, in a horizontal row, from left to right.

Rune #1:
The first rune, to the left, describes where you currently find yourself in life.

Rune #2:
The second rune reflects your primary thoughts, what is on your mind.

Rune #3:
The middle rune reveals what is in your heart, your deepest desires.

Rune #4:

The fourth rune denotes your primary intentions in life.

Rune #5:

The rune to the right signifies your future actions and deeds.

The Five Elements

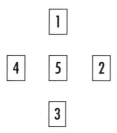

This five-rune layout delves into the elemental influences of earth, air, fire, water, and spirit, which affect the question at hand. On a deeper level, it gives more subtle insights into the question.

Follow the basic procedure outlined on page 246, and pull one rune at a time. As shown in the layout diagram, place the first rune above center, the second rune to the right of center, the third rune below center, the fourth to the left of center, and the fifth rune in the center.

Rune #1:

The rune at the top represents earth, your physical body, surroundings, and environment.

Rune #2:

The rune to the right denotes the air element, symbolizing intellectual influences related to the question. This rune reflects your present state of mind.

Rune #3:

The bottom rune indicates the creative forces at work.

Rune #4:

The rune to the left reveals your emotions in regard to the question.

Rune #5:

The center rune represents the spiritual influences and your connection to deity.

The Five-Keys Layout

Especially applicable to business decisions, this five-rune layout provides valuable insights. Begin by thinking of a question related to your work, as you follow the instructions on page 246. Focus on the question while mixing the runes. Carefully select five runes, one at a time, and place them facedown on your rune cloth according to the layout diagram. Place the first three runes in a horizontal row; then place one rune above the center, and the last rune below the center. Begin by turning over the left rune, and proceed in number order.

Rune #1:

The rune to the left denotes the actions and events that led up to your current situation.

Rune #2:

The middle rune represents the present moment and your current state of mind regarding the question. When reversed, this rune may indicate that you (or the questioner) are in a negative state of mind or deeply troubled about this issue.

Rune #3:

The rune to the right reflects future influences on the issue and the final outcome, usually showing what the next three months hold, in regard to the question.

Rune #4:

The rune lying above the center indicates help you will receive in the near future. If a reversed rune appears in this position, it may show your unwillingness to accept help from others or, possibly, delays and problems that may hinder a successful outcome.

Rune #5:

The rune below the center is the Orlog rune, representing aspects of the question that are set in place by the Fates and cannot be altered.

The Runic Cross

```
        [ 6 ]

[ 1 ]   [ 5 ]   [ 3 ]

        [ 2 ]

        [ 4 ]
```

In a receptive state of mind, mix the runes while thinking of a question that is the most important one to you personally at this moment. It is crucial to lay out the six runes in the correct order. As shown in the layout diagram, pull the first rune and place it to the left of the cross column. Next, pull a second rune and place it second from the bottom of the column, and then a third and put it to the right of the cross column. The fourth rune goes at the base of the cross, the fifth in the central position, above the second rune, and the final sixth rune goes at the very top of the cross column.

Rune #1:
The first rune reflects the past.

Rune #2:
The second rune represents the present.

Rune #3:
The third rune suggests the possible future.

Rune #4:
The rune at the base of the cross column represents the basic influences that underlie the question.

Rune #5:
The center rune describes events and factors that will either help or hinder a successful outcome.

Rune #6:
The topmost rune represents the most probable outcome.

The Career Mirror

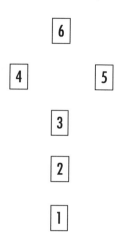

Utilizing six runes, the Career Mirror layout helps when you need to make business or career choices and decisions. This rune layout takes the shape of a traditional hand mirror with a handle.

Begin by selecting a question that pertains to your career or business—the question foremost in your mind. While thinking about it, mix the runes for a minute or two, and pull the first six that come, placing them facedown in a horizontal row on the casting cloth. Take the first rune, turning it over as you would the page of a book, and place it at the base of the mirror handle. Turn the second rune faceup and put it above the first, and the third rune, faceup, above the second. Position the fourth rune to the left, the fifth to the right, and the sixth at the top of the mirror—all faceup, as shown in the layout diagram.

Rune #1:

The first rune, at the base of the mirror's handle, reflects your current position.

Rune #2:

The second rune represents the challenge you face.

Rune #3:

The third rune, which attaches the mirror handle to the mirror, signifies your position of greatest strength and ability.

Rune #4:

The rune to the left reveals your past perception in regard to the question at hand.

Rune #5:

The rune to the right denotes your future perception.

Rune #6:

The rune at the top of the mirror represents the future outcome.

Mimir's Head

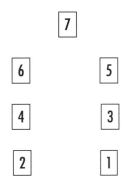

Mimir is a gigantic god of the open sea who embodies the four elements. Originally part of the Aesir, his home is Mimir's Well (the sea), beside one of the roots of the mighty Yggdrasil. Drinking from Mimir's Well confers mysterious and all-knowing wisdom. Odin once gave one of his eyes for a drink from Mimir's Well.

After the war between the Aesir and the Vanir, they exchanged two members each as a goodwill gesture. The Vanir sent Frey and Freyja in exchange for

Mimir and Hoenir of the Aesir. Hoenir was basically an oaf, and the Vanir felt insulted and angered because they had sent two of their best members to the Aesir. As a reaction to the insult, the Vanir cut off Mimir's head and sent it to Asgard. Odin preserved it with herbs, and regularly consulted Mimir's head as an oracle.

This layout works with pairs of runes, and is best used for questions that feature several unknown variables, such as beginning a new business or making an investment. After following the basic instructions on page 246, think of your question, and begin to mix the runes. Pull out seven runes, one at a time, placing them in the order shown on the layout diagram. Place the first and second runes at the bottom of the layout, from right to left. Put the next two runes in a row directly above the first two. Then, place the fifth and sixth runes above three and four, and put the seventh rune in the middle position, at the top of the head.

Runes #1 and #2:

The first and second runes signify the question or problem at hand.

Runes #3 and #4:

The third and fourth runes reflect the reasons for the question or problem.

Runes #5 and #6:

The fifth and sixth runes point to viable solutions and ways of resolution.

Rune #7:

The seventh rune, which sits at the top of Mimir's head, represents the result and final outcome.

The Seven-Rune Spread

1	2	3	4	5	6

7

The Seven-Rune Spread is ideal for offering insights as to what created your present dilemma, and for obtaining more detailed information for dealing with it. This spread is suited for more comprehensive questions. Instead of asking a "yes" or "no" question like "Would it benefit me to take the job?" or "What about this job?" you can ask such questions as "How will my life progress if I accept this job?"

This rune layout represents events and influencing factors three months into the past and three months into the future. While mixing the runes and thinking of your problem, concentrate on this time frame.

Pull seven runes, one at a time, and lay them face-up in a row of six, with the seventh and final rune below the row and centered, as shown in the layout diagram. In this seven-rune reading, interpret the runes in pairs, paying close attention to how the pairs relate to one another and to the question at hand.

Runes #1 and #2:

The first two (left) runes represent the problem or dilemma.

Runes #3 and #4:

The third and fourth (middle) runes denote the past influences and factors that have led up to the present situation.

Runes #5 and #6:

Considered most significant in this layout, the fifth and sixth runes present the advice the runes are giving you. They can point to the need to act or wait patiently, or they can indicate a complete shift of focus, moving your attention to something more pressing or crucial.

Rune #7:

The seventh rune—below the horizon—points to the probable outcome. If this is a positive rune, it will indicate a truly positive outcome only if all the other runes are also positive. If the rune pulled in this position is negative, it will only be a *truly* negative outcome if all the other runes are negative, too.

The Ve (pronounced "vee")

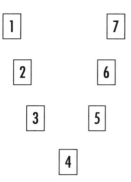

The Ve is ideal for finding the best course of action in any given situation. In this reading, the runes appear in a V-shape, named for the sacred V-shaped enclosure made of standing stones, which are primarily used for runecasting and ritual. The V-shape also honors the Norse god Ve (also called Lothur), who with his brothers Odin and Vili gave life to the first humans, Ask and Embla.

The story of Ve begins with the primal giant Ymir (the roarer), from whom the races of rime-giants sprang. The cosmic cow licked salty ice blocks and formed the first person, Buri, who was androgynous. From Buri sprang Bor, who married Bestla, the daughter of a rime-giant. Bestla and Buri were the parents of Odin (inspiration), Vili (will), and Ve (holiness). The three brothers sacrificed Ymir and shaped the world with portions of his cosmic body, thus creating the Nine Worlds of Yggdrasil and the cosmic order. These sons of Bor then fashioned the primal man and woman called Ask and Embla (ash and elm), and gave them many physical, mental, and spiritual gifts. Ve's gift to the first humans was blood, flesh, and the spark of life, the five senses, appearance, and speech.

Ponder your question while mixing the runes as usual. Draw out seven runes and place them face-down, one at a time, on the rune cloth in front of you, beginning with the top left-hand rune. Lay the remaining six runes in order until the seventh rune rests at the top right point of the Ve. Turn over the runes in the same order that you laid them down.

Rune #1:

The top left rune reflects past actions and influences affecting the question.

Rune #2:

The second rune represents present influences and actions affecting the question.

Rune #3:

The third rune points to future prospects and potential actions.

Rune #4:

The rune at the point of the Ve is called the "Key." The most important rune of this layout, the "Key" reveals the best possible course of action for a successful outcome.

Rune #5:

The fifth rune depicts the attitudes and feelings of people close to the questioner.

Rune #6:

The sixth rune suggests the delays and obstacles that can prevent a successful outcome.

Rune #7:

The upper right-hand rune represents the most likely future outcome.

Tiwaz's Shoat

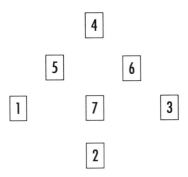

Named after the Tiwaz rune, this traditional shoat (runecast) reproduces the shape of the actual rune, each of the seven cards or stones representing one of the seven stars of the constellation Tir. Over a thousand years ago, Scandinavian seafarers used the constellations and other skylore to sail across the Atlantic Ocean, long before any other peoples.

The Tiwaz rune keeps the faithful always on course through the dark night, and even today its shape is used as a path marker by hikers. This is done by picking up seven pebbles and placing them in the shape of an arrow (Tiwaz), which points the way back to where you started. Because of its "staying on course" nature, Tiwaz's shoat often provides a clear and accurate reading, even when other rune layouts don't seem to be working for you.

Decide upon a question that needs special clarity. After mixing the runes or cards, take the first four runes that present themselves or four cards from the top of the deck. Place them facedown in a counter-clockwise cross pattern on the runecasting cloth, starting at the left, and then moving to the bottom, right, and finally the top. Mix the remaining runes or cards and pull three more. Place these in a clockwise (sun-wise) triangle shape inside the cross pattern, as shown in the layout.

Rune #1:

The left-most rune denotes the basic feelings and influences that underlie the matter at hand, as well as the origin of the question.

Rune #2:

The bottom rune symbolizes the highest level of attainment and best possible results in regard to the question.

Rune #3:

The right-most rune shows the obstacles, delays, and hindrances that can prevent a positive outcome.

Rune #4:

The rune at the top reflects those factors that can destroy a successful outcome and bring failure to the question at hand.

Rune #5:

The fifth rune, second from the top, represents influences, feelings, and events from the past that affect the question.

Rune #6:

The sixth rune indicates the present and all the influences that affect the question today, right this minute.

Rune #7:

The seventh rune, also known as the Seventh Star, describes the major future influences that will affect the question.

The Eight-Spoked Runic Wheel

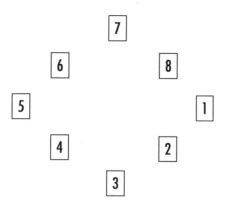

This eight-rune reading represents the Wheel of the Year, reflecting its eight quarter and cross-quarter divisions (the Sabbats), as well as the eight directional Nordic divisions of space: North, Northeast, East, Southeast, South, Southwest, West, and Northwest. Each of the eight spokes of the wheel is ruled by a rune. When you do this rune spread, the meaning of each rune you pull is determined in relation to or in combination with the rune that governs that particular spoke or house. If a rune falls into a house that is ruled by itself, then its meaning is doubled, while if it falls into a house whose rune means the opposite, both are neutralized. Because of this, the Eight-Spoked Runic Wheel is well suited for questions with many related parts.

Focusing on your question and mixing the runes or rune cards as usual, draw the first eight runes that come to you. Place them, one by one, faceup on the casting cloth in a sunwise (clockwise) pattern, starting at the east, the point furthest to the right, as shown in the layout. The reason you begin here is because the sun rises in the east. When you interpret this reading, however, you begin at the house that corresponds with your question, moving in a sunwise direction around the wheel until all of the runes are read. If, for instance, your question concerns higher learning and knowledge, you would begin in the west house of Kenaz. When asking a question about polarities in your life or sudden changes, you would start your reading at the south point, the House of Dagaz. As with any layout that utilizes rune combinations, the Eight-Spoked Runic Wheel layout takes a little more time than some of the previous ones and also a bit more thought.

Rune #1:

   The House of Berkana

   Birth, motherhood, beginnings, fecundity, the Mother Goddess

Rune #2:

   The House of Laguz

   Growth, flow, increase in energy, second sight, initiation

Rune #3:

   The House of Dagaz

   Possible sudden changes, polarities, the balance between day and night, "dawn rune" of entry

Rune #4:

   The House of Thurisaz

   Protection from enemies and personal attack, defensive and resistant powers

Rune #5:

   The House of Kenaz

   Learning, creativity, artistic mastery, inspiration, illumination

Rune #6:

The House of Hagalaz

Transformation, evolution within a fixed framework, metamorphosis

Rune #7:

The House of Jera

Rune of the yearly harvest, reward, completion, success, luck

Rune #8:

The House of Algiz

Inner strength, defense against all harmful forces, the rune of divine guidance and assistance.

The Grid of Nine

4	9	2
3	5	7
8	1	6

Used for over 3,000 years, the Grid of Nine is one of the oldest and most powerful of ancient Northern European symbols. It was associated with the "wyrd" times of the year, when the veil between the worlds was thinnest. On one such day, a Beltane (May Day) custom was to dig the nine-square grid into the ground, removing the turf on the eight outside squares and leaving the middle square of turf intact. The sacred Beltane fire was then built and lit on this middle square.

Another use of the Grid of Nine was made by Norse wise women in a form of trance-divination called "Utiseta," which means "sitting out." A wooden platform divided into nine squares was erected upon a sacred place, such as a burial mound or holy hill. A wise woman would sit on the middle square, facing north, the direction of the gods and the ancestors, until she went into a trance and received knowledge from them. In this application, the grid created a vortex of light that the wise woman could tap into.

The Grid of Nine is made up of nine squares with a central square, like a king in a chess game, which is protected on all four sides by rows of three squares each. This makes the Grid of Nine the most appropriate rune layout for questions dealing with protection from negativity and personal attack, injury, bad luck, or evildoers.

The Grid of Nine is known popularly as a Magic Square of Saturn. Notice that the numbers are placed in rows so that the sum of any one row of three is the same as that of every other row of three. All horizonal, vertical, and diagonal lines add up to fifteen, so the total of all numbers of the grid equals forty-five.

Think of a question that relates to protection from negative people or influences. Mix your runes or cards at random in the usual manner, and pull nine runes, placing them facedown in a row in front of you. Then take the first rune and turn it over from right to left, like turning the page of a book. Put this rune in square (1), the second in square (2), the third in square (3), and so on, until you have placed all nine runes in their proper grid positions according to the diagram. Read the runes in horizontal rows of three, in the following order.

Runes #8, #1, and #6:
  This row represents the past. Rune #8 reflects hidden influences from the past. Rune #1 denotes basic past influences, and Rune #6 shows the questioner's present attitude toward these past events.

Runes #3, #5, and #7:
  This row represents the present. Rune #3 reveals the hidden influences operating right now. Rune #5 stands for the present state of affairs, and Rune #7 indicates the questioner's attitude toward these present influences.

Runes #4, #9, and #2:
  This row represents the future outcome. Rune #4 shows the hidden obstacles, delays, and problems that can prevent a successful outcome. Rune #9 is

considered the "key" rune in this layout, and symbolizes the best possible outcome. Rune #2 denotes the questioner's response to the outcome.

The Loving Cup

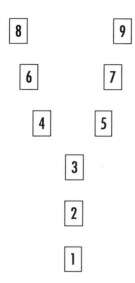

The Loving Cup uses nine runes, and is particularly useful for questions concerning matters of the heart. Traditionally made of clay, the cup is a universal symbol of water, especially the waters of the sea womb, which gave birth to the Earth and all that lives on it. As a vessel symbolic of the womb and well of knowledge, as well as of the magical cauldron of the Great Goddess, the cup embodies the essence of the mother. It depicts the source of life and the well of inspiration from whose watery depths all things spring. Once consecrated through dedication, the cup becomes a loving cup, representing the sacred union of the Goddess and God.

Think of a question regarding love. Use this layout only when asking a question in regard to your beloved—not just someone you are infatuated with, but someone for whom you feel "deep love." Mix the runes as usual while pondering the question. Pull nine runes, placing them, faceup, in position as if you were constructing a loving cup. Put the first rune at the base of the cup, the second above the first, the third above the second, and so forth, according to the diagram. The top two runes are read in combination, both representing the future outcome. If one of the top runes is positive and the other negative (Othala, for example, and Thurisaz), they cancel each other out.

Rune #1:

The first (bottom) rune represents your current position.

Rune #2:

The second rune signifies your beloved's present position.

Rune #3:

The third rune denotes the nature of the issue at hand.

Rune #4:

The fourth rune shows your desire in relation to the question.

Rune #5:

The fifth rune reveals your beloved's desire.

Rune #6:

The sixth rune shows the possible obstacles and challenges that can arise for you.

Rune #7:

The seventh rune stands for the possible obstacles

and challenges that your beloved may encounter.

Runes #8 and #9:

These two topmost runes represent the future outcome. Read them in combination with each other.

The Tree of Life

1	
3	2
5	4
6	
8	7
9	
10	

Using ten runes, this layout represents the Tree of

Life, which is the essence of all trees, ever green, and continuously blooming and bearing fruit. In the Northern Tradition this great tree was usually guarded by a serpent or dragon. A giant ash, Yggdrasil, was the World Tree that links and shelters all the worlds. Three roots in three different worlds fed Yggdrasil—one in Nifelheim by the spring of Hvergelmir "roaring kettle," which is the source of many rivers; one in Midgard by Mimir's Well (the Well of Wisdom); and one in Asgard, which is watered daily by the Norns from Urd's Fountain (the Well of Fate). Four stags representing the Four Winds and named Dain, Dvalin, Duneyr, and Durathor ran across the branches of the World Tree. They fed on the topmost twigs as dew dripped from their antlers onto the world below. Other inhabitants of Yggdrasil included Vithofnir, the golden cock, who watched Surt the fire giant; Ratotosk, the gossiping squirrel; an eagle with the falcon Vedfolnir perched on his head; and Odin's goat, named Heidrun, who supplied the divine mead. On the day of Ragnarok, when the forces of chaos would arise, Surt would set Yggdrasil on fire, but a man and woman would hide inside its trunk. They would be the only humans to survive and would begin a Golden Age.

Designed to give a concise overview of your life or that of another person, this particular layout is more advanced than the others, yet it brings quick, comprehensive, and accurate results. The runes represent the roots, trunk, branches, and top of the Tree of Life.

When doing this reading for yourself, focus your attention on your life while you mix your runes. When doing the reading for another person, focus your attention on that other person while mixing your runes. When using rune cards, let the other person mix the cards while focusing on his or her life, and then hand them back to you, the reader. Pull ten runes, one at a time, and place them facedown in a row in front of you. Then, take each rune in the order you pulled it, turn it over, and place it in the correct position, according to the diagram.

Rune #1:

The rune at the top of the tree symbolizes your highest ideals and standards of excellence.

Runes #2 and #3:

The second rune represents your current energy level, and the third your physical and mental experiences. Read these two runes as a pair.

Runes #4 and #5:

The fourth rune signifies your ethical virtues and personal moral code, and the fifth shows the area of your most recent victories and successes. Read these two runes individually and then as a pair, in combination with each other.

Rune #6:

The sixth rune represents your health, and issues with health.

Runes #7 and #8:

The seventh rune denotes personal issues of love and trust, and the eighth rune stands for creativity in the arts, crafts, and procreation. Read these two runes, in combination, as a pair.

Rune #9:

The ninth rune points to your powers of imagination and creative ideas.

Rune #10:

The bottom rune at the roots of the tree represents your living conditions and the state of your hearth and home.

The Four Quarters

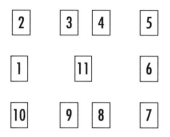

This eleven-rune layout is based on the four quarters of the year. It is ideal when you need a precise answer to a complex question as well as an overall view of your life for the past six months and the next six months.

Decide on a question about something that has been affecting you for about six months. Begin by mixing your runes and select the first eleven that come to you, placing them facedown in a horizonal row in front of you. Then turn over each rune, one at a time, and place it in its correct position according to the diagram, beginning with Rune #1 and moving in a sunwise (clockwise) pattern, ending with Rune

#11 in the center. In this layout, each row is divided into quarters and read accordingly.

Runes #1, #2, and #10:

These three runes, to the left, represent the First Quarter, and indicate your present state of mind.

Runes #5, #6, and #7:

These three runes, to the right, signify the Second Quarter, and show possible helpful or opposing influences in regard to the question.

Runes #3 and #4:

These two middle runes at the top symbolize the Third Quarter, and reveal what will happen if things continue in their current direction.

Runes #8 and #9:

The two middle runes in the bottom row denote the possible outcome of the question six months from now.

Rune #11:

The eleventh and final rune, in the center, represents the overall tone of the rune spread.

The Cosmic Axis

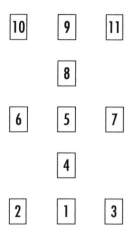

This eleven-rune layout is similar to the Grid of Nine, but with two additional linking runes that represent the cosmic axis, the passage between the three worlds (Utgard, Midgard, and Asgard).

Think of the question and mix the runes as usual. Pull out eleven runes, one at a time, and place them faceup, beginning with the first rune at the base of the central column. Then place the second rune to its left, and the next to the right of it. These three runes represent the lower level of the cosmic axis. The fourth rune is positioned directly above the first rune, and serves as the lower-link rune. Put the fifth rune or card directly above the fourth, and then runes six and seven to its left and right, respectively. These three runes create the central level of the cosmic axis. Place the eighth rune above the fifth (middle) rune. This is the upper-link rune that joins the middle tier with the upper one. Place the ninth rune just above the upper-link rune, with runes ten and eleven to the left and right, respectively.

Rune #1:

The central rune reflects the major past influence on the questioner.

Rune #2:

The second rune denotes the unconscious response to this major past influence.

Rune #3:

The third rune signifies the conscious response to this major past influence.

Rune #4:

The fourth (lower link) rune represents the results of the influences that have led to the present state of affairs.

Rune #5:

The fifth rune denotes the present.

Rune #6:

The sixth rune suggests current unconscious responses.

Rune #7:

The seventh rune shows current conscious responses.

Rune #8:

The eighth (upper link) rune reveals the results of the present influences if you do nothing to alter the flow of energies.

Rune #9:

The ninth (center) rune signifies the major outcome of the question at hand.

Rune #10:

The tenth rune shows the unconscious response to the outcome.

Rune #11:

The eleventh rune represents the conscious response to the outcome.

The Celtic Knight Cross

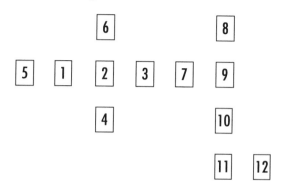

Adapted from the traditional Celtic Cross Tarot layout, this twelve-rune reading is my personal favorite. It is especially helpful for making decisions and learning more about possible changes in career, relationships, and your living environment.

In this layout, you add a Significator rune stone or card. To choose a Significator, place all the runes or rune cards faceup on the casting cloth in front of you, and then select the most appropriate rune. The Significator represents the subject of the reading—

either yourself or the person for whom you are doing the reading. You can also choose a Significator rune by simply selecting the rune with which you have the strongest affinity, one that you feel corresponds with your personal image. When doing a reading for other people, have them select the rune they feel most drawn to as the Significator. The Significator can also be a rune that reflects the matter in question. For example, in questions regarding personal credit and money, you could use Fehu. For questions relating to travel, you might employ Raidho as the Significator. For questions pertaining to disruptive or sudden change, you could select Hagalaz.

Begin by placing the first rune, the Significator rune, faceup, in the center of the layout. Then gather the remaining runes together and mix them as usual, focusing on the question at hand. Pull the runes, one at a time, and place them, faceup, in the layout as shown in the diagram, starting with the second rune, which goes to the right of the Significator rune. Place the third rune to the right of the second, and continue, following the layout, until you have pulled all twelve runes.

Rune #1:

This is the Significator rune that represents the person for whom the reading is being done.

Rune #2:

The second rune signifies the question.

Rune #3:

The third rune denotes immediate future influences, positive and negative.

Rune #4:

The fourth rune reflects childhood and other past influences.

Rune #5:

The fifth, the rune to the left, reveals present influences just about to move out of your life.

Rune #6:

The sixth rune at the top of the cross shows possible influences in the future, depending upon the polarities of the runes next to it. For example, if runes #5 and #7 were Algiz and Thurisaz, and rune #6 was Tiwaz, rune #6 may represent a potential enemy or threat.

These runes reflect influences that might come into being.

Rune #7:

The seventh rune represents future influences that will impact the question at hand.

Runes #8 and #9:

These two runes signify your hopes and fears. Read them in combination, since hope and fear are basically two ends of the same polarity. Hope and fear are polar opposites, which means they reflect one another. For example, hoping for a new love in your life may also be your fear—in this case, a fear of intimacy.

Rune #10:

The tenth rune shows influences from your family and friends, positive and negative. For example, if Thurisaz shows up here, you may be having thorny relations with your parents or friends. If Dagaz shows up in this position, you may finally be seeing daylight with a problem relationship. If Othala shows up, it may indicate an inheritance from family or friends.

Runes #11 and #12:

These are final-outcome runes. I always like to have options, which is why two runes appear in this final position. Read these runes in combination with each other.

The Futhark Layout

1	9	17
2	10	18
3	11	19
4	12	20
5	13	21
6	14	22
7	15	23
8	16	24

Using all twenty-four runes, the Futhark Layout gives the most comprehensive reading of any of the previous layouts. Because the nature of this spread is a personal overview of the next year, the Futhark Layout is the perfect reading for New Year's Day. The question you ask in this reading will relate to the influences that will affect you over the next twelve months.

The Futhark Layout also takes more time than other readings. You not only need to pull all the runes, but also to read each one in relation to the rune that rules its position in the *aett*. I suggest you write this rune reading down in your journal and take a look at it from time to time over the next few months. This will give you added perspective and help you to understand the reading fully.

Spend at least five minutes mixing the runes or rune cards while you focus on your life over the next year. Then pull the runes, one at a time, placing them faceup, in three vertical rows of eight, starting with the left row, as shown in the diagram. Each of these three rows represents one of the three *aettir*. Read the pulled runes according to the position in which they appear. For example, if Wunjo appears in position #1 (Fehu), it may point to the possibility of a joyful reward, such as the money for a new home within the next year.

Following are the rune positions and their corresponding meanings. The meanings are given in the form of a question, making it easier to see how the rune you pull relates to its position. Remember: This reading pertains primarily to the next twelve months.

Rune #1: Fehu
What will provide you with money and prosperity?

Rune #2: Uruz
What will give you inner strength and good physical health?

Rune #3: Thurisaz
What will defend or destroy you?

Rune #4: Ansuz
What will inspire you and drive your intellect?

Rune #5: Raidho
Where will you journey?

Rune #6: Kenaz
    What will you create and come to know?

Rune #7: Gebo
    What gifts will be given to you?

Rune #8: Wunjo
    What will bring you joy, pleasure, and happiness?

Rune #9: Hagalaz
    What will transform and change you?

Rune #10: Naudhiz
    What will you need?

Rune #11: Isa
    What will constrain or bind you?

Rune #12: Jera
    What harvest will you reap?

Rune #13: Eihwaz
    What choices and challenges lie ahead?

Rune #14: Perdhro

What hidden talents and abilities will come into being?

Rune #15: Algiz

What life and death issues will come up in the next year?

Rune #16: Sowilo

What will be your guiding light?

Rune #17: Tiwaz

What will be the state of your legal affairs?

Rune #18: Berkana

What will create growth and beauty?

Rune #19: Ehwaz

What partnerships and relationships will you form over the next year?

Rune #20: Mannaz

What will your social life be like?

Rune #21: Laguz

How will you feel, emotionally, over the next year?

Rune #22: Ingwaz

What form will your sexual expression take?

Rune #23: Dagaz

Where will you find balance in your life?

Rune #24: Othala

What property or knowledge will you inherit (and/or receive) within the next year?

Ceremonial Runecasting

Ceremonial runecasting differs greatly from readings using layouts. It is more complex, subtle, and requires your undivided attention. By tradition, only wooden, amber, or stone runes are used for ceremonial runecasting.

One ancient ceremonial runecasting technique is called "Raed Waen," which translates as "riding the wagon," where you visualize yourself as a rider in the divine wagon of the gods from which all things can be seen and known. The riding of the wagon is the actual ceremony while the throwing of the runes is called the "shoat."

When working indoors, you need to throw the runes along the main axis of the room, which is called the "rig," or "right line." The rig is an energetic line that crosses the room. Its direction may vary, depending on the room. To find the rig, when you're doing ritual the first thing to do is find the four corners. Then determine the rig by drawing a straight line between the north and south points and east and west points. The longest line is the rig, which, in a room, is usually the line between the east and west corners. The reason for this is that the rig parallels the path of the sun, moving from east to west. When working outdoors—the optimal setting for any rune ceremony—orient the rig so that it faces toward the sun at the time the divination takes place. This direction will of course change depending upon the time of day.

The poem entitled "Rigsthula," from the *Edda*, is the story of how Rig (another face of the god Heimdall) visited families belonging to the three classes. Rig stayed with each of the families for three days, lying with all three wives, and in this way became the father to all classes of people. Rigs were also strips of land belonging to a village that in traditional Scottish folk law were allocated using runic lots called "Runrigs," a form of lottery. Because the runes came from Odin, the allocation of land by runrigs was considered the sacred will of the gods.

THE STOL

Most people prefer to sit on a pillow while doing a runecasting. A "stol" is a pillow that has been specially crafted, often embroidered, beaded, or handpainted with runic signs. Customarily, the stol is placed at the negative end of the ceremonial rune cloth—generally next to the wall toward the west.

CEREMONIAL RUNE CLOTH

To do ceremonial runecasting, you need a ceremonial rune cloth. You can make one out of any white or ivory natural fabric, though linen is traditional. The size of the cloth is as wide as your outstretched arms, from fingertip to fingertip (a measurement called a fathom). The cloth's length is as long as the distance from your feet to your fingertips when your arms are stretched out high above your head.

Orient the cloth so that its central point is located one-third of the way up the rig. Your view along the rig is toward the longer part of the room. The wall you are facing is considered positive, and the wall behind you negative. Using a simple compass, this means that you are correctly oriented when east is positive (in front of you), and west is negative (behind you), with the north toward your left side and the south to your right. The direction along the rig toward the positive wall is "up." Moving toward the negative wall along the rig is "down." Symbolic objects may also be placed on the four corners of both the larger ceremonial cloth and the smaller casting cloth.

THE MEAROMOT

Many runecasters place another smaller cloth on the larger ceremonial rune cloth at the positive end. On this smaller cloth you can place your "mearomot," or personal talisman. Made of silk, hemp, burlap, linen, cotton, or other natural fabric, the mearomot is a pouch containing a crystal, feather, picture, and other objects you choose with which you have a sacred connection. Write the question of the runecasting on a piece of paper. The paper accompanies the mearomot and is placed underneath the pouch on the smaller white cloth. You do not always need to use this smaller cloth; you can simply cast the runes onto the larger ceremonial cloth in front of you. When you become more adept at runecasting, though, you will most likely find the smaller cloth of greater value, because it allows you to focus more effectively on the runecast.

Decorating the Mearomot

The smaller ceremonial cloth has specific symbols on it, and again usually measures nine inches (22.5 cm) square. One way of decorating it is to draw three circles on it representing past, present, and future, and the four directional points of north, east, south, and west.

Another more traditional way to decorate the smaller cloth is either to visualize or draw the Nine Worlds upon it. In Norse Mythology, when Odin, Vili, and Ve sacrificed Ymir, they arranged his remains to create the Nine Worlds. This brought about cosmic order and manifestation. Yggdrasil, the World Tree, supported the Nine Worlds, which contained countless dwellings and homes. Between and among these worlds were found the runes, their secrets, and their pathways. You may want to use the layout on page 321 to design your smaller cloth according to the *Eddas*.

Alfheim or
Lightalfheim (northwest)
(northeast) (light-elf-world)

Asgard
(Aesir-world)

WEST DIRECTION
Vanaheim
(Vanir-world)

CENTER POINT
Midgard
(Middle-world)

EAST DIRECTION
Jotunheim
(Etin-world)

 Hel
(southwest)
(silent, sleepy realm or
realm of the dead)

Svartalfheim
(southeast)
(black-elf-world
or dwarf-world)

SOUTH DIRECTION
Muspelheim

A more contemporary method for embellishing your smaller rune cloth, based on Jungian psychology, is called Three Levels of Consciousness. In Norse Mythology, creation originated from two primal forces: fire and ice (frost). The interaction of these forces is what resulted in the formation of the Nine Worlds. The Nine Worlds may then be divided into three levels of consciousness, as pages 323–324.

LEVEL ONE–HIGHER CONSCIOUS

ASGARD
Realm of the Gods
Inspiration and Spirit
Highest Plane

MUSPELHEIM
Intuition, Vital Energies
Creative Fire

VANAHEIM
Feeling, Emotion,
Water, Balance

MIDDLE LEVEL–CONSCIOUS

MIDGARD
The Personality
Humankind
Ego

SVARTALFHEIM
Sensation
The Dark Elves
Transmuting Base
  Minerals into Higher
  Minerals

LIGHTALFHEIM or
ALFHEIM
Thought
The Light Elves
Plants, Trees
Birds

LOWER LEVEL–UNCONSCIOUS

JOTUNHEIM
Giant World
Animus/Disruptive Male Energy
Chaotic Part of the Self

HEL
Realm of the Dead
Anima/Destructive
Feminine Energy

NIFELHEIM
The Fog World
The Shadow Self
Origins and Roots
Accumulated Wyrd

PROCEDURE FOR CEREMONIAL RUNECASTING

Hold the bag or box of runes and ask a question. Stir the runes around with your hand, pick a handful; the number is purely a matter of personal preference, nine being the usual number. Then cast or throw the stones onto your cloth, along the rig orientation, if possible. Take any runes that land facedown off the cloth and do not use them in the reading. These are called murk-staves. From the runes that land faceup, choose three to read—or you can read all of them, starting with the closest rune and moving to the most distant. These are called bright-staves. The patterns the letters form, their positions and relationships, point to an answer to the question. Be sure to take into account adjacent runes and how they correspond to one another. For example, if the three closest runes were Raidho, Wunjo, and Algiz, it may suggest that you will move toward your goal and achieve it, but must also be protective of that achievement. When the smaller ceremonial rune cloth is used, any runes that land off the cloth are generally ignored. Some people consider the runes that fall off the cloth representative of hidden influences at work in regard to the question.

How the runes are read is subjective, but a receptive mind and consistency are crucial. It is up to you to determine the meanings of the runes and the answer to the question from the positioning of the runes on the cloth.

You need to follow a few simple guidelines. First, the number of runes you cast need to be easy to hold in your hands. Second, very large readings tend to be more complex and can over-complicate things. Last of all, three and multiples of three are considered particularly significant and useful for divination purposes.

Runes lying in the center are the most immediately relevant, while those lying around the edges are less important or represent more general influences. Runes that are close together or even touching often complement each other, or may even represent a single thing, while runes that fall on opposite sides of the pattern frequently represent opposing influences.

Runecasting cannot always be fully interpreted in one sitting, so whenever possible, be sure to journal the casting, take a picture of it, or draw a simple sketch of it. You may only realize the true significance and meanings of the casting sometime later when you contemplate your notes and the sketch.

NINE-RUNE CEREMONIAL CASTING METHOD

A magical number around the world, nine is also the number of the worlds in Norse Mythology. This nine-rune ceremonial casting method gives an over-all view of your spiritual path, or the path of the person you are doing the reading for, presenting possible outcomes and influencing factors. With this casting also, it's a good idea to take a picture or draw a rough sketch of it, if you can, after the runecasting, so you can study it further.

Begin by turning your mind toward the spiritual path you are on, and where you would like to find yourself, spiritually, within the next few years. While thinking about your spiritual path, mix the runes and then pull nine from the pouch. Pass these nine runes from hand to hand, at least three times, pondering your spiritual path. Place the runes between both of your hands and take a few moments to focus on your spiritual path. Next, gently toss the nine runes onto the casting cloth, along the rig, in a single throw.

Take a minute to study the runes, and pull off any that land facedown or off the cloth. Then proceed to read the runes that remain. These key runes correspond directly to your spiritual path and the circumstances that led you to it. Those that lie toward the center are the most immediately relevant, while those lying around the edges of the cloth have a less direct bearing on your spirituality. When runes touch or are grouped close together, they can represent complementary energies. Runes that fall on opposite sides of the cloth may represent opposing influences.

It is your choice as to how to interpret the runes and determine what the various positions and patterns in a runecasting mean, but once you have come up with a few general rules that work for you, stick with them. The best thing you can do is to look at the patterns and relationships that appear in the runecasting and see what interpretations make sense to you.

CEREMONIAL CASTING UPON THE NINE WORLDS

This casting takes more time and utilizes all 24 runes, plus the Nine Worlds of a traditional ceremonial casting cloth. Ideally done on New Year's Day or on a birthday, this runecast is simple and complex at the same time. The more you learn about Norse mythology, the better you will understand the pattern of the Nine Worlds and the more you will enjoy this rune cast.

Begin by thinking about your present life. Slowly mix all 24 runes in the rune pouch, bag, or box. Then, cupping them in both your hands, toss them all onto the casting cloth, along the rig, in one gentle throw. Remember to use your intuition and be sure to write the runecast down for future reference.

The pattern resulting from a casting upon the Nine Worlds can be interpreted in a multitude of ways. The easiest way is to energetically, if not physically, divide your casting cloth into the Nine Worlds by means of one of the many methods mentioned previously. Where the runes land, in relation to the Nine Worlds on your cloth, is how they are interpreted. It works like this:

Nifelheim (North):
That which resists you. Things that are dormant and intangible

Jotunheim (East):
That which confuses you. Forces pressing for change

Asgard (Northeast):
That which inspires you. Your spirituality.

Vanaheim (West):
That which promotes growth. Sexual and erotic relationships

Lightalfheim (Northwest):
That which stimulates your mind. Forces that help you

Midgard (Center):
That which sustains your ego

Hel (Southwest):
That which is hidden. Influences from the past

Svartelfheim (Southeast):
That which you need to reflect upon. Creative emotional influences

Muspelheim (South):
That which vitalizes you. Active creative influences from outside

CEREMONIAL CASTING WITH RUNE-TINES

Rune-tines are similar-sized twigs or popsicle sticks inscribed with runes. You can make your own by collecting 24 twigs of similar length and size, or 24 popsicle sticks, and then painting the runes on one side of them with red paint or, in a pinch, you can use a red felt pen.

To do a runecasting with tines, hold all 24 in both your hands and toss them onto the ground, along the rig, if possible. Only read the runes that are faceup, pulling the tines that land facedown off the area or cloth. The positions of the remaining tines denote their relation to one another. For instance, two or more touching or parallel rune-tines may complement and reinforce one other. Two or more crossing tines can indicate opposing forces and obstacles. The tines that land closer to you are more influential right now, while those farthest from you reflect influences in the distant future. Consider all the groups of runes and how they relate to one another, as well as whether they point to other runes and the general direction they lie in. Use your intuition to select the three rune-tines that seem to be the key to the casting. By interpreting the three primary tines, you will most likely get a clear answer to your question.

CEREMONIAL RUNECASTING WITH STICKS

The advantage of stick casting over all other rune divination methods is that the runes only come into being after you cast the sticks and they fall across one another. In this way, the runes created by a stickcast reflect the exact moment that the casting is done, when the sticks hit the ground. The other interesting thing to note about stick casting is that the same runes may appear more than once in a single reading. This is called doubling, and it is something that never occurs when you use rune stones or cards. Runes that are doubled point to extremely strong energies.

It is customary to use birch sticks for runecasting, but other woods also work well, such as oak, madrona, fir, and pine. Take nine sticks of similar lengths and sizes, and pass them back and forth between your hands while you think of a specific question. (Some people also like to roll the sticks between their hands, but that's entirely up to you.) Feel as though you are putting the question into the sticks. Next, toss the sticks, in one motion, onto the ground or your rune cloth, along the rig. The patterns of the sticks, after they fall across one another, reveal particular runes. The sticks form shapes that resemble rune shapes. Some of these rune shapes are upright, some reversed, some backwards, and others appear doubled. The rune shapes that lie at the center of the casting, plus the doubled runes (those that appear more than once), are the ones to focus upon.

Stick casting can also be done when walking in the woods. One of my favorite activities to do with my young son is to walk down to our creek, picking up nine sticks off the ground as we go. We size them into similar shapes and then clear off a nine-inch (22.5 cm) round circle on the ground with the side of our shoe. Then we each take a turn holding the sticks, thinking of a question, and then toss them onto the ground. Generally, it's best to keep stick casting simple when just beginning, so I suggest selecting one, two, or three rune shapes to focus on. As you progress, stick casting can also become the most profound and advanced form of runecasting that you practice.

Basic Rune Meditations

Besides divination, runes can act as a medium for tapping into inner knowledge through meditation, dream work, and visualization. The following basic rune meditations will help you better understand the powerful energies of these ancient symbols.

One Rune a Day

Select one rune each day, for 24 days. Just after waking up, mix your runes, and without looking—but with intention—pull the one that you feel most drawn to. Draw the rune symbol on a few slips of paper and place one next to your bed, one on the refrigerator, one on a bathroom mirror, one on the dashboard of your car, one on a window, and one on the wall so that you will see the symbol continually throughout the day. Do this each morning for 24 days. You will begin to feel the rune resonate inside you. Sometimes the rune even seems to correspond to a part of your body. You may find that you see the rune symbol wherever you look—in road signs, the shapes of trees, the way pencils fall together on a desk, and so forth.

Each day, for 24 days, record the rune you pulled on a sheet of paper. After the 24 days, go back and look at the sheet and notice how many times certain runes were pulled during the 24-day period, and which runes were not pulled. The runes that appear most often reflect the influences that are currently the strongest in your daily life. The runes not pulled reflect energies that are not yet directly influencing your life.

RUNE AWARENESS

Place the 24 Elder Futhark runes faceup, in front of you, in the form of rune stones, squares, or cards. Arrange the runes by *aett*, grouping them in three sets of eight, yet spacing them out so you can look at each one individually. Sit or stand comfortably. Clear your mind, letting go of distracting thoughts. Take a few deep breaths, inhaling to the count of six and exhaling to the count of six, and begin looking at the runes, one at a time, making a mental note of how your mind and perception move as you see the various runes in front of you. Allow your awareness to drift slowly from symbol to symbol, focusing for a few moments on each one. Be particularly aware of your intellectual process and how it works in relation to the symbols you are studying. What does your mind do? Do you dissect the symbols, one by one, analyzing their essential elements? Do certain runes evoke sensations or memories, and do these then connect to other sensations and memories? Think about how each runic symbol relates to your present life, noticing how some seem to resonate with you more than others. As you focus on each symbol, chant the name of the rune over and over. Notice what effect this has on your perception, and any related body sensations. Take at least fifteen minutes to do this meditation. When you finish, select one rune to work with for the day and put the remainder away in your rune bag or box.

SENSING THE RUNES

This simple meditation takes only about five minutes a day, and produces excellent results. Recline or sit comfortably, in a place where you will not be disturbed for a few minutes, and if possible set a timer for five minutes. Select your favorite rune and place it faceup on the casting cloth, on your lap, or in front of you on a table, desk, or similar surface. Take a few deep breaths, relaxing your mind and body. Shift your body around a bit to get even more comfortable. Begin looking at the rune in front of you, perceiving it with all your senses, including your intuition and psychic ability. *See*, *touch*, *taste*, *smell*, and *hear* the rune. Use your imagination. Be in the moment with the rune. At the point where you feel yourself wavering and moving away from the experience, go back to the rune and again experience it with all your senses. Any time your mind tries to take over the experience, move back to the rune and sense it with another one of your senses. Do this for five minutes at a time. As you practice this technique, you will become better at staying in the moment with the rune and its essential energies. It's a good idea to apply this meditation to each of the 24 Futhark, over an extended period of time.

24-WEEK RUNE MEDITATION

This meditation takes a 24-week commitment, but the results are guaranteed to expand your mind and your knowledge of the runes. If you apply yourself, you may even hear the runes sing to you, as others have, making their messages clear through sound.

Ideally, begin this meditation on Wednesday (Woden's Dag). The first week (Wednesday through Tuesday), you will focus on Fehu; the second week, Uruz; the third week, Thurisaz; and so on, for 24 weeks, moving through one of the three *aettir* every eight weeks. Use a rune stone, card, or square for this meditation, so that you have a physical point of reference. After selecting the rune of the week, read over the rune description in the encyclopedic listing in this book (pages 35–195). During the week, from Wednesday through Tuesday, notice how the rune and its primary energies influence your life. Make a few notes throughout the week as to how you feel about the weekly rune, and also record some of your thoughts about the process. You may find that the rune will have a much stronger and more active influence when you work with it after doing this meditation.

The following is a very basic guideline for helping you focus on each of the *aettir* and 24 runes. For instance, Week One, concentrate on mobile wealth—where you find yourself financially, where you would like to find yourself financially, and how the Fehu rune can strengthen your personal wealth.

The first *aett* belongs to Freyja and Frey, and is the *Aett* of Creation.

1. Fehu—Financial prosperity and mobile wealth
2. Uruz—Health and healing issues
3. Thurisaz—Conflicts, obstacles, and psychological issues
4. Ansuz—Communications and transmissions; points things back to sources in the past

5. Raidho—The direction of your personal path
6. Kenaz—New ways of experiencing things, new opportunities, information, and creativity
7. Gebo—Issues having to do with an exchange of energies such as contracts, gifts, relationships, and partnerships
8. Wunjo—Your wishes, hopes, achievements, and accomplishments

The second *aett* of Hagalaz belongs to Heimdall and Mordgud, the goddess who guards the bridge leading to the underworld. It is the *Aett* of Humanity.

9. Hagalaz—Issues of change and transformation, sometimes disruptive, but often for the better
10. Naudhiz—Anything that restricts you, or situations that make you anxious or fearful
11. Isa—All of those things you have trouble letting go of, especially past hurts and pain, things that have crystallized. This is the rune of your conditioning
12. Jera—Your hopes and expectations, and the harvest rune that shows the results of your actions and efforts

13. Eihwaz—The driving force of motivation and your sense of purpose

14. Perdhro—Your hidden talents, intuitive abilities, and creative powers

15. Algiz—Your protective powers and spiritual connections with the divine

16. Sowilo—Your sunshine in life and the direction in which you will be guided by divine light

The third *aett* belongs to Tiwaz and Zisa, and this is the *Aett* of Divinity or Godhood.

17. Tiwaz—Your personal strengths, initiative, honor, sense of justice and fair play, and leadership abilities

18. Berkana—Your feminine power and intuitions. Issues with family and personal growth

19. Ehwaz—Your abilities of cooperation, sexual expression, and relationships with others

20. Mannaz—Your social position and the people around you, including your friends and enemies

21. Laguz—Your emotions and powers of imagination

22. Ingwaz—The way you integrate your life. Your expectations

23. Dagaz—Your balance between polarities. Issues of initiation, birth, and new beginnings

24. Othala—Your spiritual heritage and birthright

RUNE GIFT GUIDED MEDITATION

This meditation is intended to help you connect with the runes on a deeper level. It is particularly helpful to tape-record the meditation and play it just before going to sleep, and upon waking. If you tape-record it and want to use it before going to sleep, just alter the ending to take you into a restful, refreshing sleep. You can also change the meditation to use the word "god" in place of "goddess," if you prefer.

Close your eyes, breathe deeply, and relax. Get as comfortable as you can, breathing and relaxing more and more. Breathe in to the count of three, holding your breath for three counts and then exhaling completely. Do this three times or more, deeply breathing in and out, relaxing more and more, and allowing all the tension of the day to leave your body every time you exhale. Each sound you hear in the room will help you to become even more relaxed and peaceful.

Begin to breathe white light into your body from all around you. It's as if you can feel yourself breathing in the light through your skin, through the tips of your toes and the top of your head, softly and completely. As you breathe in the white light, you can feel it flowing through your body and warming you from head to toe.

Now very slowly begin to visualize yourself walking down a garden path on a warm summer's day, the sun shining brightly. The air is warm and a gentle breeze touches your face. You come to a garden gate made of wood. The gate is very ornate and carved with runic symbols. The symbols seem to come alive as the sun shines on the gate.

Slowly you open the gate, and as you do you notice the warmth of the wood on your hands. You walk slowly through the gate into the lush garden, leaving the gate open behind you. As you enter the garden the smell of roses, lavender, and jasmine fills your senses. Several tall mountain ash trees guard the entrance, and their branches suggest ancient runic symbols in the way they weave together. Oaks, pines, and fir trees surround the area, shading delicate ferns and butter-colored wild irises. Pine needles, twigs, and leaves cover the ground here and there, and their shapes, again, remind you of runes.

You can hear bees buzzing in the garden as you walk on, and the smell of water greets you as you approach a small pool fed by a natural spring. The spring bubbles softly over several large milky-white quartz stones as the water flows into the pool.

You sit down comfortably on the grassy bank next to the pool and look into the water. You can see the reflection of trees in a circle around the pool and you also see yourself in the brightly lit water. Dip your hand into the water and feel the cool sensation, perhaps even take a drink from the pool.

Noticing some very small white quartz stones at the edge of the pool, you pick up three stones in your hand and begin throwing them into the pool, one at a time. You watch the ripples from each stone move outward and finally disappear before you toss in the next stone. With each stone you toss into the water, you feel more relaxed, peaceful, and warm.

Suddenly you have the sensation and realization that you are not alone. As you look to your left, the picture and form of the Goddess appears. Study her image for a few moments, using your breath to get an even clearer picture of her. Taking a deep breath, you can see her clearly now. Communicate with her. If you know her name, call her by name. If you don't know her name, ask her and she will tell you. Merge with her and become one with the Goddess. With each breath you take, her image becomes more defined and her face more clear. She seems surrounded by a kind of golden-white luminosity that radiates from her being and melts into yours.

In her hand, she holds a rune stone. Notice which rune symbol and what kind of stone it is. Take the stone from the Goddess and notice how it feels in your hand. It may feel cool or hot, alive with energy or soothing and calm. Trace the runic symbol engraved in the stone with your fingers, feeling the indentation on the smooth surface. This rune stone is your magical gift from the Goddess, and you can use it to communicate directly with the divine.

Now it is your turn to give the Goddess something in return: a kiss, a song perhaps, or a vow—

whatever you choose. Give this gift to her now. Breathing slowly and deeply, say whatever you need to say to her, silently and completely. Breathe slowly and visualize the experience even more clearly now, sensing every feeling and thought between you and the Goddess.

Suddenly the Goddess beckons you to follow her. You carry your rune stone with you as she takes you through the garden, showing you the many trees, plants, roses, and other flowers, animals, and magical beings that live there. You notice the runic symbols in nature all around you. The bright sun shines upon everything: the leaves of the plants, the branches of the trees, the path in front of you—brightening everything with its pure light. The Goddess reminds you that you can return to this magical garden whenever you choose, and then she takes your hand and guides you through the wooden gate carved with runes, closing the gate behind you.

As you move through the gate, the Goddess becomes invisible, but she is still very much with you. You can sense her hand on yours. She is always with you. The rune stone gift that she has given you is eternal.

Slowly begin to move back into your body, remembering the rune symbol that the Goddess has given you and what you have given her, knowing that these gifts are signs of your connection with the Goddess and the divine. Moving your hands, toes, and head, come back to the present moment completely, opening your eyes and breathing deeply. Be sure to make note of the rune stone the Goddess gave you, and what you gave her in return. Look up the rune in the encyclopedic listing and study the description. Over the next few weeks, notice how this particular rune influences your life.

Rune Dreaming Techniques

The way you live is directly related to the way you dream. As you work with runes more often, you may find yourself beginning to dream about them, experiencing the symbols in your dreams. The following three rune dreaming techniques will help you integrate the runes into your dream world, allowing for a deeper understanding of these ancient symbols.

DREAMING A SOLUTION WITH THREE RUNES

About an hour before you go to bed, identify one pressing problem in your life. Pick something that you want to resolve, preferably something that you've given a great deal of energy and thought already, for example, finding a better place to live. Make a few notes on a sheet of paper. Then think of one clear question regarding the problem, such as, "How can I find the best place for me to live?" and write the question down on the same sheet of paper.

Mix the runes as usual, thinking of your question. Pull three runes from your rune bag, and place them, faceup, on your bedside table in a horizontal row, from left to right. The first rune represents the problem, the second the reason for the problem, and the third, the possible solution. Look up the meanings of the runes in the encyclopedic listing. Study their shapes, and then lie back and close your eyes, all the while still visualizing the three runes on your bedside table.

Allow your mind to begin to explore the different ways you might find a solution to the problem. Let the three runes be your keys and just let your mind wander. Even consider a few outlandish solutions.

Then amplify your intention of finding an answer to your problem by stepping into the future for a few minutes and experiencing how wonderful it feels to have already resolved your problem, to be living in the perfect place.

As you drift off to sleep, keep visualizing the three runes and the perfect solution to your problem. When you wake up, write down or record your dream and draw any dream images or rune symbols. Most people find a workable solution to their problem within a few days.

AT ONE WITH THE RUNE STONE

This dreaming technique uses a semiprecious rune stone. Hematite, clear quartz, amethyst, citrine, and rose quartz are excellent choices of stone for this purpose, or you can use a favorite stone you have found in nature and painted or engraved as a rune stone. Select the rune symbol you feel most drawn to at this moment.

Begin by closing your eyes. Breathe deeply, relaxing as much as possible. Sense yourself sinking into the rune stone. Start with your toes, feeling your toes sinking into the rune stone, into the symbol itself.

Then move your awareness slowly up your body, feeling your ankles, calves, knees, hips, stomach, back, arms, neck, and head all sinking into the rune stone and runic symbol. Let all your muscles go and feel your flesh and bones sink completely into the lattice of the stone and symbol. Melt into the stone and become one with it. Now, in your mind's eye, fully sense the runic symbol and see yourself shifting into the symbol, becoming one with the essence of the rune. Look at the runic symbol from every angle, from the inside and the outside, in your mind's eye. Move around it, see, feel, and sense the totality of it. As you continue to melt into the rune, allow yourself to drift into sleep. When you awaken, rub the rune stone in your hands and write down or record those details you recall about the dream.

DREAM SHEET RUNE

This method uses a rune dream sheet. Generally made of paper, posterboard, cardboard, or wood, the rune sheet can be used as a tool for dreaming and meditation. You can easily make your own rune sheet by cutting a piece of paper twelve inches (30 cm) long by six inches (15 cm) wide and drawing the three *aettir* of the Elder Futhark on the sheet in black ink, in three vertical rows of eight each.

Just before you go to sleep, light a votive candle, one that can safely burn down all the way as you sleep. Place the rune dream sheet on your bedside table or on the wall so that the light of the candle illuminates the runic symbols drawn on it. Move your attention completely to the rune dream sheet, and notice if one of the runic symbols seems to draw your attention more than the others. Place your finger on that rune for a few moments. Lie back, and as you drift off to sleep visualize that particular rune, repeating its name over and over silently, giving yourself the suggestion that you will see that specific rune in your dream, and that you will remember your dream when you wake up long enough to write it down. When you wake up, write down which rune you focused on and any details you recall about your dream.

You can also use this method for answering a question. Just before going to sleep, concentrate on a simple question and run your fingers over the rune dream sheet. Notice if your finger seems to stop or stick on any particular rune(s). Does any rune feel different to you as you do this? Whichever rune stands out or sticks out is the rune that is most influential in regard to your question. As you drift off to sleep, focus on the rune, repeating its name over and over in your mind.

PART 5

Magical Uses of Runes

Rune Magic

Because they involve all your senses, runes are powerful magical devices. Through sound, color, image, number, and divine powers they provide ways of moving energy toward an intended purpose. Traditionally, people used runes as talismans, charms, on rings, in candle magic, and in ritual. Because they are compact, easy to use, and versatile, runes continue to be invaluable in magic. They are also easy to carry and conceal.

On a very basic level, magic is an affirmation that divine energy will help you. All magical energy comes from a connection with divine energies, within and without. Magical things are imbued with divine love, like a cup overflowing. This is one of the signs that you are doing real magic—the deep feeling of love and divine light that fills you.

When you do magic, you are creating or influencing a pattern of energy. In fact, magic can be said to be the practice of noticing and influencing synchronicity through intention, expectation, desire, and merging. When you practice magic, you intentionally thread and weave fields of energy together in an effort to create positive change. You will it to be so, and then act upon your intention.

Magic begins with intention and expectation, together with desire. This, when merged with the divine, unleashes energies both within the individual and within the cosmic forces of Oneness. When you learn to use the power of your expectations to become clear about what you truly desire, you become more aware of the synchronicity continually taking place around you. This synchronicity is a result of the connection between everything in Oneness. By understanding these connections, you give your magical patterns added power. It's the difference between having a map showing you how to get to your destination and stumbling around blind, hoping you might get there. Synchronicity is a road map to Oneness, and magic is a process of getting where you want to go.

Fields of energy, called morphogenic fields, surround the human body. We are all powerhouses of psychic energy that emanates to and from us in all directions. Magic is being aware of and influencing these patterned fields. This means that inside you exists a great power that you can cultivate and extend. This psychic energy has the potential to influence things, and the more focused and congruent we become at gathering and directing this energy, the more successful our magic.

Knowing this, we can have faith that things will turn out the way we intend. This is our magical field of intention. We can set our field of energy to have a certain magical effect by systematically extending it, reaching new heights of experience. The strongest energy field prevails, which is why it is important to remember that we are influencing energies—not manipulating people—with magic. Keep in mind that everything you expect and turn your mind to, you bring into being, whether it is positive or negative, conscious or unconscious. In this respect, it is wise to master your thoughts.

Magic influences synchronistic change on an energetic level as well as on a physical level. The energetic level is felt in terms of your state of consciousness. The way you think has a profound effect on your reality. The physical and energetic interact constantly and affect one another, so change on one level influences change on the other. Change displaces energy, moves it around, and we can make use of this shifting of power in magic.

Nothing exists in a vacuum. Everything affects everything else. When doing magic, we need to be aware of our intentions and expectations, to take responsibility for our actions. We need to become more aware of how these intentions and expectations affect our life and the world as a whole.

The two primary kinds of magic are shamanic and ritual. In shamanic magic, the emphasis is on the individual. This system of magic is experienced and developed through teaching and practice. Shamanism relies extensively on information received in altered states of consciousness, either through dreams or "merging." Dreaming can be passive or active in nature. Merging is done while awake. In merging, the shaman moves into an altered state by using intention and desire. The merged state of being is realized when the shaman becomes one with cosmic forces and the totality of the universe.

The word "shamanism" is akin to the Vedic word *sram*, meaning "to heat oneself" or "to practice austerities." The Norse word *seidr* also means "heating" or "boiling." Seidr is a form of shamanism that is practiced mostly by females—only rarely by males. In fact, the sole male mythological figure known to have practiced it is Odin, and he did it only after Freyja taught him how.

A modern form of spirituality that stems from the Northern Tradition is called Asatru, which means "trust in the Aesir" or "faith in the gods." Asatru is a modern reconstruction of the religion that the Germanic tribes practiced before their conversion to Christianity. One of those practices was rune magic.

Referring to culture and language, "Germanic" is a collective name for the ethnic groups that originated in Northern Europe. Besides the Germans, the Scandinavians, the Dutch, the Frisians, the English, and several other ethnic groups are all descended from the original Germanic tribes. Because such a large number of cultures descended from these tribes, many people in the United States, the United Kingdom, Europe, Australia, and New Zealand have Germanic ancestry.

Those who practice Asatru feel that the natural world is sacred and alive. The sun, moon, and Earth are personified as deities. There are also local nature spirits such as dwarfs and elves. The gods and goddesses are multidimensional. Thor, for instance, is a thunder god; yet he is also a protector of the common people. The modern practice of Asatru keeps in step with the times, and Asatruars today apply their efforts to important issues such as the environment and building community.

Whatever your spiritual path, rune magic can be used to enrich your life. I am trained in the Celtic Druid tradition, which is akin to the Northern Tradition but different in some ways. For example, in the Celtic Tradition, the Goddess is emphasized, whereas in the Northern Tradition, the God is more central. Interestingly, there is evidence pointing to a strong Mother Goddess tradition that existed before the Vikings.

The rune magic methods presented here reflect my Celtic background, mixed with some of the more traditional Northern practices, and integrating these spiritual truths. In this way, the information here represents a blending of traditions and styles, the mixing of magics into very effective forms of changework.

Magical Timing

Timing is all-important when doing any kind of magic. If the proper universal energies are lacking, doing magic can become as futile as trying to hammer a nail into a stone. On the other hand, with correct timing, magical works can spread wings of their own and really take off!

As mentioned before, the eight divisions of the year represent the traditional yearly cycle of Northern Europe. The best times for magic, including runic magic, are the eight seasonal solar festivals. Each of these days has traditions that have been passed down through the years. For example, Beltane, or Walpurgis Night, was sacred to Freyja. On the winter solstice in Holland, the midwinter horn was blown and a flaming (solar) wheel was rolled down a hill to celebrate the return of the sun.

The Eight Days of Power

These eight days of power occur on the equinoxes, solstices, and four cross-quarter days. The following are the runic correspondences for these magical days.

Day	Date	Corresponding Runes
Winter Solstice or Yule	Dec 21	Isa, Jera, Eihwaz
Imbolc or Bridget's Day	Feb 2	Perdhro, Algiz, Sowilo
Spring Equinox or Hertha's Day	Mar 21	Tiwaz, Ehwax, Berkana
Beltane	May 1–5	Mannaz, Laguz, Ingwaz

Summer Solstice or Midsummer	June 21	Othala, Dagaz, Fehu
Lughnassad	1st week Aug	Uruz, Thurisaz, Ansuz
Autumnal Equinox of Hellith's Day	Sep 22	Raidho, Kenaz, Gebo
Samhain	Nov 1–5	Wunjo, Hagalaz, Naudhiz

Remember to focus on the associated rune, depending upon the time of the year. This will make your rune magic more timely and guarantee better results.

The Eight-Fold Moon Phase

The Norse peoples understood the natural cycles of the moon and used them in their lives. They knew the waxing moon was the time for building energy, while the waning moon was the time for releasing it. Traditionally, from the new moon to the first-quarter moon is a time to initiate and build, to clarify your intention and expectation. From the first quarter to the full moon is the time to cultivate what you have created and to gather the energy needed for its successful completion.

The full moon is called the High Moon, because it is then that lunar energies are strongest. The last quarter of the moon corresponds to harvest time, when you reap the rewards of your efforts. The last quarter through the dark moon and into the new moon is a time to explore the mysteries of life, rebirth, and dreams.

When doing magic with the runes, select those that correspond to the specific moon phase or day of power on which you are working. The following chart shows the eight-fold moon phase cycle and how it corresponds to the eight solar days of power, together with the primary corresponding rune.

Moon Phase	Corresponding Power Day	Primary Rune
New Moon	Winter Solstice	Jera
Crescent Moon	Imbolc	Algiz
First Quarter Moon	Spring Equinox	Berkana
Gibbous Moon	Beltane	Laguz
Full Moon	Summer Solstice	Dagaz
Disseminating Moon	Lughnassad	Thurisaz
Last Quarter Moon	Autumnal Equinox	Kenaz
Balsamic/Dark Moon	Samhain	Hagalaz

THE ELEMENTS

Using the elements of earth (north), air (east), fire (south), and water (west or all directions), with the fifth element being spirit (center), is customary in most magic traditions. Traditionally, because of the harsh environment the Norse peoples placed ice at the north and earth at the center. These key elements of earth, air, fire, and water are integrated in rituals, charms, talismans, and other magical workings.

The runes embody these elements, and you can use them to call upon elemental energies. The following list shows the runic and elemental correspondences. Refer to the encyclopedic listing for more information.

Element	Corresponding Runes
Earth	Wunjo, Jera, Berkana, Eihwaz, Ehwaz, Ingwaz, Othala
Air	Ansuz, Raidho, Gebo, Algiz, Tiwaz, Mannaz, Eihwaz
Fire	Sowilo, Fehu, Thurisaz, Kenaz, Naudhiz, Dagaz, Eihwaz
Water and Ice	Uruz, Laguz, Perdhro, Hagalaz, Isa, Eihwaz

You can also enhance your rapport with the elements by associating them with facets of your being. Keep reminding yourself verbally of your connection with the elements. The more you practice this, the closer your rapport with them will become. In respect for the Northern Tradition, I have included ice. Chant these words:

> My flesh and bones are the earth. The earth is my flesh and bones. We are one. My breath is the air. The air is my breath. We are one. My potential is thawing ice. Thawing ice is my potential. We are one. My eyes are the light. The light is my eyes. We are one. My emotions are water. Water is my emotions. We are one.

THE FOUR DIRECTIONS

Bringing the power of the four directions into your magic is essential for a successful outcome. The more divine energies—deities, magical tools, and sacred symbols such as runes—that you can bring into your sacred space, the greater your magic.

Directions and Their Associated Gods and Goddesses

- North—Odin and the Three Norns: Urd, Verdandi, and Skuld
- East—Frigga and Tyr
- South—Iduna and Thor
- West—Freyja and Njord

Directions and Their Corresponding Magical Objects

- North—Odin's Spear, Gungnir, and the Norns' threads
- East—Frigga's distaff and Tyr's sword
- South—Thor's hammer, Mjollnir, and Iduna's golden apples of immortality
- West—Freyja's necklace and Njord's ax

Directions and Their Central Ruling Runes

- North—Jera
- East—Berkana
- South—Dagaz
- West—Kenaz

Magical Focals

Focals are items used in magic to help you focus on your magical goal. They also help you amplify and direct magical energies. Select the focals that match the intention of your magic. It is a good idea to combine magical focals—candles, oils, and stones, as well as magical tools, foods, and sound—so that your senses are engaged as fully as possible.

- Auditory Focals—Music, sound, your voice, vibration, singing, chanting, drumming, humming, breathing, waterfalls, rivers, animal calls, the wind, falling rain, hail, snow, oceans, fountains, birds and rhythmic electronic sounds such as the sound of the engine of your car or a hot-tub motor
- Gustatory Focals—Food and beverages, things you taste and ingest
- Intuitive Focals—Things that represent a divine or magical experience you have had: ritual jewelry, talismans, tools, and certain symbols such as runes, serve as intuitive focals
- Kinesthetic Focals—The colors, textures, feel, and shapes of things; things you touch; runes are

ideal kinesthetic focals because you pick them up in your hands and imprint them with your personal energy

- Olfactory Focals—Things you smell: essential oils, perfumes, scented candles, foods, campfires, incense, etc.
- Visual Focals—Things you can see: photographs, symbols (including rune symbols), drawings, paintings, flowers, shells, trees, the sun, moon, stars, crystals, and the like.

RUNE *GALDR* (GALDER) SONGS

Galdr songs are the primary auditory focals in rune magic. These songs are ancient intonations that were used in seidr workings in Iceland. *Galdr* is the singing of runes and runic combinations. Forming the roots of runic incantation, which brings the powers of the cosmic breath into action, *galdr* is the vibratory embodiment of the rune. Each rune has a specific *galdr* sound, formula, or song associated with it. (See the Encyclopedic Listing for specific *Galdr* songs.)

The *galdr* is probably both the most powerful and subtle way to access the magical energy of the rune. These chants have been described as being like a soft-flowing river with a powerful current under-neath. Used in every phase of runic magic together with the form of the rune, the *galdr* is the main medi-um through which runic power finds expression. Everyone intones slightly differently, so feel free to experiment. By chanting and toning a rune, you can better experience and express its meaning.

When learning to *galdr*, focus on one rune at a time. Observe each rune's tone, form, flow, and rela-tionship to you and to the other runes. Trust your intuition, and decide when to sing each rune as a song in and of itself, complete with melody and a beginning, middle, and end, and when to sing the rune by toning only one note. There is no right or wrong way to *galdr*.

When you *galdr*, breathe from your diaphragm and really stretch out the sound of each rune, toning as many consonant/vowel combinations as possible. For example, Fehu can be sung as "Feeeeeeee, Faaaaaaaa, Fuuuuuuuuu, Faaaaaaaayhuuuuuuuuu!" (akin to the giant's "fee-fi-fo-fum" as he counts his golden coins, a symbol of mobile wealth). Draw out and expand each of the vowel sounds, exploring all registers and resonances in your voice. Discover where each rune fits in your vocal register, and note where you feel it in your body. Above all, remember *galdring* is a lot like learning how to sing for the first time. Relax and enjoy the process. *Galdring* together with your children, in the woods or at the ocean, can be great fun. As you become proficient, you can combine the chants of several runes into one song. With 24 runes in the Elder Futhark, there are many possible combinations, but generally *galdr* songs using one rune, three runes, or nine runes work best in magic. Be aware of the numerical significance of the combined runes when crafting songs.

THE ALTAR

Traditionally considered the table of the Goddess and God, your altar is your magic-working surface. It holds the tools and elements and is a primary focal in magic. Ideally, you would want to set up the altar in a forest clearing and make it of stone. The stone altar symbolizes the Earth and the north direction. Also, the stone and the earth work to ground or eliminate unwanted energies. In the Northern Tradition, a "Horgr"—meaning "holy pile of stones"–makes the ideal altar. It consists of a large, flat stone, set upon a pile of smaller, gathered stones.

Today altars can be everything from a table, chest,

or desk, to a fireplace mantel, cardboard box, or even the bare ground. Most of the time, an altar cloth covers the altar. It can be made of any natural material such as linen, cotton, silk, or wool. Generally, it is left in its natural color, but it can also be red, green, or deep blue—any color. You can also embroider or paint rune symbols on it.

You can carve or paint appropriate runes on your altar to create an even more sacred space. Altar runes are Berkana (for the Goddess), Ansuz (for Odin), Uruz (for strength), Algiz (for divine protection), and Ingwaz (designating the four quarters of the sacred circle/square).

I have always set my altar up in the north point of the room. This is the preferred placement in the Northern Tradition. Some set the altar in the east quarter to correspond with the rising sun. Still others place their altars in the center of their magical space. Try the different placements, and then select the one that feels right to you.

The right side of the altar is the active, power side, dedicated to the God. The left half of the altar is the creative, nurturing side, dedicated to the Goddess. It's best to keep your magical altar fluid, changing certain items such as runes, candles, incense, flowers, and gemstones to correspond with the seasons. Be sure to place all your tools and altar items so you can reach them conveniently.

To prepare this sacred space: Put sea salt in a bowl of water. Take a sprig of greenery and dip it into the salt water. Sprinkle your altar and ritual area in a sunwise (clockwise) motion as you say aloud with a clear voice, "Begone from here, all evil and foulness and darkness! Begone from this place in the name of the Goddess Freyja!" (You may also use the name of any primary goddesses from other spiritual traditions such as Kerridwen, Isis, or the Mother Mary.) Say this three times while visualizing a white light, edged with cobalt blue, that energetically clears out the area.

Before beginning your ritual or magical work, set your altar up with everything you will need. Some people leave their altars set up; others put everything carefully away upon completion of the work.

MAGICAL TOOLS

Although you need no special tools for working magic, the implements you gather together, consecrate, and use regularly in magic become more than just symbols that trigger your unconscious. Infused with the sacred energies of the Goddess and God, they become energetically alive and a part of you, imprinted with your energy signature.

- **Antler**—Associated with Frey, this optional Norse tool represents the horned God of the woods. The antler can be engraved with runes associated with Frey such as Fehu, Jera, and Ingwaz. I found my antler while sliding down a canyon side one day about 24 years ago. You can purchase an antler, but it is much more powerful if the antler is found in nature. It is then considered a gift from the god.
- **Bowl**—Traditionally made of clay, the bowl corresponds to the north and the earth elements. Salt, the universal purifier, usually dry but sometimes mixed with water, goes into the bowl. You may also use soil in your bowl. In the Northern Tradition, the bowl holds the last bit of the sacred mead (or apple juice), and is called the "Trygill." It is customarily made from pottery, wood, stone, glass, or metal.
- **Brisingamen**—In the Northern Tradition, this necklace associated with the goddess of love,

Freyja, is customarily made of amber and gold-colored metal. It is worn by women during magic and ritual.

- **Candle Holder**—It may be made of metal, clay, glass, stone, or crystal. The holder is the vessel, while the lighted candle represents the fire element and the creative source. You may inscribe your candle holders with runic symbols.

- **Cup or Chalice**—Traditionally made of clay or metal, the cup is associated with the west and symbolizes water. Once consecrated, the chalice becomes a loving cup, embodying the sacred union of the Goddess and God.

- **Drinking Horn**—Used to hold the sacred mead (or apple juice), the horn contains the power of the Goddess and God. This energy passes to you when you drink the mead from the horn during magic and ritual. A drinking horn was carved to enchant the drink it held and to detect poison, whereas sounding horns were carved to send true and strong tones over long distances. Traditionally, the runes Othala, Dagaz, Raidho, Ansuz, Raidho, Isa, and Algiz (in that order) are carved or painted on the horn. These runes translate as "Odhroerir," which is the name of the divine mead from the well of inspiration and from the kettle that held the divine mead.

- **Drum**—A bridge to the spirit or otherworld, and magical tool of vibration and sound, the drum is associated with air and earth elements. Drumming is one of the easiest ways to enter an altered state of awareness. The head of a person's drum is broken as a way to free the spirit when he/she dies.

- **Fetish**—Often carved of stone, wood, or made of clay, fetishes can be in the shape of animals or more abstract symbols of the Goddess, God, ancestors, or the sacred spirits of the Earth. They are usually used as a powerful focus when doing magical work. You can carve fetishes with the runes, and will find them particularly effective when working with power animals. You can use them as talismans, for example, or to trigger a certain state of consciousness.

- **Incense Burner, Brazier,** or **Fire-pot**—Also called the *glodhker*, and made of metal or earthenware, the burner needs to be large enough to burn incense, paper, and wooden rune staves in it easily. When lit, the fire symbolizes the quickening power of Muspelheim.

- **Knife**—A Sax, used in the Northern Tradition, is a single-edged knife. The "athame," used in other pagan traditions, is a double-edged ceremonial blade. The knife represents fire and is associated with the south. Available in all sizes and shapes, the knife can be used to carve runes on wood and clay. (Keep all knives in a safe place, away from young children and away from the edges of your altar table.)

- **Mead**—Made from fermented honey, mead is perhaps the oldest-known alcoholic beverage. It represents the draught of wisdom that Odin drank at Mimir's Well. If you prefer, a non-alcoholic drink such as apple juice can be substituted for mead.

- **Robe**—Your magical skin, made of any fabric, any color, any design, the robe is reserved for magic. When you put on your robe, it automatically moves you into a magical frame of mind. You may also wear a tunic, kilt (Celtic), cape, cloak (Norse), or nothing at all when doing magic.

- **Sprig**—The sprig, taken from an evergreen tree dipped in either saltwater (Celtic) or mead (Norse), is used to sprinkle your magical space and yourself. Ask permission of the tree before snapping off the sprig. Then return the sprig to the ground below the tree, after your magic is complete.

- **Sword**—Associated with the Knights of the Round Table (Celtic) and the god of justice, Tyr (Norse), the sword represents the south direction, and the element of fire. It is used for magical protection and ancestral contact. Oaths are often sworn over swords. For power and protection, engrave the Tiwaz rune on the hilt or blade of the sword. Name your sword to give it power, sureness, a fine cutting edge, and personality.

- **Thor's Hammer**—A magical tool of the Northern Tradition, the hammer is cut from wood and metal, and is often marked with the Thurisaz rune. The hammer protects and defends, keeping your magical space harmonious.

- **Wand** or **Staff**—Called a *gandr* in the Northern Tradition, the magical wand or staff is considered the most ancient of tools. It is used to move energy from one place to another, to create magical states of consciousness, and to set up sacred areas. It also bridges energies, tying them together in specific patterns.

The wand or staff is painted or carved with all

24 runes or with specific runic formulas. Often made from the wood of a fruit-bearing tree, the *gandr* can also be made from yew or ash. Associated with Odin, the earth element, and the north direction, staffs measure about as tall as you are, and are larger in diameter than wands. Wands are usually no longer than the length of your arm (fingertip to elbow), and represent the powers of the mind. Because you make them from wood that still contains the vital essence of the tree, *gandrs* are excellent for use in magic, healing, protection, and power over the elements. They are used to draw runes in the air.

Making a *Gandr* (Runic Wand)

1. Select a wood with the qualities you desire. Here are some suggested woods and their corresponding magical qualities.

- **Alder**—The "battle witch" of trees, it represents truth, as in purification by fire.
- **Ash**—The "guardian tree," dispenser of justice. The first man was an ash. The world tree,

Yggdrasil—synonymous with the yew—is commonly referred to as an evergreen ash. Ash bark is deadly to snakes.

- **Beech**—Tree of the Three Norns, its bark is also deadly to snakes. Runes were written on thin beech boards.
- **Birch**—Called the "birth-tree," and associated with the Mother Goddess, it has been used in healing and for magical besom brooms. It also symbolizes the return of spring. Traditionally you consecrate it to Thor. The birch protects against lightning.
- **Elder**—The "thirteenth tree," it represents the Great Goddess and is associated with Berkana.
- **Elm**—In the Northern Tradition, the first woman was shaped from an elm. This tree also is associated with the Mother Goddess, the light elves, and healing.
- **Hazel**—The tree of wisdom, the hazel cuts away impurities to see the self honestly.
- **Laurel**—The oracle tree of Delphi, this tree represents victory and honor.
- **Oak**—The "Forest King" of endurance, tree of the Norse god Frey, and the primary wood of the

sacred fire of the Goddess, the oak is associated with fertility, ancestry, and love. Its fruit, the acorn, is a symbol of the Goddess.

- **Pine**—Representing the cycle of life and rebirth, the pine is called "Tree of the Manifest," the sun. Pinecones are its fruits and symbolize the Goddess.
- **Rowan**—Called "Tree of Runes" and "Wood of the Sorcerer," the rowan's pliability is thought to aid in magic. The tree branches are tied with red thread to protect your home or property from enemies.
- **Silver Fir**—The fir is associated with the moon, representing feminine rebirth.
- **Willow**—The traditional tree that wands are fashioned from, the willow is flexible and excellent to use for magic and enchantment. This tree draws its power from water.
- **Yarrow**—Also called Milfoil, this is a popular wood for divining wands. It is also a healing herb called "the medicine of life."
- **Yew**—Yew is a popular wood for runic talismans and wands. It is also a tree of death and rebirth and is associated with Yggdrasil, Odin, Ymir, Uller, and the Valkyries.

2. After choosing the type of wood to use, locate a living tree from which to cut your wand. If the tree is on someone else's property, be sure to ask permission of its owner before cutting the branch. The wand is usually about 12–16 inches (30–40cm) long.

3. When you find the tree, communicate with it. Sit under the tree and feel its bark supporting you. Touch the tree with the palms of your hands. Look up at the canopy and notice how the branches weave out from the trunk.

4. Walk around the tree three times sunwise (clockwise), asking if you may have a branch from its body. You will receive some sort of feeling at this point, whether or not to proceed with cutting the wand. If it is positive, the tree will help you select the best branch. If you feel a negative response, find another tree and repeat the procedure.

5. Dig a small hole in the ground at the base of the tree and make an offering such as bread and mead, and then thank the tree. Say to the guardian, or "wight," of the tree:

Hail to thee, wight of (*insert tree name such as oak*),

I pray thee give this branch of your body!
Into it send thy speed,
To it bind the might of the bright runes.
(insert the names of the runes to be used on your wand)

Then cut your wand, while chanting or toning the runes, preferably on a day of the new moon or during the waning moon. Timing the cutting in this manner will ensure the proper amount of time—an entire moon cycle—for "curing" the wand. Traditionally, wands were snapped off the tree, not cut with metal blades.

Staffs are larger and are usually cut. If you are going to cut the branch with a metal blade, use your magical knife or sword, and take appropriate safety precautions as you proceed. Protect the tree by painting the cut area on its trunk or branch with a small amount of bituminous paint or seal it in another way.

6. Once the wand or staff is cut, thank the tree wight for its magical gift by saying:

Wight of *(insert tree name)*, accept my thanks.
Henceforth may your might be in this branch!

Magically bound to the bright runes (*insert rune names*),
Working my will with speed and wisdom.

7. Begin to shape the branch's personality. Use your knife to strip off the bark, collecting and keeping the bark shavings on a cloth or piece of newspaper. Sometime during the next 28 days (a moon phase), go back and sprinkle the bark shavings around the base of the tree in a sunwise (clockwise) circle. While doing this, touch the tree with the palms of your hands and thank it again. Create a simple blessing song or chant for the tree, and sing it as you walk around the base of the tree three times sunwise.

8. Leave the stripped wand in the sunlight and moonlight for an entire moon cycle, while working with it each day to perfect its shape.

9. After the wand's skin has dried, you can paint, write, or burn runes into the surface, but ideally cut them into the wand. When carved into the wand, the runes infuse the tool with supernatural and divine strength. The "ristir," meaning "cut," is an extremely sharp woodcarving tool customarily used for the cutting of runes. You could also use a knife. The cutting of the runes into different materials is an act of magic, one requiring your full attention. Call in the appropriate divine energies as you work, making an effort to sense the rune before you cut it. State the purpose of the rune and sense the direction of the energies. This will help you decide where to start the cutting. When in doubt, use your intuition. Chant the runes or the corresponding *Galdr* song with each rune that you cut into the wood. If the wand has a magical name, carve it on the shaft. Besides cutting runes on your wand, you can also use consecrated oil or the ashes of burned runes to trace the symbols.

Take time to think carefully before marking the tool irrevocably with the runes. Be sure the runes match the tool's intended use. The purpose of putting runes on the tool is essentially to bless and dedicate it to a specific task. The runes make the tool's attributes purer, stronger, and more reliable.

10. After carving them, the next step is to redden the runes. Traditionally, "Tiver" extracted from the madder plant, is used. As an interest-

ing side note, the word *tiver* means "magic," and the color red symbolizes magic and active energy. Red runes stimulate the circulation of the blood and the senses. You can also use red ocher, minium (red lead), dragon's-blood resin, or another reddening substance. These reddening pigments are ground with linseed oil, in a sacred manner, while you are chanting, "Laukaz, Laukaz, Laukaz," before you begin. Laukaz invokes the fertility of nature. To apply the red dye to the runes, a special tool called a "galdrstaf" is customarily used. Inscribed with the appropriate runes, it is a small veneer-thin piece of wood cut into the shape of an isosceles triangle that can easily be held in your hand. Chant or sing the runes as you redden them.

11. Use consecrated oil or beeswax to seal your wand. Match the magical qualities of the oil to the intended purpose of your wand. For example, a wand sealed with honeysuckle oil would give it qualities of protection, abundance, and strength. (Refer to the list of oils on pages 429–431).

12. Complete your runic wand with natural materials like silk ribbon, feathers, and shells, or

mount a quartz crystal in the tip. The hinder (bottom) end of the *gandr* is rounded or blunted.

CONSECRATING YOUR MAGICAL TOOLS

After your wand's skin has dried, smudge it with cedar and sage or incense to clear it of any unwanted energies. You can also use sea salt and water for this purpose, or pass the tool carefully through the flame of a sacred fire. You can also clear it out by setting it in the sun or moonlight.

Next, consecrate or hallow the tool for its particular magical function by merging deeply and invoking the divine energies of the Goddess and God, with the intention of charging the tool with the elemental qualities they embody. Become one with these divine beings, asking them to impart their energy and aspects into the object of your focus. Visualize and sense the power of the Goddess and God, and then use your breath to physically move the divine energy into the item, by breathing in and then sharply exhaling through your nose. Do this at least three times and, for better results, nine times. Your breath and focused intention are the carrier waves that move the energy into the tool. Visualize what you will be using the tool for and how it will help you. Reflect on these images and feelings, making the tool your own and fashioning its magical purpose.

Washing your altar tools in the morning dew before sunrise fills them with divine creative power and knowledge. As well as dew for consecrating your tools, you can use the water of a river, the ocean, or a lake, or any of the other elements to charge your tools with powerful energies. For example, you can use the sun to empower your tools (fire); you can rub fresh soil on them (earth); you can bathe your tools in incense smoke (air). You can also rub herbs and oils on your tools to enhance their energies.

The best time to consecrate knives, swords, staffs, and wands is at sunrise on a clear day. Use the power of the sun's birth to fill yourself and, in turn, your tools with this energy. Other ideal times for consecrating magical tools are noon, twilight, and midnight, depending upon their intended use.

You can also consecrate magical tools by using this invocation. Hold the tool in both hands, and say these words of power:

In the name of the High Ones,
In the name of the Aesir, Vanir, and the Norns,
In the divine light of Oneness,

Hail to the Ancestors, the Kin Fetch, to Life and
   Creation.
May this (*name of tool*) be made sacred.
I consecrate and hallow this (*name of tool*) to
(*name of deity*).
May you imbue it with your power and light,
May those who use it well receive the blessings of
   the High Ones,
May they be granted wisdom, strength, and good
   fortune,
And may their spirits be bright and mighty.
So mote it be! (or So shall it be!)

The Three Steps of Magic

The natural progression of the mind is to move from
intention and expectation to desire and then to merging; these are the three steps to magic. Another way
to see the steps is as 1) conceiving, 2) creating, and 3)
experiencing.

Basically a formula for patterning energy, the
three steps provide a straightforward path that moves
your mind energy from A to B to C. You can use this
process in any magical work.

First, be very clear about your intention and what

it is you expect to accomplish from the work. But most of all, you need to make sure that it is what you really want. One of the ways of making sure is to see yourself getting what you intend and expect. Go into the experience, feeling it for everything it is. Then ask yourself if this is really what you want.

Second, build a strong desire toward your intended creation—seeing it, feeling it, and touching it—until it becomes tangible reality.

Third, merge with Oneness as deeply as possible, and then a little deeper still, allowing your intention, expectation, and desire to flow out of you and circulate into Oneness. See and sense yourself releasing thought energy so powerful that this energy becomes manifested and created. All magical traditions involve gathering, moving, directing, and shaping energy into patterns, with merging the key for facilitating the magic.

Merging

Merging is the natural feeling you get when you are in love or when you look into the eyes of your newborn baby. Merging is the sensation you get when you watch the sun set slowly across the valley, walk in an old-growth redwood forest, or sit at the top of a mountain. Merging is the feeling that comes over you when you are in sync with everything and at one with it all.

Merging connects you with Oneness and is the key to all magic. You experience an awareness of Oneness when merging. Through this experience you begin to understand that Oneness is the true state of existence. In this way, merging with Oneness becomes your gateway to other thresholds and dimensions of experience.

The sensations you experience when merging range from relaxation, peacefulness, incredible calm, and well-being to spinning, flying, whirling, and either lightheadedness or heaviness. Often during merging you may find your awareness energetically floating as you feel yourself being both everything and nothing at the same time.

A few methods that can enhance your merging experience include breathing exercises, staring at candlelight, swimming, dancing, running, walking, and chanting, as well as listening to special music and drumming, and using visualization techniques. Merging is sometimes triggered by exhaustion, near-death experiences, sudden injury, illness, alcoholic drinks, and drugs.

The Sacred Enclosure

The sacred enclosure can be in the shape of a circle, a square, a sphere, an Ingwaz diamond, or a Ve. It serves as a protected space in which you can do magic; or as a vortex of light or a threshold from which you can communicate with the Goddess and God. In the Northern Tradition, men often use a square. The Ve, shaped like the Kenaz rune, and a sphere are also traditional. An Ingwaz diamond-shaped enclosure (two Kenaz runes) is also very effective for magic, especially love magic.

To cast the circle, square, or sphere, visualize a bright blue-white flame shooting out of your out-stretched hand (or the tip of your knife, *gandr*, or sword) as you spin sunwise (clockwise). See and sense the area you want your sacred space to cover as you spin around. Do you want the sacred area to extend ten feet (3m) or around the entire room, backyard, or meadow? When doing the Ve, stand in the middle of the formation and visualize the Kenaz rune surrounding you and forming the Ve enclosure as you turn in a circle. When forming the Ingwaz diamond, visualize yourself surrounded by two Kenaz runes in the shape of a diamond.

Stand at the north point of the room (where your altar is positioned), take the sprig of greenery and dip it in a bowl of water in which you have placed pinches of salt. Wave the sprig gently in the north direction, lightly sprinkling the direction with water from the sprig, and say:

> The rune-might is drawn 'round the sacred stead, unwanted wights wend away. Helpful spirits stay!

Do the same thing to the east, south, and west.

You can also use pinches of dry salt or fresh earth instead of the sprig. In this case, you take a pinch and lightly spread it in the corner. Both of these techniques purify the corner, which is the point of the action.

When working in the Ve or sphere, stand in the middle and turn toward each of the four directions, one at time, sprinkling saltwater as you go. When working in a sphere, repeat the words on page 392, and sprinkle water above your head and beneath your feet as well.

Next, face your altar and say: "Blessed be! Blessed be the gods! Blessed be all of those who are gathered here." You may add statements such as: "I consecrate this sacred space to the ancient goddesses and gods. May they bless this space with their presence and love. Hail, Odin! Hail, Frigga! Hail, Frey! Hail, Freyja!"

Finally, tap or knock nine times on the altar with your *gandr* (or knuckles) in three series of three. You might also place a red or green candle with the Berkana rune carved on it on your altar. At this point in the ritual you would light it. Your sacred enclosure is now set in place.

Traditionally, women and men had separate rites, but today things have changed for the better, and women and men work together in the circle. After all, magic is an ideal way to learn how to integrate both masculine and feminine energies into a congruent whole.

THE FOUR WARDS

The four dwarfs whom Odin set to hold up the sky are also called the Four Wards. Ancient guardians of the four directions, the dwarfs are Nordi (north), Austri (east), Sudri (south), and Vesti (west). Before doing magic, it is customary to call in these Four Wards to protect your sacred space.

To begin, face north and move sunwise (clockwise, but counterclockwise in the southern hemisphere), energetically carving and coloring the Kenaz rune (the torch) in the air. (As you probably noticed, the Kenaz and Ve shapes are the same, simply turned in different ways.) To carve Kenaz, use your *gandr* or the palm of your right hand to form the first stroke— down and to the left—and say:

I hold the light of the torch.
Then form the second stroke—down and to the right—repeating:
I hold the light of the torch.
To color Kenaz, use gold or yellow. Begin in the middle and do an upper stroke—up and to the right—and say:
I hold the light of the torch.

Then form the second stroke again—down and to
   the right—repeating:
I hold the light of the torch.

The reason for shaping the Kenaz rune in this
manner is that the energy comes down and then radiates outward. After carving and coloring Kenaz, turn
to the north direction and say:

Nordi of the North
See thee the light of the torch,
Accept its sacred flame
And pray let none pass thee by.

Turn clockwise to the east direction, and say:

Austri of the East,
See thee the light of the torch,
Accept its sacred flame
And pray let none pass thee by.

Next, turn clockwise to the south direction, and say:

Sudri of the South,

See thee the light of the torch,
Accept its sacred flame
And pray let none pass thee by.

Finally, turn sunwise, to the west direction, and say:

Vesti of the West,
See thee the light of the torch,
Accept its sacred flame
And pray let none pass thee by.

Face north again, and say, "Hu, ha, hi, he, ho."

You can also do Thor's Hammer Sign in the four directions.

THOR'S HAMMER SIGN

Raise your right hand over your head and hold it there for a moment. Make a fist and bring the fist down, visualizing it passing through a vibrant cloud of energy just over your head. Touch your fist to your forehead and say three times, "Odin! Odin! Odin!"

Now bring your fist down to your breast, mentally tracing a blazing line of white energy, and say, "Baldur, Baldur, Baldur!"

Moving your fist to your left shoulder, say, "Frey, Frey, Frey!"

Moving your fist to your right shoulder say, "Thor, Thor, Thor!"

As you do this, visualize the line of blazing energy you are tracing with your fist, and see the trail that this energy leaves in the shape of Thor's Hammer.

Finally, just before doing your magical works, say:

The circle is bound
With power all around.
In Nine Worlds I stand
Protected in all lands.
Blessed be the gods.
Blessed be all who are gathered here.
So mote it be!

Once you have established your sacred space and called in the Four Wards, stand in the center of the space and loudly chant the name of the goddess and god you have selected to help you. Chant the names of the goddess and god, three or nine times in succession, using alternating female and male deities; for example, "Freyja, Freyja, Freyja, Frey, Frey, Frey!"

Next, perform your specific magical works, such

as rune charms, rune candle magic, power animal magic, *galdr* songs, and so forth.

PULLING UP THE SACRED ENCLOSURE

When your magic is complete, take a few minutes to thank the divine energies that have helped you. Then it is time to allow the elemental energies to depart. Say aloud as you turn toward the appropriate directional point in the same pattern used previously:

Nordi of the North, depart in peace.
Many blessings and thanks for thy presence.
Austri of the East, depart in peace.
Many blessings and thanks for thy presence.
Sudri of the South, depart in peace.
Many blessings and thanks for thy presence.
Vesti of the West, depart in peace.
Many blessings and thanks for thy presence.

Holding your palms outstretched (or your knife, *gandr*, or sword), visualize the Kenaz rune and the blue-white light of the circle (square, sphere, or Ve) being pulled into your hands (or tool). Move in a 360-degree counterclockwise circle as you do this. Knock three times on the altar with your *gandr* in honor of Odin's three faces and the Triple Goddess in order to completely release the Four Wards.

Power Animals

Power animals are an expression of your wild and free nature. Certain powers of nature are vested in specific animals, as reflected in their innate qualities and characteristics. By finding and communicating with your power animal, for a specific time and for a particular purpose, you can increase your knowledge and magical ability, which in turn transforms you. Besides, it's fun!

Many a tale begins with the line "These things happened long ago, when animals could speak like men." Throughout the folk traditions and religions of the world, animals appear as reincarnated ancestors, messengers of the gods and goddesses, divine beings themselves, creators as well as supporters of the world. They assume the roles of causers of earthquakes, familiars, protectors, teachers, weather makers, life tokens, doubles, and guides of souls to otherworlds of existence. In Norse tradition, the Swedish wise women called "vargamors" were known to have wolf familiars.

Fylgia is the word in the Northern Tradition that corresponds to "power animal." It means a magical force, defined as a shapeshifting power or fetch, which is a partly separate aspect of the human self that appears in the form of a spirit beast of power.

The relationship between humans and animals is a divine one. Many traditions around the world perceive animals and people as coming from the same divine place. Because of this, some cultures believe individual people and animals share a soul. Certain people are born with the ability to understand the speech, communication, and messages of power animals. Other people acquire the faculty as a divine gift, from a specific power animal, goddess or god, or by magical means.

One simple way to connect with power animals is to use certain three-rune bindrunes. For example:

Wunjo, Laguz, and Kenaz (WLK), or Uruz, Laguz, and Fehu (ULF), for wolf,
Berkana, Ansuz, Raidho (BAR) for bear,
Kenaz, Ansuz, Tiwaz (KAT) for cat,
Dagaz, Othala, Gebo (DOG) for dog,
Dagaz, Fehu, Raidho (DFR) for deer, and
Raidho, Ansuz, Wunjo (RAW) for raven.

Be creative, and make up your own three-rune power animal bindrunes. Just make sure the runes you select match the specific animals' special qualities.

As mentioned earlier, in the Northern Tradition Odin, the Norse god of wisdom, had a pair of ravens, Hugin (thought) and Munin (memory), that perched on his shoulders. At dawn the ravens explored the Earth and at night they returned to whisper the secrets they discovered in Odin's ear. Other power animals, already mentioned, and associated with Odin, are Sleipnir, the eight-legged horse, the wolves Geri and Freki, the snake, and the eagle. Odin changed himself first into a snake and later into an eagle. Freyja's power animals were the falcon and the cat, and she was associated with the raven even before Odin. Sif, the second wife of Thor, was a swan maiden and could assume the swan's form.

Traditionally, four power animals correspond to the four directions. In a story about Harald Gormsson, King of Norway, for example, the king's wizard shapeshifted into a whale and went to Iceland on a scouting mission. When he arrived, four guardian beings warned him to leave. They were the dragon (north), the bull (east), the rock giant (south), and the eagle (west). The wizard quickly returned to the king and told of his experience. King Harald promptly called off his planned invasion of Iceland.

Finding your own power animal and communicating with it once you find it, is a uniquely personal experience. It is guaranteed to expand your understanding of the runes and the diverse interpretations of these ancient symbols. Here is one method for finding your power animal:

1) Set up your altar, and place your rune stones upon it.
2) Establish your sacred space.
3) Call in the Four Wards.
4) Light a green or blue candle.
5) Look at the flame of the candle and merge with its divine light.
6) Take your runes, mix them in their pouch, and then pull the first nine that come to you. Place these in a horizontal row, faceup, from left to right.

Interpret the runes along the following guidelines:

Rune #1:
What is the basis of my connection with my power

animal? What do I have to learn from the animal?

Rune #2:

How can I contact my power animal?

Rune #3:

Will I contact my power animal soon?

Rune #4:

How will we communicate, and to what purpose?

Rune #5:

What influences block communication with my power animal? What are the present delays and obstacles?

Rune #6:

What runic energies can help me better know my power animal?

Rune #7:

How can my power animal help me walk between the Nine Worlds of Yggdrasil and learn the powers of the runes?

Rune #8:

Will my power animal appear in physical form in the near future?

Rune #9:

What gift will be exchanged between us? What will be the outcome of my knowing my power animal?

Write down the nine runes you pull, in the order you pull them. Allow the candle to burn down completely.

In a month look back on this sheet with the nine runes written on it. Also for the next month pay close attention to animal signs in your daily life. Notice what animal names you encounter, what animals you see, what animals are in your dreams, what animals you most resemble, and what animals you admire or think about most. Also be aware of which animals you are most attracted to and which ones seem to like you. Behavioral mannerisms you display also may give you clues to your power animal. For example, do you growl, purr, or fly around a lot? Do you wear clothing with animals on it or drive a car with an animal name such as Mustang or Jaguar?

Whatever your power animal, the creature has

magical power to offer when you open yourself up to receiving its natural gifts and abilities. As you work with your power animal, you will rediscover your sacred connection with the dignity, beauty, and wisdom of the natural world around you, helping you build a more positive relationship with the Earth and her creatures.

Sending Runes

Runic energies are sent, or directed, toward specific destinations, people, and outcomes. The strength of your magical field of intention, together with the depth of your desire and merging, determines how strong the sending will be.

One of the best ways to send runes is via your power animal. You do this by calling an energetic power animal, also called "the double" or "soul-animal," from out of the "wyrd." This animal can be called, activated, and sent off to help you with your magic, heal loved ones, communicate with friends, or carry important messages to and from other worlds. The energetic power animal is then assimilated into your being, and you gain knowledge from the experience.

Shamans and others who practice magic often send forth an animal familiar to represent them in a specific undertaking. Remember always to make an effort to apply the Four Keys of Knowledge—self-honesty, self-responsibility, wisdom, and love—in every magical work you perform. Sendings of the helpful kind are almost always appreciated. Of course, never use your power animal or any other magical work to harm others.

To create a double, merge deeply with Oneness, with the Goddess and God, and deliberately project your intended energy outward. Choose your power animal; then tell, show, and communicate to this animal the runes you want to send, giving instructions on how, when, where, and why. Pay close attention to your experience. Notice how sounds seem to echo as you create the double. Also notice how your other senses alter when you send runes via this magical animal.

Runic Charms

A passage from the *Kalevala* reads:

> The cold told me a tale
> The rain blew me some poems:
> Another tale came to me in the winds,
> Carried by the swell of the sea;
> Birds added words,
> The tree tops, sentences.

The *Kalevala* is an ancient collection of Nordic magic healing charms. Through much of the *Kalevala*, the words for "to cast a spell" are interchanged with "to sing," showing the ancient bond between magic and poetry. Sound is magical and each song, validating its corresponding charm, is an integral part of its enchantment.

Since Odin shared the wisdom of the runes with humankind, runic symbols have been particularly valuable in creating magical charms for love, money, and protection, as well as for success, victory, and gaining wisdom. Charms are essential parts of folk magic and, when used properly, can assist with personal, emotional, physical, and spiritual challenges, helping ensure the success of a cure or a magical work, and improving and enriching your life.

Before you begin, make sure you have a clear intention and expectation. Build your desire for a successful and powerful outcome, and make an effort to merge as deeply as you can with deity. Effective charms are done, like all magic, using intention, expectation, desire, and merging. Remember negative magic will only come back to haunt you. It is always possible to find a way to create the results you want in a positive way. Be creative.

Thirteen Steps for Making a Runic Charm

1) Clearly state the purpose of the charm, mentally and in writing, with images such as photos, pictures, or drawings.
2) Set up your altar and gather together everything you'll need.
3) Establish your sacred space.
4) Call in the Four Wards.
5) Select a sponsor goddess and god, relying on your intuition. Keep in mind: the greater your

desire for the successful outcome of your magic, the better the chance of positive results.

6) Fashion the charm. Carve, color, and empower the runes, using chanting and the *galdr* songs. When possible, chant the runes at sunrise.

7) Send out the necessary energy to bring about the needed result by merging with the successful effect of the charm. Say these words to bind your charms:

By the might of Odin, Vili, and Ve
By the strength of ice, air, fire, land, and sea
I bind the powers within this charm.
Let it always heal and never harm,
Now this work has been wrought
With the mighty runic lot.
By the powers of the moon, stars, and sun,
I ask that this work be done.
So shall it be!
So be it!

8) Use deep breathing and visualization to direct the charm's energy toward its destination. Become one with the divine, attuning with the

Goddess and God, asking for guidance and insight. See, feel, hear, taste, touch, and intuit the successful outcome of your magical rune charm. Remember, it is your perceptions that provide the best key for unlocking the magical energies of the runes.

9) Thank the divine energies who have helped you with your magic.

10) Release the Four Wards.

11) Pull up your sacred enclosure.

12) Put everything away.

13) Several times a day visualize the runic charm being successful. Do this for as long as it takes for the charm to work.

A SAMPLING OF RUNIC CHARMS

The following runic charms reflect a blending of Northern and Celtic traditional incantations, plus some more contemporary formulas. They utilize three runes each. One of the runes is non-invertible—a rune that looks the same whether upright and reversed (Sowilo, for example)—and represents the realm from which power is drawn. When drawing these runes as bindrunes, work from the non-invertible rune outward.

Rune Money Charm

Divine Powers: Freyja and Frey, Njord and Nerthus

Three Runes: Ingwaz, Fehu, Laguz

Ingwaz—Non-invertible rune, storehouse of potential energy, a rune of the Vanir, of peace and plenty

Fehu—Mobile wealth, prosperity, and plenty

Laguz—Rune of magical power and growth

Rune Healing Charm

Divine Powers: Thor, Iduna, Eir

Three Runes: Sowilo, Jera, Uruz

Sowilo—Non-invertible rune. Strengthening solar energy, motivating healing energies

Jera—Rune that accesses the healing energies of the Earth and the yearly cycles of the sun and moon

Uruz—Strength and driving energy for healing energies

General Protection Rune Charm

Divine Powers: Odin, the Valkyries, Thor

Three Runes: Isa, Naudhiz, Thurisaz

Isa—Non-invertible rune, crystallizes and constrains energies, using the powers of ice and frost

Naudhiz—Rune of protection and deliverance from distress.

Thurisaz—The thorn of protection. Can be used in its passive mode (reversed) or in its active mode (upright), depending upon the situation

Extinguishing the Old Flame Rune Charm

Divine Powers: Frey and Freyja

Three Runes: Ingwaz, Ansuz, Perdhro

Ingwaz—Non-invertible rune, draws energies from the Vanir, especially Frey.

Ansuz—The energy to release old patterns and feelings, using breathing, chanting, or singing

Perdhro—The rune of change, synchronicity, and divine guidance

Rune Protection Charm from Negativity

Divine Powers: Odin and the Norns

Three Runes: Isa, Kenaz, and Raidho

Isa—Non-invertible rune, used to slow energies down

Kenaz—Allows you to see things coming your way, whether positive or negative. Helps you focus your attention

Raidho—Returns negative energy to its source

Rune Healing Charm for Reducing Fever

Divine powers: Nerthus, Iduna, Eir, Thor

Three Runes: Isa, Laguz, Naudhiz

Isa—Non-invertible rune, cools things down

Laguz—Cooling and soothing power of water

Naudhiz—Provides you with only the fire you "need" while you are healing. Balances the inner fire

Say aloud:

In the name of Thor,
Laukaz!
By thunder,
Thor!
Isa, Laguz, Naudhiz,
By the power of the Gods, leave (*name the patient*)
To no longer torment him/her.
I bid you begone,
The sun bids you begone, the moon bids you begone,
The stars bid you begone, the stars bid you begone,
Man bids you begone, Woman bids you begone,
Child bids you begone,
All families bid you begone, I bid you begone.

Safe Travel Rune Charm

Divine Powers: Freyja and Odin, Thor, Baldur

Three Runes: Sowilo, Ansuz, and Raidho

Sowilo—Non-invertible rune, strengthens the energies for traveling, melts the ice, lights up your path from one locale to another

Ansuz—Balances elemental powers of the wind

Raidho—Ensures a safe journey

Rune Success Charm

Divine Powers: Odin, Thor, Baldur

Three Runes: Sowilo, Othala, Jera

Sowilo—Non-invertible rune, strengthens your personal power and mental skills

Fehu—Associated with Frey and mobile wealth

Jera—The harvest rune, signifying reward and good luck

Rune Victory Charm

Divine Powers: Tyr and Zisa, Frigga, Thor

Three Runes: Sowilo, Tiwaz, Algiz

Sowilo—Non-invertible rune, strengthens and melts the ice

Algiz—A powerful protector rune for defense and victory

Tiwaz—The rune of law, justice, patterns, and courage

Rune Wisdom Charm
Divine Powers: Mimir and the Norns
Mannaz—The hugrune of memory and mental ability
Ansuz—The hugrune of inspiration.
Kenaz—The hugrune of knowledge

Rune Love Charm
Divine Powers: Freyja and Frey, Frigga and Thor
Three non-invertible runes: Gebo, Ingwaz, Dagaz
Gebo—Non-invertible rune, representing the exchange of energies and the give-and-take in relationships; also stands for the sexual union of male and female
Ingwaz—Used to invoke the blessings of the Vanir; rune of sexuality and fertility
Dagaz—Balance of male and female energies in the relationship

Rune Charm to Attract a Potential Mate
Cut out two paper or cloth hearts as a symbol of your love. On each of the hearts, draw the three

runes Gebo, Ingwaz, and Dagaz in red ink. You can make them into a bindrune, if you prefer. Next, tie the hearts together with red or pink string. Carry this love charm on the right side of your body or next to your heart for best results.

Rune Marriage Charm

Divine Powers: Frigga and Thor

Three Runes: Gebo, Ehwaz, Othala

Gebo—Non-invertible rune, represents the exchange of energies in a marriage, the give-and-take

Ehwaz—The traditional rune of marriage

Othala—Symbolizes family, prosperity, happy home, and inherited, ancestral, power

Magical Power Rune Charm

Divine Powers: Odin, Heimdall, Freyja

Three Runes: Sowilo, Kenaz, Raidho

Sowilo—Non-invertible rune, represents the sun and is associated with Alfheim (world of the light-elves), from which the energy is drawn

Kenaz—Signifies the powers of discovery and intuition, clairvoyance, and a clear mind

Raidho—The rune associated with the solar cycle

Rune Cord or String Magic

Like the ring, the knot acts as a spiritual bond. String magic is a method of harnessing energy. In fact, fishermen's nets are the original forms of string magic. Spinning and weaving the threads of the Wyrd, like the Three Norns, is an old magical tradition that you can learn. Spinning and weaving cloth are themselves magical workings. Rune chants and *galdr* songs are then woven into the very fabric of the garments for protection and power.

First, as for any magical work, choose a location in which you can completely focus on your string magic. Use red, white, and black strings to represent the Three Norns. Cut three lengths of colored string, each one yard (1 m) long, and hold them in your hands. Sit back for a moment until you get a clear and strong image of the three runic energies these strings represent. They represent the energies that you would most like to tie into your life; for example, strength (Uruz), forward movement (Raidho), and reward (Othala). You should have a positive intention and a clear expectation of what it is you want. You will be making a number of knots in the strings. The number will correspond to the runic energies you desire. (Refer to the encyclopedic listing for the numbers that correspond to the energies.)

Start by tying the ends of your strings together in a firm knot. Then, loop and slide the threads in and out of your fingers. Use both hands, cradling the threads as you slide them in and out of your fingers, and knot them in a sort of makeshift cat's cradle. There is no right or wrong way to do this. Allow your hands to weave the three threads in deliberate shapes as if sculpting the runes with the string. As you do this, chant the appropriate rune names or intone the corresponding *galdr* songs. Turn your mind completely to the runic energies you truly desire. The sound of your voice, your fingers, hands, and the threads tell the story of what you want. They form a link with the energy of your intention and expectation. The runes, the movement of the thread, your hands and fingers become one. Everything becomes connected and joined in light. Keep weaving the energy together, all the while chanting or intoning the runes.

To activate the runic energies of the string magic, burn the thread in your incense burner or fire-pot, offering it to the Goddess and God. Or you can tie the woven thread around the leg of a chair or your bedpost. Thank the Goddess and God for their gift.

Rune Script Magic

When you "spell" a word in runes, it empowers that word. It makes it magical. The Norse would often finish runic inscriptions with the statement "So-and-so wrote this" or "So-and-so made me." By doing this, the carver of the runes was magically connected to the writing.

One easy way to use runes for magic is to write out rune rows, or rune scripts. These runic mini-spells are made up of a sequence of two or more runes. For example, if you wanted to create a rune row to help enhance your magical abilities, you could use Laguz, Perdhro, Ansuz, and Kenaz.

Runic scripts may be inscribed on talismans, magical tools, and other personal belongings. They may also be carved into a piece of wood or an altar candle, or in any number of other things. Your selection of materials is important, since this will be the medium that ferries your message between worlds, adding its own signature to the energies. For example, metals, stone, and wood are excellent amplifiers of runic energies. Plastic has little or no energy.

Permanent runic inscriptions may also be carved or engraved on personal items such as jewelry, furniture, fountains, and other similar objects. Natural materials are best for the enscription runes because their elemental energies combine with the runic energies to create a stronger magical field. But never carve runes into living trees. This would indicate a foolish lack of respect for nature and would often harm the tree. To enscript runes on living things such as trees, trace the runes with consecrated oil instead of carving them.

If you are going to send the runic script energy out by burning it in your incense burner or fire-pot, use small pieces of wood, parchment, or regular paper. When using wood, scrape off the runic symbols and burn only those shavings in the fire-pot.

Rune Candle Magic

Traditionally given to us by the gods, fire has been used by people for over half a million years. From early times, candles have been used for divination, celebration, and to influence magical practice, from the simple candles on the birthday cake to elaborate rituals employing consecrated candles.

The flame of the candle touches the spirit, within and without. The fire and flickering candlelight represents the highest potential of spirit, while the smoke of the candle carries your desires and prayers to the divine. Different parts of the candle and candle holder represent different aspects of being. The flame of the candle represents the spirit. The wick, when lit, is the vehicle of transmutation. The halo of the flame symbolizes divinity, while the body of the candle represents physical properties. When lit, the candle embodies all the elements.

Using candles in rune magic is easy and effective. Customarily practiced on the eight days of power—full moons and holidays—candle magic can be a fiery change-element, helpful in obtaining love, money, protection, good health, and better luck. It can be as simple as dedicating a candle to a special god or goddess—for example, to Odin, the Allfather and god of wisdom, or to Freyja, the Norse goddess of love—bringing these divine energies into your life.

Coming in all shapes, colors, scents, and sizes, the

candle needs to be matched to the magical work. Here is a brief description of candle colors and their uses:

- Red—Power, sexual energy, love, creativity, vitality, action
- Green—Healing, growth, abundance, good luck, shapeshifting, fertility, money
- Blue—Higher wisdom, clearing out negative energies, intuition, healing, protection, flexibility, and flow
- Gold/Yellow—Personal power, creativity, sun energy, knowledge, color of the mind and conscious mental energy
- Brown—Earth energy, healing, grounding, the harvest
- Silver—Moon energy, ancestor contact, purification, astral travel, dreaming
- Purple/Violet—Spiritual awareness, balance, psychic ability, communication with the gods and goddesses, higher wisdom
- Pink—Love, romance, friendship, family, and children
- Orange—Healing, meditation, fair play, higher wisdom

- Black—The unknown, potential power, getting rid of negativity, ending relationships and partnerships, the shadow self
- White—Communication with the Goddess or God, divine inspiration and protection, motivation

Before beginning your candle magic ritual, take a ritual bath or shower, using sea salt or a scented soap, such as lavender or sandalwood. You may even sprinkle a few drops of your favorite oil into your bath. After your bath or shower, dress in your ritual robe. This robe is your magical skin, and should represent who you are. It can be any color or style. Gather together everything you will need and place the items on your altar table. The following is a handy checklist for performing rune candle magic.

RUNE CANDLE MAGIC CHECKLIST

1. Set up your altar.
2. Dress your candle by washing it in cool saltwater, drying it, and carving the runes on it. Carve each rune three times on the candle, if space permits. You can carve bindrunes upon it (see page 217), or you can carve the purpose of the candle in runes, for example, MONEY

(Mannaz, Othala, Naudhiz, Ehwaz, Jera). You can use the *ristir*, a regular writing pen, your knife, a quill, a pointed stick, or—in a pinch— your fingernail. As you do this, concentrate on your intent. See and sense yourself energetically charging the candle with the runes you are carving on it.

3. Cover the candle completely with a thin coat of scented oil.

4. Set the candle upon the altar. You can also place the 24 Elder Futhark rune stones, crystals, other stones, shells, herbs, flowers, and so forth around the candle in a circular or Ingwaz pattern to strengthen its magical energies.

5. Dim the lights and draw a protective circle or square around yourself to create a protected magical working space.

6. Establish the directional corners of north, east, south, and west, and clear them of unwanted energies.

7. Call in the Four Wards.

8. Select a sponsor god and/or goddess. Choose the goddess or god with whom you feel the strongest rapport. Ask them to help you in your rune candle magic.

9. Choose a guardian power animal, selecting an animal you have no fear of, and ask it to help you.

10. Create a simple chant or song (or use the *galdr* songs appropriate to the runes), saying specifically what it is that you want to achieve with the rune candle. Include the names of any sponsor deities and power animals.

11. Light the candle with care.

12. Merge with the flame of the candle and connect with the divine energy of the Goddess and God. Do this for at least nine minutes. Use deep breathing to intensify your focus and connection. You might also chant the runes that are being used in the work or sing the *galdr* songs that relate to those specific runes. This focuses the energy into a tightly knit band that is very powerful.

13. When the work is complete, allow the candle to burn down fully. If you leave the room, be sure the candle is positioned where it can burn down safely without being disturbed. If you need to extinguish the candle, do so with wetted fingers or a snuffer.

14. Discard the candle appropriately. If it's a

beeswax candle, you can bury it in the ground. If it's made from synthetic material, it is best to put the candle end in a paper bag and put it in the garbage. Or you can save the candle ends and melt them down to make new candles.

15. Clean up and put everything away.

16. Burn incense or smudge or scatter salt to clear and purify your ritual area.

Candles are excellent meditative aids, and burning candles works along the same lines as all other magic—through intention, expectation, desire, and merging. Wax from magical candles can also be used to seal charms and rune inscriptions.

SELF-EMPOWERMENT RUNE CANDLE MAGIC

You will need three red candles. Set up a sacred enclosure (see page 391). Then go through your runes slowly, looking at them one at a time. Pick out three runes that represent the energies you most desire at this point in your life. Place them on your altar where you can see them clearly. Carve rune symbols three times into each of the three red candles, rub them with amber or rose oil, and put them on your altar behind the runes.

Merge with the qualities of the runes in front of you, and concentrate on bringing their runic energies into your life. Call upon your favorite gods or goddesses or other divine energies or power animals to assist you. Allow the candles to burn down completely on their own. Pull up your sacred enclosure when you are done, but leave the three runes on your altar for nine days.

Essential Oils

Each concentrated essence represents the spirit of a plant and carries its energy and qualities. Plants absorb energies from the elements, from the Earth, sun, and moon; they store this vital life force that can be tapped and used in magic, especially in candle magic. You release the power of the oils by dressing your candle with them and by rubbing them into the runes you carve.

Purchase only quality essential oils and stay clear of synthetic-based oils. Use a good carrier oil, such as almond or sunflower, to dilute your essential oils before using them. To tap into the essence of the oil, place a drop or two on a cotton ball and carry it in your pocket. Also, you can burn it in incense or, if you are sensitive to smoke, use it in an aromatherapy diffuser. Putting a few drops in a small pan of boiling water also releases the powerful fragrance of oils. Some people always use the same scent whenever they do rune magic, so the fragrance immediately puts them into a magical state. You can also use your personal scent on paper and envelopes for correspondence. You can also write or rub rune symbols on the outside of gifts you give. Gebo is the rune to use for this purpose. This empowers everything with the energy of the oil and the rune.

USING RUNES TO CHARGE ESSENTIAL OILS

Decide which oil from the list below matches your intended outcome. Then look at the magical properties of runes in the encyclopedic listing, and use the rune or runes that correspond to your desired result. For example, honeysuckle or ginger essential oil would be good selections for obtaining money, and you could use Fehu when charging the oil.

To charge the oil, hold the vial between your palms for a few minutes, focusing on the rune you have selected and its inherent energies. See and sense yourself placing the runic energies into the oil, through the palms of your hands. Roll the oil vial between your hands for a few minutes, and then set it down on the altar. Position the runes you are using to charge the oil around the vial, and let them all sit overnight on your altar. This allows the oil to mature to its fullest magical strength. Here is a list of oils you can charge with runic energy, and their magical qualities.

THE ESSENTIAL OILS

- **Almond**—Prosperity and wisdom
- **Amber**—Love, happiness, and strength
- **Apple**—Love, happiness, and uplifting
- **Apricot**—Love, creativity, and mental openness
- **Balsam, Fir**—Prosperity and mental clarity
- **Bay**—Protection, purification, healing, attracting women, calming, and psychic powers
- **Benzoin**—Purification, prosperity, comforting, calming, and balancing
- **Carnation**—Protection, blessing, stimulation, and strengthening
- **Cedar**—Money, healing, protection, purification, calming, comforting, and strengthening

- **Chamomile**—Money, love, purification, calming, and relaxing
- **Cherry**—Love and divination
- **Cinnamon**—Psychic powers, protection, love-power, creativity, and antidepressant
- **Clove**—Protection, prosperity, purification, love, and mental powers
- **Dragon's blood**—Love, protection, exorcism, crown chakra, and control of energies
- **Geranium**—Love-fertility, protection, calming, balancing, and antidepressant
- **Ginger**—Prosperity, love, power, healing, strengthening, and warming the spirit
- **Honeysuckle**—Prosperity, protection, relaxing, soothing, uplifting, and psychic powers
- **Hyacinth**—Love, happiness, protection, and optimism
- **Jasmine**—Love-money, dreams, antidepressant, aphrodisiac, spiritual love, and raising vibrations
- **Juniper**—Purification, protection, love, strengthening, antidepressant, and centering
- **Lavender**—Love-peace, purification, protection, calming, balancing, strengthening, and stimulating
- **Lemon**—Purification, love, friendship, clarity, calming, and helping mental powers

- **Lilac**—Exorcism, protection, peace-harmony, mind clearing, aiding memory, and concentration
- **Mint**—Passion, protection, travel, exorcism, refreshing, clarity, increases memory and concentration
- **Orange**—Love, prosperity, divination, luck, relaxing, balancing, stimulation, and sensuality
- **Patchouli**—Prosperity, passion-fertility, aphrodisiac
- **Pine**—Fertility, prosperity, exorcism, protection, strengthening, cleansing, and regeneration
- **Rose**—Love, luck, divination protection, peace, balancing, and strengthens heart chakra and spirit
- **Rosemary**—Protection, love-passion, mental powers, purification, uplifting, mental stimulant, building strength of character and courage
- **Sage**—Wisdom, protection, purification, cleansing, balancing, and strengthening
- **Sandalwood**—Protection, exorcism, spirituality, and harmonizing
- **Vanilla**—Passion, aiding mental powers, calming, soothing nerves, and relaxing
- **Violet**—Protection, soothing, passion, wishes, reuniting and stimulating throat chakra healing

The Talisman

Frequently passed down through generations, talismans give power to the possessor. The medieval Philosopher's Stone is probably the most famous talisman in history. Possession of this touchstone enabled its owner to perform many wonders, presumably including transmuting base metals into gold.

A magical object that possesses and transmits powerful energies, a talisman contains feelings and radiates these qualities according to your desires. A talisman generally has a pattern incorporated in it—such as runic symbols—designed to assist in magic and ritual. Prepared magically to contain and radiate a specific field and tone of energy, talismans are usually small and carried on your person. They generate spectrums of energy, usually combining the four elements: earth, air, fire, and water.

Carving runes on talismans charges them with runic powers. They can be used to secure love, wealth, good health, and protection. Runic talismans, or tines, were traditionally scratched into stone, bone, and wood. Yew wood was usually used for talismans because of its long association with magic. Tines were also shaped from twigs. Today, runic talismans are made of wood, clay, metal, stone, and parchment. Parchment talismans are often carried in lockets or wallets. Pieces of jewelry large enough to have runes carved on them also make excellent talismans. Any fixed object such as a wall in your room—even a house—can be turned into a runic talisman.

Making a Runic Talisman

You create a runic talisman by moving your magical field of intention into an object. You can influence the energetic structure of the object with this field by using runes.

Runic talismans are best made during the waxing moon and, preferably, on one of the eight days of power (see page 361). Prepare the materials you will need, working out the runic inscriptions in advance on a sheet of paper. Consecrate your workplace by sprinkling it with salt and water, and then lightly smudge (with sage and cedar) or use incense. Light two candles for ambiance and to symbolize fire.

To make the following talisman, use modeling clay, which you can find in most craft stores. Select clay that's easy to fire in a regular oven. It comes in several colors, and you can match the color to the purpose of the talisman. You will also need a quill, a ballpoint pen, or something similar with which to engrave the runes on the clay. You can also use wood if you prefer it to clay, but it's more difficult to carve.

Once you have chosen the medium for your talisman, and know exactly what runic energies and feelings you are going to place in it, the next step is determining the area your talisman will influence—two feet (60cm), twenty feet (6m), or a mile (1.6km). This depends upon its intended use.

Next, set up your altar, establish your sacred enclosure (circle, square, sphere, Ingwaz diamond, or Ve), and call the Four Wards. Place the talisman between two red candles on your altar, directly in front of you, where you can look at it comfortably. (If you wish, you can carve the runes on the altar candles to double the energy.)

As you begin carving the runes, call out their names, visualizing their power entering the talisman. Sing the corresponding *galdr* song to empower the runes you are using. As you carve or draw the runes, visualize the color that corresponds to each of them. For example, when carving Laguz, you would focus on a deep green or blue-green.

Next, redden the runes you have carved with either red ocher paint, dragon's-blood resin, tiver, minium, or some other red-pigmented dye. You can also use red wax from the altar candles you are using to redden the runes carved into the talisman.

Now merge, using your emotions, sensations, or whatever works best for you, and fill your mind with the feeling, the sound, the shape, and the quality of the rune(s) you are placing into your talisman. Imagine actually planting an energetic runic symbol into the talisman, superimposed on the reddened symbol. You could do this by visualizing a laser beam of rune-shaped light moving from your forehead or your hands into the talisman. Direct your feeling, emotion, and all your attention into the object. See the pattern of your thought-energy and field of magical intention being absorbed by the molecular structure of the talisman.

When this is done, enclose the talisman in darkness, wrapping it in a dark cloth or putting it in a pouch. This symbolizes the womb. Keep the runic talisman in the dark overnight or, ideally, if you have the time, for a full moon cycle.

After keeping the talisman in the dark for an appropriate period of time, take the pouch (with the talisman inside) and carry it in a sunwise (clockwise) circle nine times. While you do this, chant its runic

name of power and the names of the gods and goddesses, and then bring the talisman into the light of
day.

A living being having Orlog from inception, the
talisman has a purpose, and when you bring it out
into the light, this symbolizes its birth. This is the
time to name and empower it. By naming the talisman, you strengthen it and give it personality.
Traditional names are kennings (poetic metaphors)
for the power within the empowered object. Choose
a name for your talisman that is related to its function. If it is for protection, you might call it "draw
wand," which is the kenning for "sword."

For the actual ritual of naming the talisman, call
upon the powers of light and life to bring its qualities
to life. Pass the talisman slowly over the flame of a
candle or through the smoke of smudge or incense in
a *glodhker* or incense burner, three times, and say:

Now, powers of fire, with speed spew forth,
lend thy quickness and life.

Then lay the talisman on the altar, sprinkle water
over it carefully, and say:

I sprinkle thee with the powers of water and give thee the name (*insert the talisman's name*).

Henceforth, when addressing the talisman, call it by its name as you would any other living thing.

Next, visualize and sense an energy field around—and radiating from—the talisman. Do this at least three times. Then give the talisman the power to carry out its task by speaking its function aloud, three times—for example, "Your function is to bring me good luck and fortune." Finish by saying:

In the name of Odin, Vili, and Ve, and by the might of Urd,
Verdandi, and Skuld, so shall it be!

Once you do this, you have activated the runic talisman. Now you can use it to tap into the runic streams of energy that have been loaded into it. Keep it on your person, or near the person it is intended for, or in a specific room, at home or at work, in your car, or in whatever location its runic powers can function best.

It's usually a good idea to wear the talisman next

to your skin, suspended by a red or black cord. After you place the runic talisman in its intended destination, say these words:

> Now the work has been wrought, with the might of mighty runes.
> So shall it be!

When you have completed these steps, thank the divine energies. Release the Four Wards and pull up your sacred enclosure. Clap your hands together and leave the area for a short time. If you are not sure that you've done the talisman correctly, then repeat the procedure until you feel satisfied with the results.

The Runic Circle (Ring)

You can create powerful amulets, called runic rings, insigils, or wheels, by using runic letters coupled with sacred geometry, namely the circle. These insigils (magical symbols) were once used on coins, and in medieval times they evolved into heraldic emblems, such as the escarbuncle used by knights to empower their shields. It was also customary to carve or write runic insigils so small that they were difficult to detect, for example, on the insides of rings or lockets, on the soles of shoes, the undersides of belts, and so forth.

The Heavenly Star, the Eight-Spoked Wheel symbolizing the eight divisions of time and space, is one of the most powerful and popular of all runic rings.

Utilizing the energies of all 24 runes of the Elder Futhark, the Helm of Awe ("Aegishjalmur") is also a particularly powerful ring. Formed from eight Algiz runes, combined with 24 cross-arms that symbolize the Elder Futhark, this insigil was one of the treasures that Sigurd (Siegfried) won by defeating the dragon Fafner.

MAKING A RUNIC RING

From the center point of the ring's circle, draw eight lines to make a star-like configuration, fashioning the lines like the spokes of the ring. These are symbolic of the divisions of heaven and the eight otherworlds of the Northern Tradition. (The ninth is the one you're standing on—Midgard.) Once you have drawn or carved the star-like configuration, draw a double ring or circle around the spokes. You can then write or carve the runes around the double ring, and also along the lines of the spokes.

You can use the runic ring in your sacred enclosure by energetically drawing it with your wand on the ground of your circle, square, sphere, Ingwaz diamond, or Ve. Or you can use colored chalk when working on surfaces such as concrete. If you make the ring of wood, clay, or metal, you can fashion it to wear around your neck. When you do, the runic ring is called a bracteate.

The kinds of runic rings you can create are virtually unlimited. Traditionally, runes have represented protection and power, but today runes are also used for growth, hope, cooperation, and love. You can use bindrunes on your runic ring or wheel to strengthen the energy. You can create a simple ring by writing your own name in runes. If you have enough runes in your name to go around the circle, you can write it once. If not, you can write it in runes as many as three times to fill out the ring and reinforce the magical energy.

PART 6

Contemporary Rune Practices

Runes in the Contemporary World

With their symbolism appearing in so many places in contemporary life, it's no wonder that many of us today feel drawn to the mysterious runes. The most widespread example is the peace sign, originally a company logo for the British Campaign for Nuclear Disarmament. Very similar to the "Yr" rune of the Younger Futhark, the peace sign also looks like a reversed Algiz rune inside a circle.

Literary interest in the runes has been strong since the late nineteenth century. Jules Verne in his book *A Journey to the Center of the Earth* (1864) wrote about Icelandic runes. More recently, author J. R. Tolkien, a professor of English at Oxford University, popularized the Anglo-Saxon or Moon runes in his book *The*

Hobbit, bringing a new awareness of runes to millions of readers. He later devised other new scripts in his Middle Earth (Midgard) trilogy, *The Lord of the Rings.* One of the scripts he devised was the Tengwar Angerthas Moria script, with characters from traditional rune rows, including Northumbrian runes, bindrunes, and a few variations of the Elder Futhark.

Now, with the resurgence of interest in pagan cultures and the Celtic and Norse traditions, the runes are reappearing, not only in books like this one, but also on rune cards, rune stones, jewelry, fabrics, and T-shirts, as well as on incense burners, magical tools, in henna art, tattoos, and even on automobile bumper stickers. In addition, runic yoga, called *stadha,* is becoming more widely known and practiced. An active system of empowerment, *stadha,* or *stahagaldr,* consists of specific runic postures or gestures.

One of the best ways to access the powers of the runes is to make your own rune set. Making your own runes fills them with your energy, marking them with your personal signature. Because of this energetic link, the runes you make yourself are often the runes that work best for you in divination and magic.

Rune Cards

Many different rune card decks are available in bookstores, new age shops, and over the Internet. Most have images that are Tarot-like, expressing the author's or artist's personal perceptions of the runes.

Use your intuition when selecting rune cards. Choose the deck that speaks to you, or the one that draws your attention more than the others. When using rune cards for divination, remember that their divination meanings are the author's interpretation of the runes, just as the information in this book reflects my opinions and experiences. Each author's interpretations are a little different.

For me, rune cards don't possess the inherent power of runes made from stone, clay, or wood. At the same time, I have found that rune cards, especially the ones I have made myself, are very useful for focusing on runic symbols, for example, in meditation. This is because the rune symbols appear much larger on cards than on stones, and you can easily see them, even in dim light.

MAKING YOUR OWN RUNE CARDS

This is one of the best ways to get to know the runes. Use index cards to make your deck; they come in many colors—choose one of your favorites. First, decide how you want the backs of the rune cards to look. You can leave them blank or decorate them by affixing patterned paper or fabric. Make sure that the backs all look the same, or at least very similar.

For applying the runes themselves, use a thick red felt marker or red paint. If you like, mix some gold metallic paint into the red to get a shimmering effect. Before drawing the rune, read over the encyclopedic listing. As you draw or paint each rune card, focus on some basic qualities, such as key words, color correspondence, and the divine energies associated with the rune. In order to use the runes proficiently, you will need to be able to visualize and know the meaning of each one.

Next, chant the name of the rune, and visualize placing the appropriate energies into each card as you create it. This imprints it with your energy.

You can either draw the rune symbol by itself on the front of each card, or you can include its name and/or key words. Other ideas include making a mini-collage on the front of each card by cutting out pictures, bits and pieces from old magazines, and so forth, and pasting them together to represent the rune.

When you are not using your rune cards, store them in a covered box or pouch.

Making Your Own Rune Sets

Requiring dedication, a block of time, and wood-working know-how, making your own wooden rune set can be a simple or very challenging project. Unless you have experience working with sharp tools and saws, approach this process slowly and with care. Take all necessary precautions when working with power tools, woodburning tools, toxic paints and dyes, and sharp carving implements. The following instructions are intended for adults. This project is also suitable for teenagers, but only with adult super-vision.

I recommend making your wooden runes as part of a ritual, but this is not absolutely necessary. The formation of the runes and the rituals surrounding them differ from person to person and from tradition to tradition. Rely on your intuition, be creative, and by all means go ahead and mix your mediums and magics!

To make a complete set of wooden runes, you will need specific materials. You may have many of them already; some you can borrow, and others you can purchase. The larger home-improvement stores or local hardware shops will carry all of the necessary tools for this project under one roof.

Here is a list of materials you will need to make your own set of wooden runes.

- A branch from a fruit-bearing tree (apple, yew, pine, cedar, redwood, olive, peach, pear, cherry). Make every effort to harvest the branch when the tree is blossoming, because then it has the strongest fruit-bearing energy and makes more powerful runes. I don't recommend using dead branches. Cut 24 (or more to allow for possible mistakes) ½-inch (1.25-cm) rounds from the branch. If you do not have access to a living tree, you can use oak boards cut to the following approximate dimensions:1½" x ¼" x 48" (3.75cm x .625cm x 120cm) oak board cut into 24 pieces 2" (5cm) in length. This will be available in the hardwood section of the lumberyard. It will save you having to saw up larger boards.

- A small saw to cut the rune disk shapes. An electric jigsaw or table saw works well.
- A clamp or vice for holding the rune disks when cutting them.
- A tool for cutting the rune symbols such as a chisel point carving knife, X-acto blade, *ristir* (scribing tool), screwdriver, ⅛" (.31cm) woodcarving chisel, Dremel tool with a narrow cutting bit, or woodburning tool with a narrow gauge bit. Be sure to consecrate the tool you cut the runes with. You do this by passing it through the flame of a candle, sprinkling it with saltwater, or bathing it in incense smoke and then dedicating it to a specific god or goddess.
- Medium and fine sandpaper
- Fine steel wool
- Reddening dye for coloring the runes, such as red pigment from tiver, minium, red india ink, red candle wax, dragon's-blood resin, red jeweler's rouge, or red enamel paint. Mixing a bit of gold metallic paint with your red pigment will create a shimmering rune symbol. If you want to be traditional, you can prick your finger and place a drop of your own blood in the red pigment. One painless way to do this is by flossing

your teeth, and using a bit of the blood in the pigment. Your blood makes the runes uniquely yours, but it is not in any way necessary, so follow your instincts.

- Linseed, lemon, walnut, or olive oil
- A rag to apply the oil
- Another rag to place the runes on after they are reddened
- A sturdy, wide-mouthed rune bag made of natural material for holding your runes. The opening needs to be large enough for you to put your hand in and mix and pull out the runes easily.

TWENTY-FOUR STEPS FOR MAKING WOODEN RUNES

1. Select a place to work where you will not be disturbed by other people, pets, or the telephone. Next, gather together everything you'll need. The entire process takes about three hours. Because of this, you might consider making your runes in three stages, one *aett* per sitting.

2. Smudge the area with cedar, sage, or sandalwood incense to clear out any unwanted energies.

3. Place your cut rune disks or tablets on the work-

table or in another safe space. Take a clean, white-colored cloth and lay it on the altar (or table) to put your finished runes on.

4. Establish your sacred enclosure (circle, square, sphere, Ingwaz diamond, or Ve (see page 391.)

5. Call in the Four Wards. (See page 394.)

6. Do the Hammer sign in the four directions, plus above, below, and center. (See page 396.)

7. Invite your favorite Norse gods and goddesses into your sacred enclosure to help you with your project. Particularly helpful would be Odin, Frigga, the Norns (Urd, Vendandi, and Skuld), Freyja, Frey, Baldur, and Heimdall. You can also invoke the energies of earth, air, fire, and water, power animals, helpful ancestors, and any other wights (spirits) to guide your hands and lend you their knowledge while you make your runes. Then, pour a cup of mead or apple juice, and place it on your altar as an offering to all the divine energies present.

8. Take your 24 disks (plus a few extras to cover mistakes) and sand all the surfaces of each piece, first with medium-grade, and then with fine sandpaper, smoothing out the corners and edges.

9. Carefully pencil the 24 runes onto the 24 disks, drawing the symbols against the grain of the wood, and downward. This draws the runic energies into the symbol itself. Chant the rune name as you draw it.

10. Put the first rune disk, Fehu, in a vise or other similar clamp to keep it stationary. With your lips next to the wooden Fehu disk, sing the corresponding *galdr* song into the rune as you visualize what Fehu means to you—for example, mobile wealth. Focus on the disk, hold your visualization, and carve the rune carefully into the wood. Or you can burn the rune into the wood with a woodburning tool.

11. Use #000 steel wool to remove any rough edges left over from the carving steps. Be careful not to rub too hard since the carving isn't that deep. Remove any remaining pencil marks with a soft, clean eraser.

12. When finished with the first rune, remove it from the vise and put it on the white cloth in front of you. Repeat steps 10 and 11, until you have carved all 24 rune disks.

13. When all the runes are on the white cloth in

front of you, gaze intently at them, one at a time, again singing the corresponding *galdr* song into the wooden disks. When you have *galdred* all 24 runes, chant the Ansuz-Laguz-Uruz phrase "Ahhhhluu!" over the rune set. This ancient rune formula means "So mote it be" or "It is sealed."

14. Redden each rune, one at a time. Be sure you have enough color for all the disks. Start with the Fehu disk and redden each part of the symbol downwards, drawing the energies into the rune. Chant "Fehu" three or nine times while reddening the disk, and feel the Fehu energies being infused into the disk along with the color.

15. Seal the energies into the rune by *galdring* the Ansuz-Laguz-Uruz phrase "Ahhhhluu!" ("So mote it be!") into the wood again. Then set the disk on the cloth to dry.

16. Repeat steps 14 and 15 until all 24 runes are reddened and completely dry.

17. Sprinkle the runes with spring water.

18. Pass the runes through smudge made of cedar, sage, lavender, copal, or amber resin. As you pass each disk through the smoke, say:

In the name of the Aesir, Vanir, and the Norns,
By the might of Odin, Vili, and Ve,
By the strength of ice, air, fire, land, and sea
I bind the powers of this rune.
Clear its purpose and true its voice.
Ahhhhluu!

Say the name of the rune, and dry it completely. Do this with each disk, and return it to the cloth.

19. Seal your wooden runes using ¼ cup olive oil with 24 drops of lemon oil in it. You can also add a few drops of the essential oils that correspond to the energies of the runes, or oils that induce visions, such as sage, amber resin, dragon's-blood, mugwort, and vervain. Stir these oils into the olive-oil base.

20. Work the oil into each of the wooden disks, while singing the corresponding *galdr* song. Think about the rune's meaning as you rub. Buff your runes to a soft, satin finish.

21. Apply linseed oil to one side of each of the disks, and let it dry. Apply linseed oil to the other side, and let it dry. Do this a couple of

times, wiping off any excess. (*Note:* Apply lin-seed oil to your runes once a year—homemade or not—to keep them well sealed.)

22. After completing this process, hold each rune over your heart and chant the rune name three times. Feel the sound resonate throughout your heart area and into the individual rune. Dedicate your runes to the main purpose for which you wish to use them, for example: "By Odin, Vili, and Ve, and the Norns, I dedicate these runes to helping and healing others and myself."

Spend some time thinking about the dedication. Finish sealing the runes by *galdring* the Ansuz-Laguz-Uruz formula, "Ahhhhluu!"

23. Thank the divine energies present, release the Four Wards, take down your sacred enclosure, and put everything away. If you are outdoors, pour the cup of mead or apple juice from the altar onto the ground, preferably under the tree from which you took the branch, thanking the tree and the wight of the tree.

24. Be sure to do your first reading with your new rune set for yourself. This sets the energy of your personal "Wyrd" into the runes.

Your Own Stone Runes

You can also use 24 similar stones to create your own set of runes; for example, stones from the ocean or smooth river rocks that you collect on a walk. (You could also use similar-sized shells that you find on the beach.) Omit steps 8–12 (unless you will be cutting the stone). Paint (redden) your rune stones with a mixture of gold metallic and red paint. Be aware that the paint will most likely rub off with frequent use.

Purchasing Runes

You can purchase wooden, stone, ceramic, and other types of runes from a variety of places, including new age shops, gift shops, at craft fairs, and over the Internet. When selecting runes, use your intuition as to how a particular set of runes feels to you, which means taking the time, if possible, to "test drive" the runes for a few minutes. Tune in to your inner feelings, asking yourself if this is the rune set for you. How do the runes feel in your hands? Do they seem to speak to you? Can you feel the divine energy flowing through them?

In some ways it is preferable to have more than one set of runes so that you can use one set for readings and another for meditation or dreamwork. You will most likely want a set that no one's energy touches except your own.

My favorite rune stones are a set of hematite runes that I got from Lost Mountain in Northern California. One of the main reasons I prefer these runes is that, unlike rune cards, which can be damaged from continuous mixing, the stones are extremely durable. Their inherent energies also play in, and act as a conduit for, the runic energies. I prefer using wooden runes when I'm traveling, because they are lightweight. I have seen magnificent sets made of amber, which feel very different. Also small metal sets can be effective divination tools.

Runic Awareness, Healing, and Protection

RUNIC YOGA (*STADHA*)

Throughout the world, gestures and postures are ways to commune with divine energies, from the simple folding of hands in prayer to the extremely complex system of asanas in the Indian hatha yoga school.

The early twentieth-century German runemasters Friedrich Marby and Siegfried Krummer developed runic yoga as a means of harnessing the streams of power present in and surrounding the Earth. You do this by taking on the shape of the rune, focusing your attention on the rune's meaning, and sounding out the rune, either by chanting or *galdring*.

Originally called rune gymnastics, runic yoga was derived from a combination of Indian yoga and Russian theater director Vsevolod Meyerhold's bio-mechanical exercises for training actors.

In runic yoga, you experience the five cosmic zones of the universe:

1) inner-earth space—a very large, contained zone of tranquil space that radiates energy,

2) material earth space—the physical matter of the planet, filled with ancient forms of patterned energy coursing through it,

3) wave space—the zone just above the surface of the earth that our bodies inhabit, and also the area where energy patterns received from above and below are most freely exchanged,

4) cosmic space—a very large zone of radiant energy,

5) super cosmic space—the zone charged by the

radiant zone of cosmic space, and influenced by celestial bodies such as stars, planets, moons, comets.

The idea is to receive and send patterns of energy to and from all five of these zones, by tuning in to runic energy waves. It sounds pretty complicated, but it's not. It takes practice, but by using the runic yoga posture you can gather energies and then reshape and guide them. Runemasters say that by becoming aware of the interplay of runic energies within these zones, engaging them, and guiding them consciously, we can actively participate in the evolution and restructuring of the cosmos. The runes act as keys to the reception, absorption, and projection of these energies. Their first effect is on the transformation of the individual.

Called *stadha* or *stadhagaldr*, runic yoga not only integrates your body, mind, and spirit, but it also increases your vital energy and mental faculties—which help you to act and think more effectively. In addition, it brings many health benefits, including improved posture, firmer stomach muscles, and increased flexibility. As a form of moving meditation, the postures can be useful for deepening relaxation and relieving stress. These low-impact exercises also promote healthy natural breathing, helpful to asthma sufferers and others with respiratory problems.

Stadha can be practiced by everyone, no matter what age, and modified to compensate for physical disabilities or injuries. Those with joint and muscle stiffness and other restrictions to their movement can gain increased mobility from performing the postures on a regular basis.

For best results, practice each runic yoga posture and its corresponding *galdr* song for at least a week or two, for 15 minutes in the morning and evening. After finishing with one posture, go on to the next. This takes quite a while, but it is well worth the effort. Plus, you can make the whole thing a family experience as a way to bring everyone together for a few minutes twice a day.

Do the *stadha* postures in this order to begin with:

Isa
Kenaz
Mannaz
Uruz
the Cross
Naudhiz

Ehwaz
Sowilo
Tiwaz
Laguz
Ingwaz
Fehu
Hagalaz

When you have done each of these 13 postures for 14 days each (a total of 182 days), then you can move on to the other *stadhas*, incorporating them into your runic yoga practice. After mastering all 24 *stadhas*, plus the Cross, do a few of them in the morning and in the afternoon. Add the corresponding *galdr* songs to each rune as you practice the *stadha* postures. This expands your ability to absorb, gather, and direct the runic energies.

Remember to keep the six primary concerns of runic yoga in mind as you strike the poses and sing the *galdr*. They are:

1) control of the body through posture (*stadha*)
2) control of thought through song (*galdr*)
3) control of breath (being aware of the pattern of your breathing)

4) control of emotion

5) becoming aware of the rune realms of the self and the world(s)

6) control and direction of the will.

It helps to have a reliable compass so that you know which way you are facing when you do the postures.

THE TWENTY-FOUR RUNIC YOGA POSTURES (*STADHA*)

First *Aett*

Fehu—Face the sun with both arms slanted upward, left arm slightly higher than the right arm, fingers and palms pointed out for drawing and directing power, imitating the Fehu shape. Make the sound fffffffff, and visualize the runic energy flowing in through your head, hands, and arms as you breathe in, and flowing out as you exhale. Sing the corresponding *galdr*.

Uruz—Take a deep breath, exhale, and then bend at the waist, your back parallel to the ground. With your head toward the east, point your arms and fingers toward the ground and sing uuuuuuuu to draw the runic in through the soles of your feet, through your body, and then out through your fingertips. Sing the corresponding *galdr*.

Thurisaz—Face east or south, standing upright with your left arm bent at the elbow, your left hand resting on your left hip. Your palm grasps your hip bone. Make the sound thththththththth, and sing the corresponding *galdr*, feeling the runic energy moving through you.

Ansuz—Face north or east, standing upright, with both arms stretched outward and slightly downward, left arm lower than the right, imitating the shape of the rune. Make the sound aaaaaaaa, while visualizing the runic energy flowing in through your head, hands, and arms as you breathe in, and flowing out as you exhale. Sing the corresponding *galdr*.

Raidho—Face south, standing straight, with your left arm bent at the elbow, left palm resting on your hip bone. Slant your left leg out, lifting it slightly off the ground. Pull your right arm tightly to your right side. Make the rrrrrrr sound, and sing the corresponding *galdr*.

Kenaz—Face north, standing upright with your right arm raised at a 45-degree angle, forming a "V" shape. Your right palm faces outward, drawing in runic energy and letting it flow out through the fingers of your left hand. Chant the sound kaaaaann, while visualizing the runic energy flowing through you. Sing the corresponding *galdr*.

Gebo—Face north or east, standing upright, your legs spread apart, feet pointed outward and knees locked. Stretch your arms to either side, forming an "X," positioning your hands directly over your feet. Sound gaaaffff, and breathe the runic energies through your right hand, down your left leg, and then pull the energy through your left hand and down your right leg. Sing the Gebo *galdr*.

Wunjo—Face north, standing straight with your legs together. Put the fingertips of your left hand on the top of your head, imitating the form of the rune. Your right arm remains straight and tucked against your right side. Sound wwuuu-unn, and sing the Wunjo *galdr* song.

Second *Aett*

H **Hagalaz**—This is the last one of the 13 progressive runic-yoga postures, as outlined by Krummer. It takes more practice to do the Hagalaz *stadha* properly, because it uses a combination of runes. Begin by emptying your mind of all distracting thoughts. Face north, standing upright in the position of a cross, arms parallel to the ground, palms outward. Breathe in nine times, and then turn sunwise (clockwise), singing hu ha hi he ho in each of the four directions, ending again to the north. Next, do the Naudhiz *stadha*, turning clockwise, singing nu na ni ne no (on the first complete turn), and hu ha hi he ho (on the second complete turn). Then, do the Ehwaz *stadha*, singing eeeeeeee on the first turn, and hu ha hi he ho as you do the second turn. Continue with the Isa *stadha*, singing iiiiiiii on the first turn and hu ha hi he ho on the second. Next comes the Mannaz *stadha*, toning mmmmmmmm as you turn once, and hu ha hi he ho as you turn clockwise a second time. Do the Tiwaz *stadha*, singing Tiwaz, Tiwaz, Tiwaz on the first turn and he ha hi he ho as you turn again. Finally do the Gebo rune, singing gu ga gi ge go on the first clockwise turn, and hu ha hi he ho as you turn the second time. You do a total of 13 turns.

Naudhiz—Face north or east. Standing straight, your right arm pointing upward at a 45-degree angle and your left arm pointing downward at the same angle, forming a line and imitating the rune shape. Chant the sound nnnnnnnn, while visualizing the runic energy flowing into your right arm and head, and flowing out through your left arm and feet. Sing the Naudhiz *galdr*. Next, do the Cross *stadha*, and lower your hands to your hips.

Isa—Begin by facing north and standing perfectly straight, your hands by your sides. Then, chant the sound iiiissss, and feel the runic energy moving into your body both through your feet and the top of your head. Next stand straight, arms over your head, the palms of your hands touching one another. Sing the Isa *galdr*.

Jera—Stand erect and face east or south. Bend your right arm so the thumb of your right hand touches the top of your head. Bend your left arm at the same angle with the fingertips of your left hand touching your left hip bone. Sing the Jera *galdr*.

Eihwaz—Face north, standing upright, and stretch both your arms downward at a 50-degree angle. Lift your right (or left) leg backward at the same angle as your arm to imitate the Eihwaz symbol. Sing the corresponding *galdr* song.

Perthro—Face west, sitting on the ground, your back straight. Bring your knees up, keeping your feet flat on the ground. Rest both your elbows on your knees, your forearms slanted up forward. Sing the Perthro *galdr*.

Algiz—Face north, standing upright, arms stretched upward to form the runic symbol. Next, keep your arms in the same position, but kneel and sit on your heels. Your body needs to remain straight, with your head tilted slightly back.

Keeping the same arm position, kneel with your right knee on the ground and your left foot out in front of you, your thigh parallel to the ground. Sing the Algiz *galdr*.

Sowilo—Facing east, squat as if you are kneeling to the sun, heels together, your arms to your sides, resting on your thighs. Chant the sound sssoooll, while visualizing the runic power flowing in through the top of your head and out through your feet.

Third *Aett*

Tiwaz—Facing north, stand straight, arms slanted out and downward, palms downward, imitating the form of the rune. Hum the sound tttttttttt, while visualizing the runic energy flowing upward from your feet to the top of your head.

Berkana—Stand straight, left arm bent at the elbow, left palm resting on your hip. Bend your left leg at the knee with your heels touching. Your left arm and left knee form the rune shape. Sing the Berkana *galdr*.

Ehwaz—Stand straight, left arm raised and right arm lowered. This is basically the opposite of the Naudhiz posture. Chant the sound eeeeeeee as you visualize the runic energy flowing from your left arm and your head into your right arm and feet. You can also do this posture with another person by facing one another, each in the Laguz posture, forming the Ehwaz symbol. Sing the Ehwaz *galdr*.

Mannaz—Standing erect, raise both your arms outward and away from your body to a 45-degree angle, palms upward. The runic energy moves through your head and palms, and flows into your body, down to your feet. Sing the Mannaz *galdr*.

Laguz—Standing straight, hold your arms out in front of your chest at a downward 45-degree angle to imitate the rune shape. Your palms point downward. You can also do this posture with your palms pointed upward. Visualize the runic energy moving up through your feet, and out your fingertips while you sing the Laguz *galdr*.

Ingwaz—Stand with your feet slightly apart, toes pointed outward. Put your hands over your head, pressing your palms and fingertips together, your elbows angled in the form of the rune. Make the sound ooooooo, feeling the power moving from your feet to your fingertips. Also you can stand with your fingertips touching at your pelvis and your elbows forming the appropriate angles. Sing the Ingwaz *galdr*.

Dagaz—Face east, standing erect, and cross your arms in front of your chest in the form of the rune. Your right fingers touch your left shoulder, and your left fingers touch your right shoulder. Sing the Dagaz *galdr*.

Othala—Stand with your feet spread wide, arms bent at the elbows and fingertips touching at your pelvis. Next, bend your elbows in the form of the rune, fingertips and palms touching overhead. Sing the Othala *galdr*.

The Cross—Stand upright, stretching both your arms outward at right angles to your body. Your body is the vertical axis, and your arms are the horizontal axis. There is no chant. As you do the posture, visualize energy flowing in through your head and right hand, and out through your feet and left hand.

Because the stances mirror the shape of the runes, runic yoga is the ideal way to teach young children the symbols. Have them strike the pose that resembles each rune, and you'll find that they catch on very quickly, figuring out new ways to make the rune symbol with their legs, arms, hands, and fingers. The postures are varied enough to be expressive of the wide variety of runic forces present, but none of them requires extensive training or straining of the body.

Rune Mudras

Runic yoga also has mudras, symbolic gestures that depict the runic forms with the hands and fingers. They are used in inspirational and physical healing by touching the body in certain ways in the shape of the appropriate runes—for example, Fehu for fever, head ailments, or bone injuries. This is yet another way to tap into the energies of the runes. The hand mudras are best made about one foot from your face, your hands positioned at an equal distance between your forehead and throat.

Our family likes to do the hand mudras as a secret language, spelling out words to one another, for example, across a roomful of people. My son is always finding new ways to create the runes with different finger combinations. You can also sing the *galdr* associated with the hand mudra you are signing.

RUNE DANCING

Contemporary runemasters have devised runic dance methods that induce altered states of consciousness. Influenced by Rudolf Steiner's "Eurhythmy," runic dancing is a system of balanced body movement. When done properly, this form of dancing has an effect similar to the Sufi whirling dances. It brings you to merged and magical states of mind that facilitate healing miracles and visionary experiences.

One method of runic dancing involves taking a runic posture and moving clockwise. Take very short steps while humming or *galdring* the rune whose shape you are posturing. Move clockwise faster and faster. By dancing all the runes in this manner, you can reach a higher state of awareness.

I like to do runic dancing with my husband and son, often just to get energized, on full moons and the eight days of power. Much less structured than some of the established forms of runic dance, my method blends the runic symbol with a sort of Irish jig. The ideal music is that of the folk group of Swedish-speaking Finns called "Gjallarhorn," especially the album entitled, "Ranarop, Call of the Sea Witch" (Finlandia Music/Warner Music Group). You could also use your favorite dance music.

Begin by getting into a festive state of mind. Let go of your worries and tensions, turn the dance music on, and start to rune-dance. If you want, you can trace the rune symbol with chalk on the floor, but I have found that spontaneity adds to the intensity and enjoyment of the experience.

Next, breathe deeply a few times to center yourself. Listen to the music and make an effort to feel it in your body. You may have to turn up the volume and the bass in order to do this. Turn your mind to the runic symbols (have them in front of you for reference, if you like) and take small jig-like steps. With your feet, trace or dance the first rune symbol that pops into your head. Let your feet feel their way around the symbol. You can dance each rune for several minutes, or only for a few moments. I dance the runes one at a time as they come to me. You can also dance the same rune holding hands with a partner or in a group, circle, or serpentine line. As a general formula, start at the top of the runic symbol and dance downward. This steps or dances the energy down into the symbol, which is then absorbed by you as you dance, charging your batteries. With the proper focus, you will experience a sense of euphoria after dancing this way for a few minutes.

The best thing about this kind of dancing is its spontaneity. It also acts as an intuitive, divination dance as certain runes come to mind before others. Often some runes aren't danced at all in a session. By noticing this runic dance pattern, you not only become more aware of the energies present in any situation but also how you can harness them and use them to enrich your life.

When you're dancing the runes spontaneously, be aware of how the runes feel. You may also see the energetic shape of the rune on the ground on which you're dancing. Notice the flow of the energy—like the current of a river—and any associated colors and other qualities (texture, scent, sound, images, or memories) that strike you as interesting. Frequently I sense images and colored streams of energy when doing runic dancing. Dancing certain runes can make you feel as if you are floating (Laguz), while other runes weigh you down and ground you (Uruz). The rune you focus your dancing on is the one most influential in your life at that time. Also, children love to dance the runes with you, and they are constantly inventing new ways to do it.

RUNE ENERGY EXERCISE

Select three runes to use in this activity. Do it by mixing your runes and pulling the first three that come to you. Place them faceup, in a horizontal row from left to right in front of you. Begin by drawing the first rune onto the palm of your right hand with an essential oil or with olive oil. (Use your left hand if you're left-handed.) With your palm up, *galdr* the rune into your hand, your lips almost touching your palm so that you can feel the resonance of your voice on the skin. Transfer the loaded runic energy from your right palm to your left palm by slowly chanting the rune. As you begin to chant, raise your loaded palm upward into the air, gathering energy. When you feel the energy peaking, slam your loaded right palm down onto your left palm with deliberation, but not necessarily with physical force. While you do this, explosively utter the last breath of your rune chant into it. Feel your hands, and notice how they are different. You can also do this on other parts of your body; with other people; on pets, trees, large rocks; and on the bare ground. In fact, this is one of the best ways to use the runic energies for healing and revitalizing your body.

RUNE SCENTS

Draw your favorite rune on your forehead with essential oil. Good oils for this purpose are sage, rosemary, dragon's-blood, and amber. Make sure you like the scent of the oil. Mix one drop of essential oil to eight drops of light olive oil. Feel the rune's essence soaking into your forehead, and savor the scent of the oil. Breathe the scent deeply into your being, and notice any images, thoughts, or impressions that come to you. *Tip:* Use the same oil scent whenever you work with the runes. This will put you into a magical state of mind whenever you smell that particular scent.

Rune Pitching and Catching

You can play this runic game with an adult or a child. Stand facing one another, about nine feet (2.7m) apart. The pitcher holds her/his hands out, waist high, palms upward, cupped into a ball shape. The catcher holds her/his hands out, palms facing outward as if to catch a ball. The pitcher then loads the first rune into her/his hands by visualizing, feeling, and intuiting, and chanting the corresponding *galdr* either silently or aloud. When the energy peaks, the pitcher then "throws" the runic energy into the catcher's cupped hands, and afterward grounds her/his energy by touching the floor. The catcher remains still until all the runic energy has been thrown.

After doing this three or four times, switch positions, the pitcher now catching and the catcher pitching. Notice the image, smell, color, texture, feel, sound, and other energy signatures of the different runes. Try this with different people and notice how the energy changes.

Rune Telepathy Cards

You can work this activity with one or more people, or you can challenge yourself. Select four of your favorite runes. On same-color index cards, draw or paint these four runes, one to a card, until you have six cards with the same rune, 24 cards altogether. Number the cards 1–24. Make sure you can't see the rune from the opposite side of the card. You may have to double the index cards if you use dark paint or a heavy felt tip pen. Leave the opposite side blank.

Mix the 24 cards, and place them facedown in front of you. You will need a sheet of paper and a pen, pencil, or crayon for each participant in the game. Facing your partner (or group), pull the first card off the top of the deck and look at the rune. Don't say anything, and make an effort to keep your face muscles and body as still as possible. Send the rune by feeling or intuiting the rune symbol on the card to the person(s) across from you. Ways to enhance this process are:

1) tracing the rune shape in your mind
2) going over the meaning of the rune and the correspondences in your mind
3) using deep, deliberate breathing to "breathe" the rune to your partner
4) merging as deeply as you can with Oneness,

completely letting go of all preconceived notions for a few moments.

Take about a minute or so with each card, and then let your partner or group write down the rune symbol they feel you are sending them. Place the cards facedown in a neat stack, in the order that you pulled them. When you have sent all 24 cards, turn the stack over and check to see how many cards match your partner's answers. If you get four or more matches, you are demonstrating genuine telepathic powers. With practice, my son and I have discovered you can get better and better at this game. Plus, it's a great way to connect with another person on a deep, intuitive level.

SOLO TELEPATHY CARDS

When you play this game by yourself, write down the rune that you feel will come up before you pull the card. To do this, pull the first card and leave it facedown. Study it, apart from the other cards, without turning it over. Sense the rune symbol on the opposite side. Then turn the card over and see if you have intuited correctly. Ideal for building psychic ability, the solo method gives you immediate feedback. When you are correct, you can hone in on that feeling or sensation when the card comes up again.

Singing a *Galdr* Circle

You can do this alone, with one other person, or with a group of people. Begin with Fehu, and sing and *galdr* and circle around, going through all 24 runes and ending with Othala. You can add percussion instruments like bells, tambourines, drums, and shakers. You can also dance the runes as you sing them. Do this every morning and evening for personal empowerment, protection, and just for fun! You will find that daily *galdring* has the ability to improve your state of mind, increase your energy level, and promote your general well-being. Children love to sing *galdr* circles, too.

Rune Activities to Do with Children

Rune Ostara (Easter) Eggs

This is a great activity to do with your kids. After you dye your spring Easter eggs, use non-toxic color felt pens or paint to add the appropriate runic sym-

bols such as Sowilo, Berkana, and Laguz. You can
also cut out paper runes and glue them onto the eggs,
or draw the runic symbols on paper egg holders or
egg hats.

MAKING RUNE COOKIES

Cookies are always a big hit with children and
adults alike. Use one of your favorite recipes and
make your own rune cookies, each one bearing one
of the 24 Elder Futharks. Redden the rune symbol
with red icing after the cookies have cooled. You can
eat them in *aett* order (1–24), or you can eat your
favorite runes first. Before you eat the cookie, load it
with the rune, and sing the corresponding *galdr* song.
While you eat the cookie, focus on the rune's meaning and qualities. Notice how you feel as you eat each
rune.

MAKING RUNE FLASH CARDS

Making a deck of simple rune flash cards is a great
way to teach yourself and your children the 24 runes
of the Elder Futhark. Making rune flash cards along
with your child can be a rewarding experience on
many levels. You will need a stack of index cards.

Have your child draw or paint the rune symbol on

one side of the card, and then afterward you can write some factual information on the reverse side, while you both talk about the qualities of the rune. For Gebo, the G-rune, for example, you would talk about the concept of a gift in terms of both giving and receiving and the mutual exchange of energy. You can either do one *aett* at a time or the entire Elder Futhark, depending upon your child's attention span and level of interest.

To make the flash cards, use a wide-tipped red or black felt pen (or a calligraphy pen), red paint or crayon, to draw the rune. On the other side of the card, write the rune name, a corresponding letter and number, plus a few key words (refer to the following list):

Sample Key Words for Flash Cards:
• First *Aett*
Fehu—Mobile Wealth
Uruz—Auroch/Structure
Thurisaz—Thorn
Ansuz—Ancestral God/Odin
Raidho—Solar Wagon
Kenaz—Torch/Fire

Gebo—Gift
Wunjo—Joy

• Second *Aett*
Hagalaz—Hail/Cosmic Egg
Naudhiz—Need-Fire
Isa—Ice/Slow-Moving Structure
Jera—(Good) Year/Cycles
Eihwaz—Yew Tree/Transcendence/Rebirth
Perthro—Dice Cup/Knowledge
Algiz—Elk/Protection
Sowilo—Sun/Divine Spirit

• Third *Aett*
Tiwaz—The Sky God Tyr/Justice
Berkana—Birch Goddess/Nurturing
Ehwaz—Horse/Twins/Nature
Mannaz—Humanity
Laguz—Body of Water (Laukaz/Leek)
Ingwaz—The Earth God Ing/Fertility/The Seed
Dagaz—Day/The Lifting of Darkness
Othala—Ancestral Property/Oneness

MAKING CLAY RUNES WITH CHILDREN

You can use modeling clay, readily available in crafts stores, to make rune squares. Femo is perfect for this purpose and comes in many colors. I had my son select the color he wanted, and then we shaped 24 similar-sized rune squares, letting them harden a bit before carving the symbols into them. We used a regular medium-tipped ballpoint pen to mark the runes, while chanting their names and making up silly songs about them. We even consecrated the pen. My son also danced many of the runes while we were working. Afterward we oven-baked the squares, let them cool, and reddened the carved symbols with red enamel paint that was especially made for the modeling clay. We painted the corresponding letter on the opposite side of the carved runes, for example, "H" on the Hagalaz rune. I recommend that you create your own formula for making clay runes with children—something that matches your child's attention span and personality.

GLOSSARY

Aegir A giant god of the sea
Aegishjalmur The Helm of Awe, a powerful runic ring
Aesir The family of gods governing human events, such as agri-
culture, trade, battle, and law. The Aesir include Odin, Frigga,
Thor, Tyr, and Heimdall.
Aettir Plural of *aett*, usually referring to all three families of runes
Alerunes Runes used for protection
Alfheim One of the nine worlds, home of the white or light elves
Alfrig Dwarf
Algiz Primary rune of protection
Alsvin Steed that pulls the chariot of the sun ("quick-footed")
Alvismal 12th-century Icelandic poem
Alviss Leader of dwarfs
Anda Breath
Ansuz The god rune, representing Odin
Argud Icelandic name for Frey ("year god")
Arvakr Steed that pulls the chariot of the sun ("early riser")
Asatru A modern reconstruction of the religion Germanic tribes
practiced before their conversion to Christianity. Includes rune
magic.
Asgard One of the nine worlds, land of the gods and goddesses
of the Aesir, above Midgard
Ask The first man, whose name means "ash tree"
Asynjur The name for the goddesses of the Aesir

Athame Double-edged ceremonial blade used in magic

Audhumla A giant cosmic cow who began the life process

Austri Dwarf, one of the Four Wards, ancient guardian of the East

Baldur Son of Frigga, god who rules the light half of the year, brother of Hodur

Belskirnir Palace of Thor

Beltane Traditional May Day, astrologically May 5

Berchta Goddess of childbirth

Berkana Rune of the Earth Goddess

Berlingr Dwarf

Bestla Giantess, mother of Odin

Biargrunes Runes used in childbirth

Bifrost Bridge The rainbow bridge between Asgard and Midgard

Bindrunes Several runes put together for greater effect

Blithgund Oldest name written in runic script

Blodug-hofi Frey's horse

Bor God, father of Odin

Bracteate Runic ring worn around the neck

Bridget's Day *See* Imbolc

Bright-staves Faceup runes read in ceremonial casting

Brisingamen Freyja's necklace made by the dwarfs

Britsum, stave of Preserved runic talisman

Brunnhilde Valkyrie, and one of Odin's daughters

Brunrunes Weather-magic runes

Buri First giant, father of Bor, making him Odin's grandfather

Carl Free-person class of humankind

Clog almanacs Ancient English wooden runic calendar

Dagaz One of the last two runes, representing the light of the sun

Dain Stag, one of four, representing the four winds

Duneyr Stag, one of four, representing the four winds

Durathor Stag, one of four, representing the four winds

Dvalin Stag, one of four, representing the four winds

Dvalin Dwarf

Dvergar Name for the dwarfs

Earl Noble class of humankind

Eeyeneerde "Own earth" or "own land"—another name for the Othala rune

Ehwaz The horse rune

Eihwaz Rune of transcendence and rebirth

Einheriar The bravest fallen warriors

Eir The goddess of healing, Frigga's attendant, taught medicine to women

Elder Futhark The oldest known form of runes, using 24 symbols

Eldhrimnir Cauldron used to prepare meat at Valhalla

Elhaz Another name for Algiz

Elvidnir Hall of misery in which Hella lives

Embla The first woman associated with the elm tree

Escarbuncle A medieval sign that is a version of the Aegish-jalmur

Etin-world Land of the giants

Fafner Dragon defeated by Sigurd (Siegfried)

Fathom Measurement from fingertip to fingertip of outstretched arms

Fehu The first rune, the primordial fire

Fenris Wolf One of the forces that brings about the end of the world

Fetch An aspect of the self that appears in the form of a spirit beast of power

Fire-giants Giants from Muspelheim

Forseti God of justice and law, son of Baldur (light) and Nanna (purity)

Freki Wolf of Odin

Frey God of the first *aett,* ruling fertility, prosperity, kingship, Vanir, nature, and the weather

Freyja Goddess of the first *aett,* ruling over plant and animal life on Earth, love, magic; leader of the Valkyries

Frigga Second and primary wife of Odin, mother to Baldur, Hoder, Hermod, and Tyr

Futhark Runic writing

Fylgia Power animal

Fyorgyn The Earth, mother of Frigga

Galdr Singing the sounds of a rune, or song of the rune, magical incantation

Galdrstaf Small veneer-thin piece of wood cut in the shape of a triangle, used to apply red dye to runes

Gandr Wand or staff

Gebo The rune symbolizing the gift of life

Gefn Norse goddess, the bountiful giver

Gerd Frey's wife, giantess, daughter of frost giant Gymir

Geri Wolf of Odin

Ginnungapap Primordial energetically charged void

Gjallar Horn of Heimdall

Gjoll River that leads to Hel

Glitnir Palace of Forseti, means "shining"

Glodhker A burner or fire-pot used in magic

Glory twigs Symbols connected with magic, used for divination

Grer Dwarf

Gullinbursti Golden-bristled boar ridden by Frey

Gullveig (Goldlust) Woman who introduced the negative side of gold. She began as a Vanir wise woman, the triple goddess, the negative side of Freyja.

Gvesti Dwarf, one of the Four Wards, ancient guardian of the west

Gymir frost giant, father of Gerd

Hachel Wise woman

Hagalaz First rune of the second *aett*, the crystal rune of transformation and change

Hahalrunar Hook runes

Hamingia A field of energy around the body that can move at will ("good luck and guardian spirit")

Hati Wolf that pursues and catches the sun and moon during Ragnorok

Havamal Ancient Norse poem from the Elder or Poetic Edda

Heid A variation of Freyja, mother of the Valkyries

Heidrun Odin's goat

Heimdall God of light who guards the rainbow bridge Bifrost

Hel One of the nine worlds, home of Hella and those who die from natural causes, below Midgard

Hella Giantess and daughter of Loki, half white, half black, protectoress of Hel

Hellith's Day September 22

Hermod Son of Odin and Frigga

Hertha Nerthus

Hertha's Day March 21

Hinder Bottom end of the gandr

Hoarfrost Giants from Nifelheim

Hodur Twin of Baldur who kills him and then rules the dark part of the year

Hoenir Brother to Odin (Vili)

Hof marks Symbols for specific groups

Holde Sky goddess, water goddess, earth goddess, a counterpart to Frigga

Horgr "Holy pile of stones," altar

Hugin Raven of Odin, representing thought

Hugrunes Runes connected to the intellect

Hvergelmir "Roaring kettle," a spring in Nifelheim

Iarn Greiper Thor's magic gauntlet

Iarnsaxa Giantess, first wife of Thor, mother of Modi and Magni

Iduna Wife of the god Bragi. She guards the golden apples of rejuvenation.

Iis Secret runic code system

Imbolc February 2

Ing Another name for Frey

Ingun A form of Ing

Ingvaeons Tribes along the North Sea belonging to Ing

Ingvio Son of Mannaz, and another name for Frey

Ingwaz Rune of energy, named for god who is the male consort of the Earth Goddess

Insigils Magical symbols

Irmio Son of Mannaz

Isa Rune of frozen, very slow-moving energy

Istio Son of Mannaz

Jera Rune of the yearly cycle

Jotunheim One of the nine worlds, in the east, home of the frost giants

Kalevala An ancient collection of Nordic magic healing charms

Kenaz Rune of light, knowledge, and creativity; the artist rune

Kennings Poetic symbolism and metaphors

Kloprunes Rune codes using sound

Lagu runes Secret runic code system

Laguz Rune of water and flow

Laukaz Runic name for power and pure energy

Lightalfheim Another name for Alfheim

Limrunes Runes that draw upon the healing energies of trees

Lodur Brother of Odin (Ve)

Loki God of darkness, chaos, and trickery, who helped bring about the end of the world

Lonnrunor Secret runes

Lorride Son of Thor by Sif

Lothur Another name for the god Ve

Lughnassad Great day occurring in the first week in August

Magni Son of Thor by Iarnsaxa

Malrunes Runes that enhance memory, mental ability, and speech

Mani (Moon) Charioteer of Odin

Mannaz The rune of humankind

Mead Oldest known alcoholic beverage, made from fermented honey

Mearomot Personal talisman, sacred pouch with crystal, feather, picture, and other objects

Megen-giord Thor's girdle

Merging Becoming one with the divine

Midgard Middle Earth, one of the nine worlds

Milfoil Another name for yarrow

Mimir God of the open sea, son of the elements, son of Bolthorn, giant

Mithra (MithOdin) God of mystery

Mjollnir Name of Thor's hammer

Modi Son of Thor by Iarnsaxa

Mordgrud Giant Asynjur goddess who guards the entrance to Hel

Mother runes Fehu, Hagalaz, and Tiwaz

Munin Raven of Odin, representing memory

Murk-staves Runes that land facedown on the cloth and are not used in ceremonial runecasting

Muspelheim The fire land, one of the nine worlds, in the south

Nanna Goddess of purity, mother of Forseti

Naudhiz Rune of necessity

Nerthus Goddess of the Earth, mother of Frey and Freyja, sister of Njord

Nidhog Dragon who paws at the roots of Yggdrasil

Nifelheim "Fog world," one of the nine worlds, in the north

Njord God of the wind and sea, father of Frey and Freyja, husband of Skadi

Njord's glove The sponge

Noatun Seaside palace of Njord

Nordi Dwarf, one of the Four Wards, ancient guardian of the north

Nornir *See* Norns

Norns Aspects of time: what was, what is becoming, what will be; the 3 fates; the Weird Sisters

Odhr Inspiration, genius

Odhroerir Divine mead from the well of inspiration

Odin God of wisdom, son of Bor and Bestla, the All-Father who discovered the runes

Odur The sunshine

Ond The breath of life

Orlog The primal energy that makes up everything

Oski Another name for Odin, "fulfiller of wishes"

Othala The last rune, representing the DNA coding of human beings and the element of air

Othroerir The mead of inspiration and the vessel that contains it

Perdhro Rune of chance

Phosphenes Geometrical images that stem from the brain's visual cortex and neural system

Ragnarok The end of the world

Raidho Rune of forward movement and natural cycles

Rainbow bridge Another name for the Bifrost Bridge between this world and the world of the gods

Ramrunes Runes empowered by magical ritual

Ran Goddess of the stormy sea and the drowned, called "the robber," wife of Aegir

Ratotosk Gossiping squirrel

Rig Another name for Heimdall

Rigsthula Poem from the Elder or Poetic Edda

Rime giants First humans in the universe

Rimstocks Wooden calendars

Ristir Sharp woodcarving tool customarily used to cut runes

Rune-tines Twigs or sticks inscribed with runes

Runrigs Lots allocating land in Scottish folk law

Sabbats Eight quarter and cross-quarter divisions of the year

Saehrimnir Odin's boar

Samhain Great day occurring in the first week of November

Sax Single-edged knife used in magic in the Northern Tradition

Seidr A type of love magic

Shoat Runecast

Siegfried Hero (Sigurd)

Sif Second wife of Thor, mother of Lorride and Thrud, mother of Uller

Sigrunes Runes used to gain success and victory

Skadi Goddess of snow

Skinbladnir Frey's magical ship

Skirnir Frey's servant

Skoll Wolf that would pursue and catch the sun and moon during Ragnorok

Skuld The third Norn, the future, who pulls apart the weave of life

Sleipnir Odin's eight-legged steed, born of Loki and the stallion Svadilfari

Sol (sun) Charioteer of Odin, originally the female goddess of the sun, called the Glory of the Elves

Sowilo The rune representing the sun

Spae-wives Travelling fortune-tellers of medieval Iceland

Stadha Runic postures in a form of yoga

Stahagaldr *See* Stadha

Stick-casting Runecasting using ordinary sticks

Stol Pillow used during runecasting

Sudri Dwarf, one of the Four Wards, ancient guardian of the south

Sunwise Clockwise

Surt Fire giant who killed Frey at Ragnarok

Svadilfari Stallion, father to Sleipnir

Svalin Shield that protected Sol and horses from the rays of the sun

Svartalfheim One of the nine worlds, home of the dark elves or dwarfs

Swartrunes Black runes, used to speak with the dead

Tanngniortr One of the goats that pulled Thor's wagon

Tanngrisnr One of the goats that pulled Thor's wagon

Thor Agriculture and thunder god

Thrall Slave class of humankind

Thrud Daughter of Thor by Sif

Thrudheim Land of strength in Asgard

Thurisaz The third rune

Thursars Giants, also called rime-thurses or frost-giants

Tines *See* rune-tines

Tir The pole star, known as "Frigga's Spindle"

Tiver A dye extracted from the madder plant, used to redden runes. The word *tiver* means magic.

Tiwaz Rune of justice, law, and war

Tjaldrunar Tent runes

Trygill Sacred bowl used in magic

Tyr Chief god of law, justice, and war, who rules the third *aett;* son of Odin and Frigga; god of heaven

Uller The sky god, second husband of Skadi; god of winter, hunting, and archery; son of Sif; god of the straw death; Thor's step-son

Urd Norn of the past and guardian of the well, who spins the thread of existence

Urdar *See* Urd

Uruz The second rune, the eternal ice

Utgard One of the divisions of Jotunheim

Utiseta "Sitting out," a trance-divination

Valfreya Another name for Freyja

Valhalla Home of the gods of Asgard, over the rainbow bridge

Valkyries Helmeted female riders who honor the bravest fallen warriors

Vanaheim One of the nine worlds, in the west, home of the Vanir

Vanir The nature gods, including Njord, Frey, and Freyja

Vargamors Swedish wise women

Vaxspajalds or **vasapjald** Handheld writing board covered in wax on one side

Ve God of holiness, brother of Odin

Vedfolnir Falcon that lives in Yggdrasil

Veraldar Gudh Another name for Frey ("god of the world" in Swedish)

Verdandi The second Norn, who weaves thread into the Web of Wyrd

Vili God of will, brother of Odin

Vithofnir Golden cock who watches Surt, the fire giant

Volsunga Saga Icelandic poem

Volva Wise woman, sorceress

Weird *See* Wyrd

Wendrunes Runes written backwards

Wights The spirits in all things

Wodan Another name for Odin

Worlds Alfheim, Asgard, Hel, Jotunheim, Midgard, Muspelheim, Nifelheim, Svartalfheim, Vanaheim

Wuldor Another name for Uller

Wuldortanas Glory twigs

Wunjo Rune embodying the Golden Age

Wyrd The interconnectedness of all things, the web of the present pattern of existence

Ydalir "Yew grove," Uller's home in Asgard

Ygg Another name for Odin

Yggdrasil The World Tree, the cosmic axis that links all the worlds of creation

Ygg's horse Yggdrasil

Ymir Original rime giant

Yngvi Another name for Frey

Zisa Harvest goddess who rules the third *aett*

Index

496   INDEX

About the Author

Sirona Knight, coauthor of the best-selling "Shapeshifter Tarot," is a contributing editor for *Magical Blend* magazine. The author of eleven books on magic, Celtic shamanism, and the Goddess, she lives in Chico, California.

Her website is www.dcsi.net/bluesky.

If you liked this book, you'll love this series:

Little Giant Book of Optical Illusions • Little Giant Book of "True" Ghost Stories • Little Giant Book of Whodunits • Little Giant Encyclopedia of Aromatherapy • Little Giant Encyclopedia of Baseball Quizzes • Little Giant Encyclopedia of Card & Magic Tricks • Little Giant Encyclopedia of Card Games • Little Giant Encyclopedia of Card Games Gift Set • Little Giant Encyclopedia of Dream Symbols • Little Giant Encyclopedia of Fortune Telling • Little Giant Encyclopedia of Gambling Games • Little Giant Encyclopedia of Games for One or Two • Little Giant Encyclopedia of Handwriting Analysis • Little Giant Encyclopedia of Home Remedies • Little Giant Encyclopedia of IQ Tests • Little Giant Encyclopedia of Logic Puzzles • Little Giant Encyclopedia of Magic • Little Giant Encyclopedia of Mazes • Little Giant Encyclopedia of Meditations & Blessings • Little Giant Encyclopedia of Names • Little Giant Encyclopedia of Natural Healing • Little Giant Encyclopedia of One-Liners • Little Giant Encyclopedia of Palmistry • Little Giant Encyclopedia of Puzzles • Little Giant Encyclopedia of Runes • Little Giant Encyclopedia of Spells & Magic • Little Giant Encyclopedia of Superstitions • Little Giant Encyclopedia of Toasts & Quotes • Little Giant Encyclopedia of Travel & Holiday Games • Little Giant Encyclopedia of UFOs • Little Giant Encyclopedia of Wedding Toasts • Little Giant Encyclopedia of Word Puzzles • Little Giant Encyclopedia of the Zodiac

Available at fine stores everywhere.